Skillstreaming

Children and Youth with High-Functioning Autism

A Guide for Teaching Prosocial Skills

Ellen McGinnis
Richard L. Simpson

RESEARCH PRESS
PUBLISHERS

Champaign, Illinois ■ (800) 519-2707 ■ www.researchpress.com

RESEARCH PRESS
P U B L I S H E R S

Copyright © 2017 by Ellen McGinnis and Richard L. Simpson

9 8 7 6 5   23 24 25 26 27

Copies of this book may be ordered from Research Press at www.researchpress.com.

Composition by Jeff Helgesen
Cover design by Linda Brown, Positive I.D. Graphic Design, Inc.
Printed by Seaway Printing

ISBN 978-0-87822-683-2
Library of Congress Control Number 2016944910

To Carl Smith, for his career-long dedication to improving services for youth with disabilities
—E. M.
To Janice, a devoted source of feedback and inspiration
—R. L. S.
To the children and youth with high-functioning autism disorders, their teachers, and families,
who have informed and motivated
—E. M. and R. L. S.

Contents

Skill Outlines and Homework Reports   29

Homework Reports follow each skill.

Group I: Relationship Skills   31

Beginning Relationship Skills

Advanced Relationship Skills

Figures and Tables

Figures

Tables

Preface

Skillstreaming is now over 40 years old. Starting with its introduction in 1973 as one of the very first social skills training approaches, it has been widely used in the United States and beyond and is now in place in hundreds of schools, agencies, clinics, and residential treatment centers serving children and youth.

The origins and development of the Skillstreaming approach afford an interesting context with which to understand the program described in this book. The prevailing therapeutic approaches of the 1950s and 1960s (psychodynamic, nondirective, and behavior modification) held that an individual possessed effective, satisfying, or healthy behaviors but that these behaviors were simply unexpressed. In contrast, Skillstreaming represents a psychoeducational approach, viewing the individual in educational terms, as a person in need of help in the form of skills training. Instead of providing therapy, the task of the skills trainer or teacher is the active and deliberate teaching of desirable behaviors to replace those less productive in nature.

Skillstreaming differs from the approaches of behavior theorists such as Albert Bandura (1973), who described the processes of modeling, behavioral rehearsal, and reinforcement inherent in the Skillstreaming approach but who exclusively emphasized operant procedures such as prompting and shaping of behaviors. A strictly behavioral approach increases the frequency of a behavior, albeit that behavior is frequently believed to already be within a person's repertoire.

If the person does not have a grasp of the needed skill, rigidly interpreted operant procedures may be insufficient to add that skill to the person's behavioral options.

The deinstitutionalization movement of the 1960s, which resulted in the discharge of approximately four million persons from mental health and other institutions into local communities, set the stage for acceptance of an alternative way of providing treatment. The realization was that the more traditional therapeutic interventions, which focused on looking inward to correct one's nonproductive actions (i.e., in-sight-oriented approaches), were ineffective for many individuals from lower socioeconomic environments, who constituted the majority of individuals discharged from institutions. The lack of effective methods to reach this population led Dr. Arnold P. Goldstein to develop Structured Learning Therapy (Goldstein, 1973), the precursor to Skillstreaming. Structured Learning approached aggression, withdrawal, and other nonproductive patterns in a new way—as learned behaviors that can be changed by teaching new, alternative skills.

In addition to the growing importance of such structured learning methods in applied clinical work and as a preventive focus in community mental health, parallel developments in education clearly encouraged skills training. Specifically, a number of other approaches grew from the personal development context of certain educational movements—for example, progressive education (Dewey, 1938) and char-acter education (Chapman, 1977). The goal of these approaches was to support the teaching of concepts and behaviors relevant to values, mo-rality, and emotional functioning—in particular, values clarification (Simon, Howe, & Kirschen-baum, 1972), moral education (Kohlberg, 1973) affective education (Miller, 1976), and, more re-cently, social-emotional learning (Collaborative for Academic, Social, and Emotional Learning: CASEL). These approaches, as well as other per-sonal growth programs, combined to provide a supportive climate and context for skills train-ing. These programs share a concern for personal development, competence, and social effective-ness. Clearly, education had been broadened well beyond basic academic content to include areas traditionally the concern of mental health prac-titioners.

Since its initial development as an inter-vention prescriptively targeted to low-income adults deficient in social skills, Skillstreaming has increasingly been used with many other populations. In the 1980s and beyond, Dr. Gold-stein's skills training program, now known as Skillstreaming, was adapted to meet the needs of adolescents (Goldstein, Sprafkin, Gershaw, & Klein, 1980; Goldstein & McGinnis, 1997; Mc-Ginnis, 2012a) , elementary children (McGinnis & Goldstein, 1984, 1997; McGinnis, 2012c), and preschool and kindergarten children (McGin-nis & Goldstein, 1990, 2003; McGinnis, 2012b) who exhibited aggression and other problematic behaviors. In addition to its use with children and adolescents, the Skillstreaming approach has been employed successfully with elderly adults, child-abusing parents, industrial manag-ers, police officers, and others. Over more than 40 years of program use, a considerable amount of evaluation research has been conducted and reported, including its success with youth with Asperger's syndrome (Lopata, Thomeer, Volker, & Nida, 2006; Lopata, Thomeer, Volker, Nida, & Lee, 2008; Tse, Strulovitch, Tagalakis, Linyan, & Rombonne, 2007). The results of these studies support the efficacy of Skillstreaming and have suggested means for altering and improving its procedures and materials.

Acknowledgments

Professor Arnold P. Goldstein (1934–2002), along with Robert P. Sprafkin and N. Jane Gershaw, developed Skillstreaming in the early 1980s. Used initially to improve the lives of youth and adults with high levels of aggressive behaviors, Skillstreaming has expanded to enhance the social interactions of preschool and elementary age children, adolescents and young adults both with and without disabilities. Through Dr. Goldstein's research, evaluation, and nurturing of Skillstreaming, this learning strategy is now used throughout the United States and in numerous other countries. Many people, ourselves included, cannot thank him enough for his efforts to help youth and adults with aggression and other challenging behaviors change to improve their lives and the lives of those who interact with them.

Judy Parkinson from Research Press provided the encouragement needed to expand Skillstreaming to improve services for children and youth with high-functioning autism disorders. Without her understanding and support, this project would not have been possible. Special appreciation and thanks for Karen Steiner, our editor, for her talent in bringing our ideas to life in a clear, sensitive, and understandable way.

Introduction

High-functioning autism disorders are neurologically based conditions (Myles & Simpson, 1998) characterized by social skills deficits (Zager, Wehmeyer, & Simpson, 2012). Children and adolescents with high-functioning autism and similar disorders such as Asperger disorder typically possess normal cognitive and language abilities but struggle with a variety of social skills deficits in interactions with others (American Psychiatric Association, 2000, 2013). Social interaction deficits include difficulties reading subtle social cues, forming and maintaining age-appropriate adult and peer relationships, understanding nonverbal behavior, social reciprocity, and following fundamental social standards. These learners also tend to engage in stereotypic activities, including fixating on narrow areas of interest. It is not unusual for such youth to be described by others as socially stiff and uncoordinated, inflexible, and lacking in tact and empathy (Baron-Cohen, 1995; Simpson & Myles, 2011).

As these children become older, and especially during their adolescent years, social difficulties are often intensified by changes with puberty and complicated by teenage social norms and expectations. While these youth often improve their skills in basic communication, they frequently continue to struggle with social communication (Schall & McDonough, 2010). As a result, even when they actively try to engage with others, they often experience rejection and social isolation. These social challenges have a profound impact not only on the individual who is struggling, but also on teachers, peers in the classroom, parents, and the community.

WHY TEACH SOCIAL SKILLS?

Despite the challenges children and youth with high-functioning autism disorders face, there is strong reason to believe that, with appropriate education and support, they have the potential to lead effectively normal lives (Simpson & Myles, 2011). Indeed, many attend college and have successful careers (Harpur, Lawlor, & Fitzgerald, 2004).

Research and experience tell us that individuals with high-functioning autism disorders who receive training in social skills and who are provided support in doing so are better able to respond to social demands, interact with greater social ease, and become more resilient (Baker, 2004; Garcia Winner, 2008; Koegel, Kuriakose, Singh, & Koegel, 2012). Specifically, learning socially desirable skills has been shown to positively impact academic and school-related success, employment success, independent living, and overall quality of life (Chan et al., 2009; Cotugno, 2009; Stichter, O'Connor, Herzog, Lierheimer, & McGhee, 2012), while the failure to learn and use appropriate social skills is associated with more negative outcomes (Lee, Odom, & Loftin, 2007; Simpson, Ganz, & Mason, 2012).

Skillstreaming has been employed successfully with a wide range of individuals and in a wide range of settings. This volume extends the Skillstreaming approach to social skills instruction to address the specific social learning needs of this group of children and adolescents. The same skill-learning procedures as for other Skillstreaming programs—modeling, role play, feedback, and generalization—provide the foundation for instruction with this population. However, a significant difference concerns the presumption that Skillstreaming instruction will be integrated into existing overall educational and therapeutic plans for these learners, and that, to the degree necessary, they will receive individualized skills instruction and one-to-one coaching from mental health providers, teachers, peers, and families.

HISTORICAL BACKGROUND

In 1943, Leo Kanner first identified what he called "early infantile autism" in 11 children in whom he observed high intelligence, a profound preference for being alone, and an obsessive insistence on the preservation of sameness. In 1944, Viennese physician Hans Asperger observed a group of children who displayed some typical autistic behaviors, such as self-stimulation and insistence on environmental sameness. In his description, he identified these individuals as socially odd, socially uninformed, and awkward, but with at least average intellectual ability and normal language development. Asperger contended that this newly identified disorder had a neurodevelopmental cause.

Through the 1960s, psychiatrists continued to view autism as a form of childhood schizophrenia. Also popular through the 1960s was the now-debunked idea that autism resulted from emotionally distant mothering. The 1970s brought understanding that autism stemmed from biological differences in brain development. Objective criteria for diagnosing autism followed in the 1980s, as did increased interest in Asperger disorder, when Wing (1981) brought the disorder to the attention of researchers and clinicians by translating Asperger's original work into English. Wing further clarified the disorder through extensive clinical descriptions and case examples.

Until recently, Asperger disorder and other high-functioning autism disorders were included as subcategories of pervasive developmental disorder in the two common diagnostic manuals used by mental health clinicians and others: the fourth edition of the *Diagnostic and Statistical Manual of Mental Disorders* (DSM–IV; American Psychiatric Association, 2000) and the corresponding international classification system, the *International Statistical Classification of Diseases and Related Health Problems* (World Health Organization, 2007).

Although some have advocated approaching these two disorders as separate and distinct (e.g., Polirstok & Houghteling, 2006), over time the two conditions have been increasingly viewed as existing within a single classification. Today, autism, Asperger disorder, and other related disorders are commonly included on the continuum of autism-related disabilities known as the autism spectrum. The fifth edition of the *Diagnostic and Statistical Manual of Mental Disorders* (DSM–V; American Psychiatric Association, 2013) lists Asperger disorder as a component of the autism spectrum, no longer identifying it as a separate diagnosis.

It is important to note that this diagnostic reclassification is somewhat controversial among those who feel that Asperger disorder is in fact a separate entity. However, as is consistent with the most current conceptual understanding and usage, Asperger disorder, high-functioning autism, and related disorders are referred to throughout this book as *high-functioning autism disorders.*

POPULATION CHARACTERISTICS

Each child and adolescent with a high-functioning autism disorder is unique, with highly variable intellectual, cognitive, language, behavioral, adaptive behavior, and social abilities (Heflin & Alaimo, 2007; Thompson, 2007). However, learners with high-functioning autism disorders do tend to express their differences across the following main areas.

Social Skills

By definition, children and youth with high-functioning autism disorders demonstrate social excesses and deficits that frequently persist into adulthood. These youth are typically socially motivated and are interested in interacting with others. Their interactions, however, tend to be unskilled, and often these individuals struggle in carrying on age-expected social interactions, including participating in organized group activities and appropriate play. These deficits appear to be more a function of a lack of understanding of social customs and poor skill in participating in social interactions than a lack of interest in or fear of social contact. Learners with these disorders, for example, may appear ill-mannered or odd because they do not take turns in play and conversations or fail to understand a peer's social cues. These individuals, whether school-age or adult, are often easy targets for bullying and teasing (Simpson & Myles, 2011). Often by the time they are adults, these children and youth have become unwilling to engage socially with others, perhaps due to social rejection and other negative responses to their attempts to connect with others.

Some individuals in this group may be socially gregarious and socially active; others may withdraw from social interaction. Still others are often able to participate in routine social interactions (e.g., join and participate in an assigned cooperative group in a classroom) yet find it difficult to engage in extended contact and unstructured social interactions or form close friendships based on shared interests. Wherever they fall on the social continuum, they are typically perceived as socially stiff, emotionally blunted, self-centered, rigid, and lacking in social understanding. In spite of their frequent lack of social awareness, many of these individuals are aware of their social differences, and as a result may suffer from feelings of poor self-worth.

Emotional and Behavioral Characteristics

It is common for those with high-functioning autism disorders to experience emotional vulnerability and high levels of anxiety and stress, and to communicate these feelings through inappropriate or aberrant behaviors. A variety of stressors impact emotions and behaviors, including changes in routines and schedules, being unexpectedly thrust into unfamiliar social surroundings with unknown people, pressure to perform within a set time or within a performance standard, and feeling a loss of control or inability to predict what may happen (e.g., in unstructured or new situa-

tions). In other words, when persons with these disorders experience behavior problems it is most likely due to social ineptness, obsessive interests, high stress, or anxiety. Furthermore, these feelings and problems are likely to reduce their motivation for further social interaction and contact.

As these individuals get older, they are also likely to develop additional social and mental health problems, such as depression (Attwood, 2007; Barnhill, 2001; Tantam, 2000) and increased distress and anxiety in social situations (Cesaroni & Garber, 1991; Ghaziuddin, Weidmer-Mikhail, & Ghaziuddin, 1998). Other conditions that commonly co-occur with high-functioning autism disorders include obsessive-compulsive disorder, bipolar disorder, anxiety, affective disorders, attention-deficit/hyperactivity disorder, and psychosis (American Psychiatric Association, 2013; Bregman & Higdon, 2012; Volkmar & Klin, 2000). Such comorbid conditions may further complicate social performance.

Language and Communication Characteristics

Unlike children and youth with classic forms of autism, those with high-functioning autism disorders typically do not display clinically significant language delays (American Psychiatric Association, 2013; Thompson, 2007), and, in general, they acquire and use words and phrases within generally expected developmental norms. Their communication, however, may be described as "odd in its use" (Frith, 1991, p. 3). While there is some disagreement among professionals related to language delays and deficits (American Psychiatric Association, 2013; Mesibov, Shea, & Adams, 2001; Wetherby & Prizant, 2000), there is little argument that these children and youth manifest a variety of abnormal communication characteristics, particularly in their pragmatic, social, and conversational language skills (e.g., one-sided monologues). For example, a child may repeat the same phrase over and over; talk with exaggerated inflections or in a monotone; discuss at length a single topic that is of little interest to others; or have difficulty sustaining conversation unless it focuses on a particular, narrowly defined topic of their interest. The adult-like, pedantic speaking style of some children and adolescents may further lessen their appeal to their peers.

Nonverbal communication deficits such as standing closer to another person than is customarily accepted, making unusual gestures or movements while talking, intensely staring at another person for long periods, maintaining abnormal body posture, failing to make eye contact or displaying an inexpressive face, failing to use or interpret conventional gestures and facial expressions, and paraverbal deficits (abnormal voice quality, monotonic voice) further impact the social acceptance of these individuals.

While a child with a high-functioning autism disorder may develop language commensurate with his or her nondisabled peers, other language and communication challenges exist that further complicate both social and academic learning. For example, learners may have difficulty comprehending theoretical, conceptual, and abstract ideas; understanding and correctly using figures of speech such as metaphors, parables, and idioms; and grasping the meaning and intent of rhetorical and metaphorical questions (Shore, 2003). Because these conventions and language styles are commonly used by teachers and occur in school texts, these deficits may have a negative effect on students' academic success. Inappropriate behaviors, anxiety, or avoidance may also be responses in reaction to the lack of understanding and confusion in both academic and social situations.

Cognitive Characteristics

As previously noted, a defining characteristic of high-functioning autism disorders is average or above-average intellectual capacity (American Psychiatric Association, 2013; World Health Organization, 2007). Several researchers have reported that these individuals display an uneven cognitive profile on measures of intelligence and cognition, including the widely used Wechsler intelligence scales (Wechsler, 1989, 1991). For example, significantly higher scores on performance

items (and thus Performance IQ scores) when compared with verbal performance and Verbal IQ scores have been noted (Ehlers et al., 1997; Lincoln, Courchesne, Kilman, Elmasian, & Allen, 1988). More specifically, the individuals assessed obtained their lowest scores on the Comprehension subtest, which assesses understanding of social mores and interpersonal situations and is related to one's social judgment, common sense, and grasp of social conventionality.

Several theories have been proposed to explain the uneven cognitive performance. One theory suggests that individuals with high-functioning autism disorders have a theory of mind deficit (Baron-Cohen, Golan, Wheelwright, & Hill, 2004; Baron-Cohen et al., 1985). "Theory of mind" refers to an individual's ability to think about and use information related to one's own and others' intentions, beliefs, and mental states. A theory of mind deficit may also help explain the weaknesses in perspective taking and empathy characteristic of individuals with these disorders.

Academic and Learning Characteristics

While the vast majority of these learners have average intellectual abilities, they often experience difficulties in academic performance (Zager & Dreyfus, 2012). Specific difficulties include communication deficits, in combination with obsessive and narrowly defined interests; concrete, inflexible, and literal thinking styles; poor problem-solving ability; weak organizational skills; and difficulty in discriminating relevant from irrelevant information. As a result, some children and youth with these disorders are diagnosed with learning disabilities (Attwood, 2007; Frith, 1991; Siegel et al., 1996). These learners also have a tendency to resist academic subjects that don't align with their special interests, further impacting their academic success.

Students with high-functioning autism disorders may demonstrate notable capability to comprehend factual material (Church, Alisanski, & Amanullah, 2000), yet this strength does not always translate into high academic achievement. For example, Griswold, Barnhill, Myles, Hagiwara, and Simpson (2002) reported that academic achievement scores in their sample of youth diagnosed with Asperger disorder and high-functioning autism ranged from significantly below average to significantly above average. Relative strengths were found in oral expression and reading recognition; relative weaknesses were identified in listening comprehension and written language. Low mathematics scores were also found, especially in using math skills to solve application problems. Students who participated in the study also had significant difficulties in the areas of critical thinking and problem solving.

Finally, these learners also frequently have difficulty applying and generalizing previously learned knowledge and skills to new situations and problems. Thus, even when they have mastered specific subject matter such as math facts and principles, they frequently have difficulty using what they have learned to solve problems.

Sensory Characteristics

Kanner (1943) and Asperger (1944) both observed that children with autism and those with Asperger disorder were prone to unusual responses to sensory stimuli. These reactions have been validated by researchers (Dunn, 2008) as well as regularly confirmed by countless teachers and parents who watch, sometimes with anguish, as students struggle to deal with loud and unpredictable sounds, unanticipated touch from others, and so forth. Some children have an obsessive insistence on wearing a particular type of clothing (e.g., comfortable sweatpants), prefer certain foods or food textures, or engage in self-stimulatory responses such as repeatedly spinning objects, especially when they experience stress, fatigue, or sensory overload (Myles, Cook, Miller, Rinner, & Robbins, 2000). Such behavioral excesses impact both their ability and willingness to participate in planned school, family, and community activities.

Physical and Motor Skills

Wing (1981) observed that children with high-functioning autism have a tendency to have poor motor coordination and balance problems. These observations have been confirmed by others (Attwood, 2007; Dunn, 2008; Smith, 2000; Smith & Bryson, 1994). Thus, many children and adolescents with these disorders are clumsy and uncoordinated, making it difficult for them to participate successfully in games that call for good motor skills. These problems significantly affect their ability to interact in social situations and may contribute to poor self-esteem and lack of acceptance from others. Fine motor skill problems have implications for a variety of school activities, such as handwriting and art (Todd & Reid, 2007).

NEW SKILLS AND SKILL GROUPINGS

Existing Skillstreaming curricula have been used successfully with a variety of children and youth, including individuals with Asperger disorder and high-functioning autism (Lopata et al., 2006, 2008; Tse et al., 2007). Why, then, are new skills presented to guide work with learners with high-functioning autism? In brief, youth with these disorders respond best when complex social behaviors are separated into small amounts of information. For example, when teaching how to deal effectively with anxiety, a youth must first recognize anxiety, decide what has created this emotion, and then plan to deal with it. It is more effective for these youth, then, to learn three discrete skills: Recognizing Anxiety (Skill 34), Deciding What Causes Your Anxiety (Skill 35), and, finally, Dealing with Anxiety (Skill 36).

In addition, the skills included in this curriculum have been designed to relate directly to the needs of learners with high-functioning autism. Specifically, skills are organized according to the following six groups: Relationship Skills (Beginning and Advanced), Social Comprehension, Self-Regulation, Problem Solving, Understanding Emotions, and School-Related Skills. Table 1 lists the 80 skills in these categories; the rationale for teaching the skills in these groupings is next discussed.

Table 1: Skillstreaming Curriculum for Youth with High-Functioning Autism Disorders

Group I: Relationship Skills

Beginning Relationship Skills

1. Listening Without Interrupting
2. Greeting Others
3. Responding to a Greeting
4. Asking a Question About the Topic
5. Staying on Topic
6. Responding to Questions
7. Taking Turns
8. Complimenting Others
9. Helping Others
10. Encouraging Others
11. Cooperating with Others
12. Sharing
13. Asking a Favor

Advanced Relationship Skills

14. Starting a Conversation
15. Continuing a Conversation
16. When to Introduce a New Topic
17. Accepting a Topic Change
18. Ending a Conversation
19. Responding to Offers to Join In
20. Asking to Join In
21. Communicating Preferences
22. Accepting Another's Opinion

Group II: Social Comprehension

23. Reading Others
24. Reading the Environment
25. Using a Friendly Voice
26. Using a Respectful Voice
27. Giving Information Nonverbally
28. Attending to a Model
29. Respecting Another's Boundaries
30. Showing Interest in Others
31. Understanding Differences
32. Taking Another's Perspective

Group III: Self-Regulation

33. Regulating Your Attention
34. Recognizing Anxiety
35. Deciding What Causes Your Anxiety
36. Dealing with Anxiety
37. Checking Your Voice and Interests
38. No Means No
39. Using Self-Control
40. Dealing with Change
41. Dealing with Boredom
42. Responding to Authority
43. Checking Your Behavior
44. Affirming Yourself

Group IV: Problem Solving

45. Determining Private Information
46. Understanding Rules of Swearing
47. Understanding Rules of Touch
48. Planning for Stressful Situations
49. Defining a Problem
50. Considering Alternatives
51. Choosing an Alternative
52. When to Change Strategies
53. When a Rule Doesn't Work
54. Giving Feedback
55. Seeking Attention
56. Accepting Attention
57. Making a Complaint
58. When You Don't Understand

Group V: Understanding Emotions

59. Knowing Your Feelings
60. Feeling Different
61. Expressing Your Feelings
62. Calming Your Feelings
63. Showing Affection
64. Recognizing Another's Feelings
65. Showing Concern for Another

Relationship Skills

Relationships with both peers and adults are hampered by the social characteristics of high-functioning autism disorders. Interactions with others are often one-sided, with the learner's attempting to control the play or conversation. When a peer desires to change the topic or engage in another play activity, the learner often becomes distressed and may act out or withdraw. Social rules, when learned, are often applied universally. Lacking the social nuance of "tact," the learner may make comments that offend or irritate others without understanding that doing so creates embarrassment for the other person. Friendships are a protective factor and help build resiliency to deal effectively with life's stressors. However, while improvements in many areas have been found as youth with these disorders grow older, friendships are the area with the least improvement (Seltzer et al., 2003).

Social skills within this group, organized into beginning and advanced categories, focus on improving a range of prosocial behaviors. Beginning relationship skills include Listening Without Interrupting (Skill 1) and Sharing (Skill 12), whereas more advanced skills include Communicating Preferences (Skill 21) and Accepting Another's Opinion (Skill 22). Skills included are intended to provide learners with new behaviors in order to successfully participate in a variety of social activities and settings.

Social Comprehension

Social comprehension is defined by Weiss (2013) as "the complicated social responses and initiations that are part of navigating the social world. Individuals are required to understand social rules, engage in behaviors that are expected in given contexts, and interpret social nuances" (p. 36). Often, as a result of misinterpreting social cues and nonverbal messages, learners with high-functioning autism disorders have difficulty understanding and adapting to differences in people, situations, and settings. Lack of social comprehension leads to communication challenges for these learners, including the tendency to interpret simply what was stated versus considering the context and other variables (Bolick, 2001). In other words, these individuals interpret what was said rather than what was meant. This deficit may be due in part to their inability to understand nonverbal language or nonverbal social cues. These learners further find it challenging to focus on more than one thing at a time and as a result often miss salient nonverbal information (Moyes, 2001). For example, they typically find it difficult to attend to an event, activity, or object that a social partner is attending to and at the same time monitor the other's attention to the object (Jones & Carr, 2004). Two components are included in such "joint attention": following the gaze of another person to an object or activity (responding to joint attention) and using the direction of one's gaze to direct another's attention

(Mundy et al., 2007). Other social communication challenges noted by Bolick (2001) relate to lack of abilities in "reading between the lines" of an exchange, knowledge of unspoken rules, and expression of modesty and discretion.

As previously discussed, theory of mind refers to an individual's ability to infer the mental state of another person—the other's feelings, desires, beliefs, thoughts, and perceptions (Bolick, 2001; Weiss, 2013). Through theory of mind, we are able to make sense of the world around us to better understand various social situations and predict the behavior of others (Bellini, 2006; Ozonoff & Miller, 1995). Some consider deficits in theory of mind as defects in the drive for coherence, or the way in which pieces of information are shaped into coherent pictures (Baron-Cohen, 2001). These deficits contribute to the challenge in determining what is useful information versus what is not useful. Also referred to as "mindsight," this ability is often absent in youth with high-functioning autism disorders (Goleman, 2006). These youth often appear "mind-blind," or insensitive to what others are thinking or feeling (Baron-Cohen, 2001).

Addressing deficits in theory of mind involves teaching learners perspective taking, thus addressing what is perhaps the central social deficit of autism (Weiss, 2013). Without this skill, it is quite improbable that learners will express empathy toward others. Grizenko et al. (2000) found more lasting improvement from social skills instruction when social perspective taking was added. Specifically, students who are able to show empathy and understanding of others and their perspectives are less likely to act out aggressively toward others, are more accepted and sought after in social situations, are more able to participate in resolving interpersonal disputes, and tend to be more satisfied with themselves.

The purpose of this group of skills, then, is to teach "social thinking skills," such as understanding and reacting to others on the basis of their thoughts and perceptions. Skills within this section emphasize nonverbal (e.g., Skill 24, Reading the Environment) and paraverbal (e.g., Skill 25, Using a Friendly Voice) communication, as well as perspective taking (e.g., Skill 32, Taking Another's Perspective; Skill 30, Showing Interest in Others).

Self-Regulation

Learners with high-functioning autism disorders are often hypersensitive to sound, sight, taste, smell, and touch (Rosaler, 2004) and show strong preferences for certain foods, types of clothing, or textures. Many are also fearful that they may be exposed to unpleasant stimuli (Foley & Staples, 2003) and may therefore respond in a negative manner even without direct exposure. Myles and Southwick (1999) refer to this type of response as a "defensive panic attack," resulting from a lack of social understanding, high stress level, lack of environmental control, or perseverating on a certain interest. Such attacks may occur without obvious warning. Safran, Safran, and Ellis (2003) further note that problematic behaviors in need of self-monitoring include off-task questioning, lack of monitoring voice level, not attending to personal space, and frequent interrupting. Toward the goal of dealing with these and other issues, the skills in this grouping therefore focus on behaviors that teach learners to self-monitor and manage their own behaviors.

Skills to develop and improve self-regulation include Checking Your Voice and Interests (Skill 37), No Means No (Skill 38), and Dealing with Change (Skill 40). Other skills, such as Recognizing Anxiety (Skill 34) and Affirming Yourself (Skill 44), help mitigate internal emotional states that contribute to disregulation.

Problem Solving

Learners with high-functioning autism disorders tend to see issues and events as bound by rules such as "right or wrong." This characteristic poses stress and confusion when dealing with complex feelings such as embarrassment or sexual feelings. Such learners also tend to desire rules without exceptions, which creates challenges in problem solving through difficulties, holding onto the facts of a situation, and mentally testing possible solutions to the problem (Bolick, 2001). Furthermore, it is typical for these learners to have only one strategy to solve a problem. They may persist with this strategy, even though unsuccessful, which may result in a behavioral outburst (Myles & Simpson, 1998). As stated by Weiss (2013), "Children with [these disorders] often have difficulties with deciphering the ambiguity of social problems and evaluating options for a course of action. They may fail to see the range of options or respond impulsively" (p. 44).

Social problem solving skills permit learners to function in a variety of settings and circumstances and with different individuals (Garcia Winner, 2008). Examples of problem-solving skills include Determining Private Information (Skill 45), When a Rule Doesn't Work (Skill 53), and Making a Complaint (Skill 57).

Understanding Emotions

Many learners with high-functioning autism disorders deal with their feelings in inappropriate ways. Understanding the emotions of others, as well as their own, proves challenging, and expressions of feelings often are incongruent with their behavior. For example, a learner who is frustrated may have a meltdown and become aggressive toward property. Another learner who has positive feelings about another person may invade personal boundaries and appear aggressive. Just as these youth have difficulty recognizing and interpreting social cues, they are challenged in understanding and responding appropriately to the context (or "big picture") of an interaction or feeling. Learners need both motivation and opportunity to use these types of skills (Flavell, Miller, & Miller, 1993).

This group of skills focuses on the emotions that create stress for the individual learner and contribute to negative behaviors and interactions. Skills such as Knowing Your Feelings (Skill 59), Calming Your Feelings (Skill 62), and Feeling Different (Skill 60) help to mitigate this concern. Other skills in this group create a basis for some of the skills included in the Social Comprehen-

sion group, such as Recognizing Another's Feelings (Skill 64) and Showing Concern for Another (Skill 65).

School-Related Skills

As previously noted, learners with these disorders are often challenged by classroom and learning expectations. Executive functioning skills such as self-management, organization, and regulating one's attention are often lacking. Shonkoff and Bales (2011) refer to these skills as "air traffic control" in the brain. As these authors state, "Being able to focus, hold, and work with information in mind, filter distractions, and switch gears is like having an air traffic control system at a busy airport to manage the arrivals and departures of dozens of planes on multiple runways" (p. 1). The lack of such skills creates difficulties in a variety of school and classroom-related behaviors, such as regulating or shifting attention and identifying what to listen to or look for (Bolick, 2001), transitioning, changing routines, sensitivity to stimuli, organization (Batesko, 2007), revising plans as needed, and controlling impulses (Shonkoff et al., 2011).

Because these learners generally have strong skills in some academic areas, teachers and others in the school setting may not understand why their requests to make corrections on assignments, contribute appropriately to class discussions, or follow adult directions are not easily achieved. They may make the assumption that these learners "could do it if they wanted to." This is a faulty assumption, inasmuch as the skills that enable these learners to accomplish these goals are not within their repertoire.

Skills such as Organizing Materials (Skill 76), Dealing with Transitions (Skill 79), and Completing Assignments (Skill 73) are included for instruction within this skill group.

Skill Combinations and Context

Many learners experience negative reactions from others when challenged with complex social situations. Single-skill responses, even when performed correctly, prove inadequate. Suppose, for example, Keisha wants to have a conversation with a classmate and uses Starting a Conversation (Skill 14) effectively. However, when the classmate becomes bored with the discussion and changes the topic, she becomes angry and frustrated, walking away while remarking, "I didn't really want to talk with that stupid kid anyway! He knows nothing!" In another example, Jordan has successfully learned to communicate preferences (Skill 21) but remains socially isolated because he is unable to accept another's preference or opinion (Skill 22). Or in her desire to be accepted, Isabel frequently offers to help others (Skill 9), but often invades the other person's boundaries by touching them or standing too close (Skill 29).

Some useful skill combinations include the following:

▶ Listening Without Interrupting (Skill 1) and Responding to Questions (Skill 6)

▶ Starting a Conversation (Skill 14), Continuing a Conversation (Skill 15) and Ending a Conversation (Skill 18)

▶ Reading Others (Skill 23) and Showing Interest in Others (Skill 30)

▶ Understanding Differences (Skill 31) and Taking Another's Perspective (Skill 32)

▶ Recognizing Anxiety (Skill 34), Deciding What Causes Your Anxiety (Skill 35), and Dealing with Anxiety (Skill 36)

▶ Using Self-Control (Skill 39) and No Means No (Skill 38)

▶ Using Self-Control (Skill 39) and Dealing with Change (Skill 40)

▶ Defining a Problem (Skill 49), Considering Alternatives (Skill 50), and Choosing an Alternative (Skill 51)

▶ Defining a Problem (Skill 49) and Making a Complaint (Skill 57)

▶ Knowing Your Feelings (Skill 59) and Expressing Your Feelings (Skill 61)

▶ Recognizing Another's Feelings (Skill 64) and Showing Concern for Another (Skill 65)

▶ Using Self-Control (Skill 39) and Dealing with Another's Anger (Skill 67)

▶ Ignoring Distractions (Skill 69) and Completing Assignments (Skill 73)

▶ Staying on Topic (Skill 5) and Contributing to Discussions (Skill 70)

▶ Reading Others (Skill 23) and Checking Your Voice and Interests (Skill 37)

The context for skill use is also important. For example, the target of skill use (parent, teacher, peer, etc.) may not respond in a manner that helps the learner resolve the conflict or otherwise meet the learner's needs. At other times, the learner may use a skill proficiently but attempt it with a person not in a position to accept this skill (e.g., starting a conversation with an adult in a manner more appropriate with a peer). In still other cases, a learner may correctly use a skill but choose a poor time or misperceive the appropriateness of the social context. Skill instruction must therefore involve not only individual skill competency but also coaching to perform the skill (or skill combination) at the right time, in the right place, and with the right persons.

SKILLSTREAMING PROGRAM ARRANGEMENTS

Because the needs and abilities of each child and youth with a high-functioning autism disorder are unique, it is impossible to present a standard set of required training supports or to specify hard-and-fast guidelines for the duration or intensity of instruction and generalization efforts. However, the following discussion outlines some important considerations for those implementing Skillstreaming with these learners. Readers may also wish to consult the other Skillstreaming program guides (McGinnis 2012a, 2012b, 2012c) for additional detail, as is appropriate for their learners' age and developmental level.

Instructional Settings and Team

Skillstreaming instruction may take place in either the school or clinic setting. Typically, in a school setting, the Skillstreaming team consists of a person in a school leadership role, one or two support staff members (e.g., school psychologist, school counselor, paraprofessional), a classroom teacher, a special educator (if the learner receives special education services), and parent(s). If the learner receives special education services, the intervention team may include members of the learner's Individual Education Program (IEP) team. Many youth with high-functioning autism disorders attend treatment clinics outside the school setting. Health centers and autism specialty clinics often provide small-group Skillstreaming instruction in the form of "friendship groups," with the goal of fostering peer interaction and friendships among these learners. In some cases, learners' behavior, attention span, and learning needs indicate that instruction is initially best in a clinic setting. In other cases, if a learner with a high-functioning autism disorder is one of few in the school or has particular needs (e.g., requires low level of distraction or activity), a clinic setting may the only option. In a clinic setting, a member of the treatment team (e.g., therapist), parent, and a school representative (e.g., support staff member) usually compose the team. In either setting, individuals with high-functioning autism disorders can serve as self-advocates and can be encouraged to participate to the greatest extent possible.

In general, it is the responsibility of the intervention team to do the following:

1. Gather and review Skillstreaming assessment data

2. Determine the learner's social goals (if not selected by the IEP team)

3. Suggest the specific social skills, or sequence of skills, to meet the learner's social goal

4. Monitor the learner's progress in skill learning and skill use

5. Suggest opportunities for the generalization of skills

The Skillstreaming leader plays a central role in the success of intervention efforts. Teachers, counselors, and psychologists in the schools; youth care workers in treatment facilities; and social workers and therapists in mental health and other community agencies have been successful Skillstreaming group leaders. Typically, with this population, the primary group leader will be a school- or clinic-based professional—that is, an individual who spends the majority of time in the school or clinic. This is necessary to observe and develop a relationship with learners and to communicate with others regarding the learners' skill performance. Often the primary group leader is a special education teacher, school psychologist, therapist, or case manager.

The individuals working directly with the learners, as well as others who have regular contact with them, should receive training as needed to provide support within the scope of their roles. The intensity and comprehensiveness of the training will depend more on the function or type of involvement they have in Skillstreaming, rather than on their school or clinic role.

Program Implementation

As noted previously, Skillstreaming instruction for these learners will be highly variable due to the wide range of individual needs and depending on the context of existing therapeutic and educational plans. However, some general steps in implementing a program are as follows:

1. Establish and prepare the instructional team

2. Select participants

3. Assess participant skill need

4. Determine logistics: setting, time factors, and materials

5. Conduct individual orientation sessions

6. Determine group and individual supports

7. Conduct Skillstreaming sessions

8. Provide ongoing learner support

9. Assess skill acquisition and program effectiveness

It is important to note that this sequence is not invariable and that steps are not necessarily discrete. For example, the need for learner support and assessment of skill acquisition and program effectiveness are ongoing.

Establish and Prepare the Instructional Team

The first step is to establish and then prepare the individuals who will be involved in Skillstreaming instruction. It is presumed that each learner will have a team composed of those who interact with him or her on a regular basis: classroom teacher(s), support staff, families, Skillstreaming group leader, and peers. Team composition will vary based on the setting and learners' individual needs; there may be overlap with existing IEP or clinical teams that provide service.

Select Participants

If only a small number of youth with high-functioning autism disorders (i.e., up to five) attend a school or reside on a unit, all may be included in the same Skillstreaming group, as many will have similar skill needs. If a larger number (i.e., more than five) attend, skill groups may be planned based on common, priority learner skill needs. The Skill Grouping Chart, listing all 80 skills and included in the appendix, is helpful for this purpose. One benefit of this chart is providing a visual for the Skillstreaming leader to select skills for instruction needed by the majority of group members.

The participation of peers from the general population will be essential to the success of Skillstreaming instruction for this group. Across several settings, peers have been successfully used in modeling and prompting social skills (Chan et al., 2009; Matson, Matson & Rivet, 2007; Owen-DeSchryver, Carr, Cale, & Blakeley-Smith, 2008). In particular, they have been found to accelerate the learning of prosocial behaviors by youth with

high-functioning autism disorders (Simpson et al., 2012; Thiemann & Kamps, 2008).

Peer strategies include teaching peers to initiate interactions, respond to social overtures, and sustain social interactions. In addition to increasing learners' prosocial skills, use of such strategies has been found to increase peer acceptance and development of helpful peer relationships (National Autism Center, 2009). In fact, peer involvement may be the single most significant factor in generalizing skill use and long-term learner outcomes (Thiemann & Kamps, 2008).

It is best if the peers selected for Skillstreaming groups are those the learners like and want to emulate and are included in the learners' same classroom, unit, or social group. In addition, they should display positive social skills; be supportive of individual differences and the needs of learners with high-functioning autism disorders; be able to initiate, respond, and support social interactions with peers with disabilities; and be willing to participate in training and direction from the Skillstreaming team. A small number of peers may initially be recruited to participate, with additional peers included at a later time or to substitute for some or all of those initially selected. However, the more who are trained as supportive peers, the more opportunities learners will have to receive positive and encouraging feedback for skill use.

Assess Participant Skill Need

Prior to instruction, the specific skill needs of the learners must be identified. A variety of tools are helpful in pinpointing these needs for instruction, including direct observations and skill checklists. Checklists specific to Skillstreaming are included in Appendix A. The Teacher/Staff Checklist is completed by a teacher or another person in the school or clinic environment who has ongoing contact with the learner in multiple situations or settings. The Parent Checklist is completed by one or more parents or guardians. With both checklists, the rater (e.g., parent, teacher) is asked to gauge the frequency of the learner's use of each of the 80 Skillstreaming skills according to a five-point scale from "almost always" to "almost never." These checklists also provide an opportunity for raters to identify situations in which skill use is particularly problematic, information that will be useful for later modeling scenarios. The numerical value assigned to each skill prioritizes the most important skills for the learner. The Learner Checklist assesses participants' perceptions of their own skill use by asking how often they use the skill. The five-point rating scale is the same as that used in the other checklists. Ratings for each learner may be summarized on the optional Skill Checklist Summary. This summary form reveals strengths, needs, and rater discrepancies.

Determine Logistics: Setting, Time Factors, and Materials

Skillstreaming leaders, along with other members of intervention teams, will next need to decide on the logistics necessary for group instruction. Where will group instruction occur and when? What is an appropriate time frame for instruction? What materials are necessary? These considerations include desirable settings in the school, when to implement Skillstreaming in a clinic setting, frequency of sessions, when to introduce new skills, program duration, and options for support materials.

Conduct Individual Orientation Sessions

Many youth with high-functioning autism disorders will likely be reluctant—and perhaps even resistant—to learning new social behaviors or participating in a group setting to do so. Therefore, it is productive to meet individually with group members to explain why they need to learn alternative skills, describe the purpose of the group, and discuss the activities in which they will participate.

Determine Group and Individual Supports

Structuring both group and individual learning supports is necessary to maximize the effectiveness of instruction. These supports, important to include in not just Skillstreaming but all learning opportunities for these youth, may include environmental structure (e.g., clear expectations and routines); group supports (e.g., journaling, visual cues, supportive peer networks); and individual supports (e.g., visual schedules, social narratives, reinforcement, consequence maps, self-management strategies, priming, video modeling). The specifics of such efforts are highly dependent on individual learner needs and beyond the scope of this book; each learner's intervention team will be instrumental in defining necessary supports.

Conduct Skillstreaming Sessions

Core Skillstreaming learning procedures and specific steps in conducting Skillstreaming sessions are detailed in subsequent sections of this introduction. Two sample Skillstreaming sessions, one for an elementary group and one for an adolescent group, are provided in Appendix B to illustrate these learning procedures and steps. As shown in these sessions, a co-leader is a desirable (if not essential) part of instruction.

Provide Ongoing Learner Support

During Skillstreaming instruction, learners receive a great deal of support, encouragement, and reward for their efforts. However, between sessions or after instruction ends, many learners receive far less support for skill use. As a result, the social skills learned in the group often fail over time, with new people, and in varied situations and settings. Therefore, continued adult support at a level individualized for each learner will be critical to continued use of learned skills.

Assess Skill Acquisition and Program Effectiveness

Ongoing assessment of both learners' skill acquisition and program effectiveness is a requirement for Skillstreaming program success. (Discussion of assessment concerns appears at the end of this introduction.)

CORE SKILLSTREAMING LEARNING PROCEDURES

The individual Skillstreaming learning procedures of modeling, role-playing, feedback, and generalization are strongly supported by research and have been successfully employed when teaching prosocial behaviors to both children and older youth with high-functioning autism disorders (Gerhardt & Crimmins, 2013; Simpson et al., 2012; Stichter et al., 2012). Briefly, these procedures may be described as follows.

Modeling

Modeling is defined as learning by imitation. Learning from modeling typically involves an individual's acquiring the skill to perform a new behavior or strengthen an existing behavior by watching someone perform the response. There is strong evidence that individuals with Asperger disorder prefer and learn best when shown such visual stimuli (Ganz, 2007). Therefore, a visual demonstration of a skill is a necessary tool for these learners.

Research on modeling has successfully identified a number of modeling enhancers, or circumstances that increase the degree to which learning by imitation occurs. These modeling enhancers are characteristics of the model, the modeling display, or the observer (the learner). Such variables affect learning, as does illustrating a coping model.

Role-playing

Role-playing, the "practice" component of Skillstreaming, involves having learners enact the skill steps under the supervision of group leaders. As Mann (1956) noted, role-playing is helpful when an individual is asked to demonstrate behaviors that are not typical or that do not already exist in the person's existing repertoire. Learning is improved when the learner has the opportunity and is encouraged to rehearse or role-play the behaviors and is rewarded for doing so. The use of role-playing to help a person change behavior or attitudes has been proven useful over many years. However, as for modeling, behavior or attitude change through role-playing will occur and be more lasting only if certain conditions are met. Specific role-play enhancers include choice on the part of the group member regarding whether to take part in the role-play; public commitment to the behavior; improvisation in enacting the role-played behaviors; talking oneself through the skill (verbal mediation); and reward, approval, or reinforcement for performing the behaviors.

Feedback

Feedback is defined as providing the learner with information on how well he has done during role-playing. It may take such forms as constructive suggestions for improvement, reteaching, material rewards, coaching, and social reinforcement such as praise and approval. Social reinforcement has been shown to be an especially potent influence on behavior change. In addition, positive feedback from peers has been shown to increase peer acceptance as well as appropriate behavior (Jones, Young, & Friman, 2000; Moroz & Jones, 2002; Skinner, Cashwell, & Skinner, 2000). In addition, many learners with high-functioning autism disorders would welcome positive comments from peers instead of the many negative ones they typically receive.

Generalization

The main interest of any intervention program and where most programs fail is not the performance of the learner during instruction but, instead, to what degree the learner uses newly learned skills in natural contexts and experiences to improve his or her quality of life. The goal of Skillstreaming is successful social functioning in school, at home, and in the community.

In brief, generalization training assists the learner in identifying where, when, and with whom skill use is desired or necessary. Although a detailed discussion of the principles involved in this complex topic cannot be provided here, program planners may find the suggestions listed in Table 2 helpful in planning for and evaluating the success of skill generalization.

Table 2: Methods for Enhancing Generalization in Skillstreaming Instruction

Before Instruction

1. Group members include peers with whom the learners interact outside of the group.

2. One instructor has ongoing, regular contact with the learners.

3. Additional supports are implemented to reduce the likelihood of competing behaviors hampering learning and generalization.

During Instruction

4. Learners know the specific behavioral skill steps and can perform them well.

5. Attempts made to create similarities between the instructional and real-life situations and settings.

6. Numerous trials of correct skill performance provided.

7. Variability of situations (range of settings, various people, variety of reasons for skill use, various cues) provided.

8. When possible, instruction occurs in the real-life environment where the skill is to be used.

9. Some flexibility allowed in order to meet individual learner needs and settings.

10. Positive reinforcement provided often, then gradually reduced as the learners gain proficiency.

11. Prompts (e.g., cue cards) are gradually faded as the learner gains skill proficiency.

12. The learners are taught self-reinforcement for skill performance (e.g., positive self-talk).

After Instruction

13. Homework assignments provided after learners competently perform role-plays.

14. Skill use prompted or coached when daily situations suggest skill use, then gradually faded.

15. Skill use continues to be reinforced with gradual thinning and delaying of reinforcement.

16. Instruction in self-mediated generalization (e.g., self-recording, self-reinforcement) provided as appropriate to learner need.

17. When needed, booster sessions (e.g., group review, individual coaching) are provided for skills not frequently used.

18. Natural opportunities for skill use planned and implemented.

STEPS IN THE SKILLSTREAMING SESSION

Carrying out the core Skillstreaming teaching procedures—modeling, role-playing, performance feedback, and generalization—involves leading the group through a specific nine-step procedure. These steps are summarized in Table 3 and described in the following discussion.

Step 1: Define the Skill

The Skillstreaming leader presents a skill poster, skill card, or both, on which the name of the skill and the skill steps are listed, then leads the group in a discussion of the skill to be taught during the remainder of the session. The goal of this discussion is to help learners understand the meaning of the skill, its corresponding skill steps, when, where, and with whom the skill could be used, and the potential positive consequence that will result from skill use. This process can typically be achieved in just a few minutes; a long lecture is not required. The following dialogue shows a group leader briefly defining Skill 45, Determining Private Information.

> **Leader:** Good morning. I'm so glad you are here today because we are going to work on another very important skill. It's called Determining Private Information. Can anyone tell me what private information is?
>
> **Josie:** Is it something not to tell?

Step 1: Define the skill

1. Select skills relevant to the needs of the learners.

2. Discuss each skill step and any other relevant information pertaining to each step.

3. Use skill cards and/or a poster or white board or easel pad on which the skill steps are written so all group members may see the skill and skill steps.

Step 2: Model the skill

1. Use at least two examples for each skill demonstration.

2. Select situations relevant to the learner's real-life needs.

3. Use clear, brief modeling displays that demonstrate all the behavioral steps of the skill in the correct sequence.

4. Use modeling displays that depict only one skill (or skill sequence) at a time. (All extraneous content should be eliminated.)

5. Show the use of a coping model.

6. Have the model "think aloud" steps that ordinarily would be thought silently.

7. Depict only positive outcomes.

8. Reinforce the model who has used the skill correctly by using praise or encouraging self-reward.

9. Use modeling supports (e.g., simplify the information as needed, point out the skill steps as they are modeled, use supportive peers as model).

10. Follow the modeling with supports (e.g., draw attention to nonverbals and to reinforcement received by the model).

Step 3: Establish learner skill need

1. Elicit from learners specific situations in which the skill could be used or is needed.

2. List the names of the group members. The leader (or co-leader) may then list the situations identified by each learner and record the theme of the role-play.

Step 4: Select the first role-player

1. Select as the main actor a student who describes a situation in his or her own life in which skill use is needed or will be helpful.

2. Provide encouragement and reinforcement for the learner's willingness to participate as the main actor.

Step 5: Set up the role-play

1. Have the main actor choose a coactor who most reminds him or her of the other person involved in the problem.

2. Ask the main actor to provide relevant information surrounding the real event (i.e., describe the physical setting and events preceding the problem).

3. Use props when appropriate.

4. Review skill steps and direct the main actor to look at the skill card or the skill steps on display.

5. Assign the other group participants to watch for specific skill steps.

Step 6: Conduct the role-play

1. Instruct the main actor to "think out loud."

2. As needed, assist the main actor (e.g., point to each behavioral step as the role-play is carried out; have the co-leader, if included, sit among the group members, directing attention to the role-play).

3. As needed, use supports (e.g., carefully guide the selection of the coactor, coach the learner through the skill steps, make sure the environment is encouraging and pleasant, allow learners to show their uniqueness).

Step 7: Provide feedback

1. Seek feedback from the co-actor, observers, leader(s), and main actor in turn.

2. Provide reinforcement for successful role-plays at the earliest appropriate opportunity.

3. Provide reinforcement to the coactor for being helpful and cooperative, and praise the coactor's use of a prosocial skill.

4. Praise particular aspects of performance (e.g., "You stood an arm's length away from the person. Good for you!").

5. Provide reinforcement in an amount consistent with the quality of the role-play.

Step 8: Select the next role-player

Ask, "Who would like to go next?"

Step 9: Assign skill homework

1. Assign homework to the main actors who have successfully role-played the skill.

2. Provide the main actors with the appropriate Homework Report.

3. Discuss with each main actor when, where, and with whom he or she will use the skill in real life.

4. Discuss and arrange for needed supports, noting these on the reports.

Leader: Yes, it's information you shouldn't just tell anyone. Anyone else?

Donovan: Maybe you should never, ever talk about it.

Leader: Yes, you shouldn't talk about it with whom?

Max: Um. Maybe anybody.

Leader: Thanks for participating, Max. Private information is something that is personal to you or someone else. It's not public information, to be shared with just anyone. But if it's related to your safety or someone else's, you could tell a trusted adult, like a parent or a teacher. Who would you tell if the information could hurt you or someone else?

Lucy: I'd tell my mom.

Leader: Yes, she would be a good person to tell. What if the information isn't a safety concern, but just something people don't have a right to know? One example would be how much money your parents make. Is this anyone else's information to know?

(The group shake their heads "no.")

Leader: Good. When we learn this skill, we'll be able to decide what things are private and shouldn't be shared with others.

Step 2: Model the Skill

Before the session, leaders should plan their modeling displays. Displays that relate to the group's real-life concerns and needs will always be most effective as long as these displays incorporate the following guidelines:

1. Use at least two examples for each skill demonstration. If a skill is used in more than one group session, develop two new modeling displays.

2. Select situations relevant to learners' real-life circumstances.

3. The model (i.e., the person enacting the behavioral steps of the skill) should be portrayed as an individual reasonably similar to the group members in age, socioeconomic background, verbal ability, and other characteristics.

4. A coping model should be portrayed with skills that typically elicit strong emotion.

5. The model should "think aloud" what would normally be thought to oneself as the modeling display unfolds.

6. Modeling displays should depict positive outcomes. In addition, the model who is using the skill well should always be reinforced.

7. Modeling displays should depict all of the behavioral steps of the skill in the correct sequence without extraneous or distracting content.

8. Modeling displays should depict only one skill at a time.

Group members are asked to watch and listen closely as the modeling unfolds. Particular care should be given to helping learners identify the behavioral steps as they are being modeled. The leader can do this by pointing to the steps in the course of the modeling. As the model follows the behavioral steps, he or she "thinks out loud" what would normally be thought silently. At the conclusion of each modeling vignette, leaders ask "Did I follow the first step?" and "How do you know I did this?" The model may also provide self-reinforcement, such as "Yes, I followed all of the skill steps! I think I did a good job using this skill!"

Learners with high-functioning autism disorders may find focusing on more than one element of a modeling display or attending to relevant details difficult. If so, modeling supports are necessary for these learners. These supports include simplifying the information, pointing out specific key behaviors that need to be learned, using supportive peers as models, drawing attention to nonverbals (e.g., facial expressions, tone of voice), and drawing attention to potential reinforcement.

Step 3: Establish Learner Skill Need

Before group members begin role-playing, it is important to identify each learner's current and future need for the skill. Reenactment of a past problem or circumstance is less relevant unless the learner predicts that such circumstances are likely to reoccur in the future. Current learner needs will likely have been established earlier as part of the selection and grouping process through use of the Skillstreaming Checklists. Nonetheless, an open discussion within the group is needed to establish realistic and meaningful role-plays. If a learner is unable to identify a situation in which the skill could be used, information from the parent and teacher Skillstreaming checklists may help provide prompts. For example, "Many students have challenges staying on topic in a conversation with a friend. Is this a time when the skill of Staying on Topic (Skill 5) could be used?"

Each group member in turn is asked to describe briefly where, when, and with whom he or she would find it useful to use the skill just modeled. To make effective use of this information, it is often valuable to list the names of the group members on a whiteboard or easel pad at the front of the room and to record next to each name the theme of the role-play and the name or role of the person with whom the skill will be used.

Step 4: Select the First Role-Player

All members of the Skillstreaming group will be expected to role-play each skill taught, and therefore it is not of great concern who does so first. Typically, group leaders ask for volunteers to begin the role-play series. If there are group members who appear to be reluctant to role-play a particular skill on a particular day, it is helpful not to ask them to role-play first or second. Observing other learners do so first can be reassuring and may help ease their way into the activity. For a few learners, reluctance may turn into resistance and refusal. In such cases, coaching the learner through skill performance on a one-to-one basis (priming) prior to role-playing in the group may be helpful.

Step 5: Set Up the Role-Play

Following the selection of the role-player, he or she is designated as the main actor. The main actor chooses a second person (the coactor) to play the role of the other person (e.g., teacher, peer, parent) with whom he or she will use the skill in real life. The main actor should be encouraged to select as the coactor someone who resembles the significant other in as many ways as possible—in other words, someone who most reminds the main actor of the actual person.

The group leader then elicits from the main actor any additional information needed to set the stage for the role-play. In order to make role-playing as realistic as possible, the leader should obtain a description of the physical setting, the events immediately preceding the situation, and the mood or manner the coactor should portray, along with any other information that would enhance realism. Initially, providing such information may be challenging for the learner, as he or she may not be used to attending to these characteristics. The group leader may need to provide more concrete prompting, such as "Does the person's face look more like this (angry), or this (neutral)?" It may be helpful to some learners to plan their description of the role-play setting and target person prior to the group session. Props may be used if available and appropriate.

Role-play supports may include coaching from either the Skillstreaming leader or co-leader, in the form of verbally guiding the learner through performing the behavioral steps to the skill as the role-play unfolds. Coaching behaviors should be individualized to fit the needs and preferences of each learner. For example, some learners prefer or learn best when a coach uses a "physical prompting" approach that walks the learner through the required actions. In contrast, a learner who is hypersensitive to touch or grimaces when another person comes into close proximity would respond best to a coaching approach relying on no or minimal physical contact. In this case, for example, placing tape on the floor to mark where the student should stand when role-playing would be helpful. Other learners may be more receptive to coaching from a supportive peer. Still others may have certain sensitivities (e.g., noise level; difficulty performing two actions simultaneously, such as "looking at someone while talking") that must be taken into consideration.

The leader should also be very active in making sure the main actor (and the coactor, as appropriate) does not deviate from the skill steps. Instead, the leader should intervene as necessary with verbal or physical reminders (e.g., "The next step is to…" or pointing to the written step on a skill poster or skill card).

Step 6: Conduct the Role-Play

At this point the group leader reminds the learners of their roles and responsibilities:

▶ Main actor: Follow the behavioral steps and "think aloud" what would normally be thought silently.

▶ Coactor: Stay in the role of the other person and be helpful to the main actor.

▶ Other learners: Watch carefully for the enactment of the behavioral steps.

It is useful to assign each observer a specific behavioral step, have observers watch for the display of the skill step, and then report on the performance of the step during the feedback session that follows. Observers will also need to be coached regarding the kinds of cues to observe (e.g., posture, words chosen, tone of voice, facial expression). It is helpful to ask the observers to attend to specific cues that they themselves have been working to improve.

Then the role-players are instructed to begin. It is the leader's responsibility to provide the main actor with any help or coaching needed to keep the role-play going according to the behavioral steps. Learners who "break role" to offer other information should be urged to get back into the role and explain later. If the role-play is clearly going astray from the behavioral steps, the scene can be stopped, needed instruction provided, and the role-play resumed. If both the group leader and a co-leader are present, one should be positioned near the skill poster, if one is used, and point to each of the behavioral steps as they are enacted. Doing so will help the main actor, as well as the observers and coactor, follow each of the steps in sequence.

Role-playing should be continued until all group members have had an opportunity to participate in the role of the main actor. Sometimes this will require several sessions for a given skill.

Each session, however, should begin with two modeling vignettes for the selected skill, even if the skill is not new to the group. It is important to note that, although the framework (behavioral steps) of each role-play remains the same, the content can and should change from role-play to role-play. Each learner should display a level of proficiency in performing the skill as the main actor (e.g., follow all the behavioral steps in sequence; understand the purpose of the skill and when, where, and with whom the skill can be used; display acceptable nonverbal behaviors throughout the role-play) before being asked to complete a homework report.

Other strategies may be used to increase the effectiveness of the role-plays. For example, role reversal is often useful. If the main actor has a difficult time perceiving the coactor's point of view, having the two exchange roles and resume the role-play can be helpful. On occasion, the group leader can also assume the coactor role in an effort to give learners the opportunity to handle types of reactions not otherwise role-played during the session. For example, it may be important to have a difficult adult role realistically portrayed or to help less verbal or more hesitant students. The leader, serving as coactor, may also be indicated with particular skills such as Understanding Another's Intentions (Skill 66) or Dealing with Another's Anger (Skill 67), which otherwise would require the group member to engage in inappropriate or attention-getting behaviors as the coactor. Finally, in some circumstances it is also helpful for a supportive peer to play the role of the coactor, particularly if the supportive peer is a part of the same classroom or unit as the main actor.

In many cases the coactor is also role-playing a skill. For example, when the main actor attempts Greeting Others (Skill 2), the coactor in turn should greet the main actor (Responding to a Greeting, Skill 3). And when the main actor uses the skill When to Introduce a New Topic (Skill 16), the coactor will use the skill of Accepting a Topic Change (Skill 17). If there is not a group participant who can effectively perform a companion skill in response to the main actor, a supportive peer or group leader should initially serve in this role.

Step 7: Provide Feedback

Feedback follows each role-play. The purpose of the feedback is to let the main actor know how well he or she followed the behavioral steps, evaluate the impact of the role-play on the coactor, and give the main actor encouragement to try the behavior in real life. For this population of learners, it is particularly important that feedback also be provided regarding the main actor's use of nonverbal behaviors.

Feedback is presented in the following order: The coactor is asked to react first. Asking questions such as "How did you feel when she said that to you?" and "What were the facial expressions and manner that showed you she was friendly?" may be needed to prompt the coactor's feedback. The coactor should be thanked for being helpful to the main actor and also praised for positive behavior displayed during the role-play, including the specific skills he or she may have used.

Next, each observer in turn comments on whether or not the skill step he or she was assigned to watch for was followed and on other relevant aspects of the role-play. When asking for this feedback, it is useful to ask questions such as "Did he follow the first step?" and "How do you know he did this?" If the first step is to think about the situation, many group members will likely explain that they heard the main actor talk about his or her thinking (think aloud).

Then the group leaders comment in particular on how well the behavioral steps were followed and provide social reinforcement (praise, approval, encouragement) for close following of the skill steps and other aspects of the role-play as appropriate (e.g., nonverbal behaviors, voice tone).

After listening to the feedback from the coactor, observers, and group leaders, the main actor is asked to make comments regarding the role-play and, if appropriate, to respond to the comments of others. In this way, the main actor can learn to evaluate the effectiveness of his or her skill performance in light of others' viewpoints.

Leaders should provide enough role-playing for each group member to have sufficient opportunity to be reinforced. The leader should not provide reinforcement when the role-play departs significantly from the behavioral steps (except for "trying"). However, reinforcement may be provided for an individual learner's improvement over previous performances.

In all aspects of feedback, group leaders must maintain the behavioral focus of Skillstreaming. Leader comments must point to the presence or absence of specific, concrete behaviors and not take the form of general evaluative comments or generalizations. Feedback may be positive or take the form of suggestions for improvement. Positive feedback should always be given first; otherwise the student may be concentrating on the suggestion or what the learner may feel is a negative comment and not hear other feedback. Group leaders will need to model constructive comments before allowing group members to give this type of feedback. Teaching the skill of Giving Feedback (Skill 54) will also help the group learn how to provide helpful feedback.

Whenever possible, learners failing to follow the behavioral steps in the role-play should be given the opportunity to repeat the same behavioral steps after receiving constructive comments. At times, as a further feedback procedure, the role-play may be videorecorded. Doing so gives the learners the opportunity to observe themselves, enabling them to reflect on their own verbal and nonverbal behaviors in a private setting with the Skillstreaming leader.

Because a primary goal of Skillstreaming is skill flexibility, role-play enactment that departs somewhat from the behavioral steps may not be "wrong." That is, a different approach to the skill may actually work in some situations. Group leaders should stress that they are trying to teach

effective alternatives and that learning the behavioral steps as presented will increase positive outcomes.

Step 8: Select the Next Role-Player

The next group member is selected to serve as main actor, and the sequence just described is repeated until all members of the group are reliably demonstrating proficiency in using the skill in the group setting.

Step 9: Assign Skill Homework

Skill homework constitutes the generalization component of Skillstreaming and is key to facilitating skill use outside the training situation (Frankel et al., 2010). Following each successful role-play, learners are instructed to try in their own real-life settings the behaviors practiced during the session. It is most useful to begin with relatively simple homework assignments using situations that occur in the training setting. Doing so will allow for providing the support needed (e.g., coaching) to assure this practice is successful. As mastery is achieved, more complex assignments can be given (e.g., using the skill in the home or community setting). This sequence provides the leader and others who have been trained in Skillstreaming with the opportunity to reinforce each approximation toward proficiency. The learner should not be expected to perform the skill perfectly when first using it in real-life contexts. Reinforcement should be given as the learner's performance becomes closer to the ideal. Successful experiences when beginning to use the skill in the real world and rewards received for doing so are critical in encouraging future attempts to use the skill.

Homework assignments begin with the leader and learner together deciding when, how, and with whom the learner will use the skill and progress to the stage where the student independently records the skills practiced. One of three levels of homework can be assigned. It is best to begin with Homework Report 1 for each skill and gradually progress to more independent levels, providing help for those who may have difficulty with reading, writing, or comprehension as needed.

Homework Report 1

When using Homework Report 1, the learner thinks of a situation (either at home, at school, or with peers) in which he or she feels the need to practice the skill. For some learners, especially initially, the group leader may need to suggest situations and allow the student to choose one. It is especially useful if the selected situation is one the learner has role-played, as having prior practice will likely increase the learner's comfort level in trying the skill. As shown on the sample in Figure 1, the learner or leader lists the learner's name and the date the assignment is made. Together, the leader and learner decide on and enter the name of the person with whom the skill will be tried and the time the learner will make the attempt (e.g., during recess, in a specific class, at home). The leader may decide independently the supports that are needed to facilitate a successful practice attempt or may make this decision jointly with the learner. The support to be provided is marked in the second section of the report. Typically, both coaching and practice with a supportive peer are the supports most often used and are therefore listed here along with space to identify the name of the coach or peer. Other supports may also be noted. It is important for this section to be completed prior to the practice opportunity, lowering anxiety for the learner and assisting the leader in planning additional homework assignments and reporting learner progress.

After skill use, the learner writes what happened, then evaluates skill use by circling a number corresponding to one of evaluative comments on Homework Report 1. In many cases, it is initially helpful for the learner and leader to discuss the reason for this evaluation. The learner then writes or dictates the explanation on the report. It is important to convey to learners that this evaluation pertains to how well they performed the

skill steps, rather than how well the skill actually worked.

Group leaders may also use the blank Homework Report 1 form in Appendix A. Having the learner list the skill steps on the blank form can be a good way to enhance skill learning, provided that handwriting is not a struggle.

Homework Report 2

The learner who has nearly achieved mastery of a given skill (i.e., who knows the steps well and shows success with the assignments on the first level of homework) is ready to attempt self-recording, or monitoring skill practice more independently. Following a Skillstreaming session, the learner is given a Homework Report 2 (see sample in Figure 2). Then, throughout the course of the day or week, the learner lists the times of skill practice and completes the self-evaluation portion of the homework report according to the same criteria used in earlier homework assignments. It is important to note that supports (e.g., coaching, prompting) may continue to be necessary at this level. Therefore, the section at the end of this report lists the supports provided during homework and should be completed by either the learner or leader. Again, this record provides data to assist with monitoring progress, as well as provides reinforcement. A blank version of this form is provided in Appendix A.

Homework Report 3

Following mastery of each of the skills independently, it's time to put them together for a more complex social interaction. Homework Report 3, therefore, provides for practice of a sequence of skills. The learner's name and date of plan are noted on the form. Then the situation in which the skill sequence is needed is described and written. The most appropriate skills needed for the situation are then defined, with the steps to each skill listed. As in the other levels of homework, supports necessary to facilitate success of the practice are

Skill 30: Showing Interest in Others

Name___**Sammi**_____Date___**11/18**_____

SKILL STEPS

1. Look at the person or group.

2. Describe what the person or the group is doing.

3. Decide what to do next.

FILL IN NOW

With whom will I try this? **Kids in my class**_____

When? **Recess**_____

_____

SUPPORTS

✓ Coaching with *(name)* __**Ms. Crawford**_____

☐ With supportive peer *(name)* _____

✓ Other *(specify)*___**Choices for Step 3 listed on cue card**_____

☐ None

FILL IN AFTER YOU PRACTICE THE SKILL

What happened? __**I watched. I got closer. I said hello.**_____
They asked if I wanted to play. I said yes._____

How did I do? *(circle the number)*   4   3   ②   1
               Really good!   Pretty good.   So-So.   I need to try again.

Why did I circle this? __**I said it but didn't play with them.**_____
I will try again._____

Skill 36: Dealing with Anxiety

Name _____Sebastian_____ Date _____3/1_____

SKILL STEPS

1. Think of your choices.
2. Make a plan.
3. Say, "I can follow my plan."
4. Follow your plan.

When did I practice?	How did I do? *(circle the number)*			
	Really Good!	Pretty good.	So-So.	I need to try again.
1. School assembly	4	3	2	①
2. Substitute teacher	4	3	②	1
3. Noisy classroom	4	③	2	1

SUPPORTS

	Practice Situation *(circle)*		
With prompting	①	2	3
With coaching	1	②	3
With supportive peer	1	2	③
Other support *(specify)* Video modeling	1	②	3
None	1	2	3

decided upon and noted. Following homework practice, the learner writes what happened, evaluates how well he or she followed all of the steps to the skill sequence, and writes why this evaluation was made. Figure 3 shows a sample Homework Report 3. A blank form is provided in Appendix A, with skill names and steps to be added as appropriate.

Recording Progress

Two tools to document and record Skillstreaming progress include the Homework Data Record and the Group Self-Report Chart, provided in Appendix A. Following completion of each homework assignment, the Skillstreaming leader records the learner's performance on the Homework Data Record. Both the learner and leader are identified, along with the skill (or skill sequence) and date the practice was completed. Then the level of the homework assignment is circled and the learner's self-evaluation and specific supports provided are noted. Finally, a space for comments is provided. This record is a useful way to share data with individual student support or IEP teams, monitor the learner's social skill progress, and plan future homework assignments.

Following learners' successful skill performance on Homework Reports 1 and 2, the Group Self-Report Chart may be used in the classroom or other group setting to enhance continued use of learned skills. The teacher or other staff member assists each group member in making a tally mark on this form next to each skill he or she practiced that day. Teachers or staff members praise skill use liberally; as time permits, learners may be asked to describe the specific situations in which they used a skill or skills. As group members become used to this self-reporting method, they may be record their skill use on the chart independently. If group members do record their own skill use, it is important for teachers or staff members to continue to comment on the self-reporting, thus providing reinforcement. Although the primary purpose of this chart is to encour-

age the continued use of skills taught in earlier Skillstreaming sessions, the chart also provides a record of the skills learners are continuing to practice. If learners do not report using specific skills, leaders will know which areas need review or reteaching.

ASSESSMENT

Because each learner's Skillstreaming experience will necessarily be highly individualized, assessing variables in skill acquisition may be complex. However, when administered before and after instruction, the Teacher/Staff Checklist, Learner Checklist, and Parent Checklist—or similar checklists derived from them—will be helpful in gauging skill learning. The Skillstreaming Rubric, also included in Appendix A, provides another measure from which to assess the degree of learners' skill proficiency.

Measuring implementation integrity is necessary to derive accurate conclusions regarding the effectiveness of an intervention and to understand outcomes such as the behavior change of the target individuals (Lane, Menies, Barton-Arwood, Doukas, & Munton, 2005; Wood, Umbreit, Liaupsin, & Gresham, 2007). To know whether the Skillstreaming program is producing the desired behavior change, monitoring the quality and quantity of the instruction is essential.

Both the Leader's Session Implementation Checklist and the Observer's Session Implementation Checklist, included in Appendix A, are helpful in ensuring that Skillstreaming session procedures are conducted as intended. The leader's checklist is completed by leaders at the completion of each session when first beginning Skillstreaming instruction. When leaders are consistently implementing all of the steps, this checklist may then be used every two or three weeks. The checklist may also serve as a planning guide to coach leaders through a Skillstreaming session. The observer's checklist is designed for use by a highly skilled trainer of Skillstreaming leaders to provide feedback to improve performance in implementing Skillstreaming

Figure 3: Sample Homework Report 3

Name ___T.J._____ Date ___3/1_____

Situation (describe) ___My little brother keeps bothering me and___
___I cannot think._____

With whom will I try this? ___Joshua my brother_____

When? ___On Saturday when he comes home_____

SKILLS NEEDED AND SKILL STEPS

Skill __49__	Skill __50__	Skill __51__
__Defining a Problem__	__Considering Alternatives__	__Choosing an Alternative__
Steps	Steps	Steps
1. Think about what happened.	1. Think of options to help resolve the problem.	1. Decide on one alternative.
2. Decide on your part in the problem.	2. Think of the consequences of each option.	2. Decide if you can do this.
3. Say, "The problem is _____."	3. Decide whether the consequences are positive, negative, or neutral for you and others.	3. Make a plan to do this.
		4. Follow your plan.

SUPPORTS

☑ Coaching with (name) ___My mom_____

☐ With supportive peer (name) _____

☐ Other (specify) _____

☐ None

FILL IN AFTER YOU PRACTICE THE SKILL

What happened? ___I said I would play a game with him at 4:00 PM___
___if he would not talk to me until that time._____

How did I do? (circle the number)   ④   3   2   1

                     Really good!   Pretty good.   So-So.   I need to try again.

Why did I circle this? ___I made a plan and followed the plan I devised.___

26

instruction. This observation form should be used frequently to provide feedback when leaders first begin as Skillstreaming instructors. This form also has been used by leaders to observe one another, thereby providing feedback to enhance their own skills.

Skill Outlines
and Homework Reports

Group I: Relationship Skills

Skill 1: Listening Without Interrupting

SKILL STEPS

1. **Look at the person.**

   Explain and demonstrate what looking at the person means (i.e., looking at the person's face, looking away briefly, then looking at the person again). Explain the difference between appropriate eye gaze and staring.

2. **Carefully listen.**

   Encourage the learner to think about what is being said. The learner may want to say to himself or herself, "I know I can listen."

3. **Nod your head.**

   Discuss both verbal (e.g., "Yes," "I see") and nonverbal messages that show someone is listening.

SUGGESTED MODELING SITUATIONS

School: Your teacher is presenting a lesson.

Home: A brother or sister is telling about an incident at school; your parent is telling you about her day.

Peer group: A friend is talking about his weekend.

Community: The coach is explaining what you will do at practice.

COMMENTS

This skill is also useful for a variety of other skills. Through modeling, role-play, and coaching, point out the verbal and nonverbal behaviors that show someone is listening. This skill focuses only on the nonverbal behaviors of the learner.

Skill 1: Listening Without Interrupting

Name_____Date_____

SKILL STEPS

1. Look at the person.
2. Carefully listen.
3. Nod your head.

FILL IN NOW

With whom will I try this? _____

When? _____

_____

SUPPORTS

☐ Coaching with *(name)* _____

☐ With supportive peer *(name)* _____

☐ Other *(specify)* _____

☐ None

FILL IN AFTER YOU PRACTICE THE SKILL

What happened? _____

_____

How did I do? *(circle the number)*   4   3   2   1

                                  Really good!   Pretty good.   So-So.   I need to try again.

Why did I circle this? _____

_____

Skillstreaming

From *Skillstreaming Children and Youth with High-Functioning Autism: A Guide for Teaching Prosocial Skills,* © 2016 by E. McGinnis and R. L. Simpson. Champaign, IL: Research Press (www.researchpress.com, 800-519-2707).

Skill 1: Listening Without Interrupting

Name_____Date_____

SKILL STEPS

1. Look at the person.
2. Carefully listen.
3. Nod your head.

	How did I do? *(circle the number)*			
When did I practice?	Really Good!	Pretty good.	So-So.	I need to try again.
1. _____	4	3	2	1
2. _____	4	3	2	1
3. _____	4	3	2	1

SUPPORTS

	Practice Situation *(circle)*		
With prompting	1	2	3
With coaching	1	2	3
With supportive peer	1	2	3
Other support *(specify)* _____	1	2	3
None	1	2	3

From *Skillstreaming Children and Youth with High-Functioning Autism: A Guide for Teaching Prosocial Skills,* © 2016 by E. McGinnis and R. L. Simpson. Champaign, IL: Research Press (www.researchpress.com, 800-519-2707).

Skill 2: Greeting Others

SKILL STEPS

1. **Look at the person and smile.**

   Explain that looking at the person means to look at the person's face (distinguish looking at the person from "staring" at the person). Explain that the learner may look at the person while continuing to walk. If learners are being asked to perform two actions at the same time (e.g., looking and walking), practice of this skill step in isolation may be needed.

2. **Say "hi" or "hello" and the person's name.**

   Explain to the learner that if he/she does not remember the person's name, it's okay to leave this out. However, if the learner does remember and use the person's name, the person will appreciate it.

3. **Walk on if you don't want to have a conversation.**

   Discuss appropriate times to walk on (e.g., the learner doesn't know the person well, it's time for class or otherwise not an appropriate time to have a conversation) and appropriate times to have a conversation with the person.

SUGGESTED MODELING SITUATIONS

School: You are in the hallway walking to class.

Home: You come home after school and greet your parent.

Peer group: You greet a friend after school.

Community: You see a friend's brother or sister at grocery store.

COMMENTS

It is important to distinguish between greeting adults, peers the learner knows well, and classmates he or she does not know well. Taking a walk around the school and practicing greeting others, with coaching of these social nuances, will assist in building the skill.

If learners desire to have a conversation after a greeting, Skill 14 (Starting a Conversation), Skill 15 (Continuing a Conversation), and Skill 18 (Ending a Conversation) should be taught following this skill.

Skillstreaming

From *Skillstreaming Children and Youth with High-Functioning Autism: A Guide for Teaching Prosocial Skills,* © 2016 by E. McGinnis and R. L. Simpson. Champaign, IL: Research Press (www.researchpress.com, 800-519-2707).

Skill 2: Greeting Others

Name_____Date_____

SKILL STEPS

1. Look at the person and smile.

2. Say "hi" or "hello" and the person's name.

3. Walk on if you don't want to have a conversation.

FILL IN NOW

With whom will I try this? _____

When?_____

_____

SUPPORTS

☐ Coaching with *(name)* _____

☐ With supportive peer *(name)* _____

☐ Other *(specify)* _____

☐ None

FILL IN AFTER YOU PRACTICE THE SKILL

What happened? _____

_____

How did I do? *(circle the number)*   4   3   2   1

                           Really good!   Pretty good.   So-So.   I need to try again.

Why did I circle this? _____

_____

From *Skillstreaming Children and Youth with High-Functioning Autism: A Guide for Teaching Prosocial Skills,* © 2016
by E. McGinnis and R. L. Simpson. Champaign, IL: Research Press (www.researchpress.com, 800-519-2707).

Skill 2: Greeting Others

Name_____Date_____

SKILL STEPS

1. Look at the person and smile.

2. Say "hi" or "hello" and the person's name.

3. Walk on if you don't want to have a conversation.

	How did I do? *(circle the number)*			
When did I practice?	Really Good!	Pretty good.	So-So.	I need to try again.
1. _____	4	3	2	1
2. _____	4	3	2	1
3. _____	4	3	2	1

SUPPORTS

	Practice Situation *(circle)*		
With prompting	1	2	3
With coaching	1	2	3
With supportive peer	1	2	3
Other support *(specify)* _____	1	2	3
_____			
None	1	2	3

Skillstreaming

From *Skillstreaming Children and Youth with High-Functioning Autism: A Guide for Teaching Prosocial Skills,* © 2016 by E. McGinnis and R. L. Simpson. Champaign, IL: Research Press (www.researchpress.com, 800-519-2707).

Skill 3: Responding to a Greeting

SKILL STEPS

1. **Look at the person and smile.**

   Learners may need practice in producing a "natural" smile.

2. **Say "hi" or "hello" and the person's name (if known).**

   Discuss other options specific to the person (e.g., say, "How are you doing?"). Explain that the learner may want to wave or hold up a hand for a high-five or fist bump if desired. The latter actions should be reserved for peers whom the learner knows well. Such options may be listed as choices for the learner and will differ according to both the person he/she is greeting and the comfort/style of the learner.

3. **Walk on.**

   Explain that the person who is greeting the learner may want to start a conversation. If so, he/she will likely stop walking and begin speaking about a topic.

SUGGESTED MODELING SITUATIONS

School: A peer new to the school greets you in the hallway; your teacher greets you as you enter the classroom.

Home: A parent greets you when you come home from school; a friend who is visiting greets you as she enters the house.

Peer group: A teammate greets you at bowling practice.

Community: The server at a restaurant greets you; your neighbor greets you while walking past your house.

COMMENTS

The learner should maintain eye contact throughout this brief interaction.

Skill 3: Responding to a Greeting

Name_____Date_____

SKILL STEPS

1. Look at the person and smile.

2. Say "hi or "hello" and the person's name (if known).

3. Walk on.

FILL IN NOW

With whom will I try this? _____

When? _____

_____

SUPPORTS

☐ Coaching with *(name)* _____

☐ With supportive peer *(name)* _____

☐ Other *(specify)* _____

☐ None

FILL IN AFTER YOU PRACTICE THE SKILL

What happened? _____

_____

How did I do? *(circle the number)*　　　4　　　　　　3　　　　　　2　　　　　　1

　　　　　　　　　　　　　　　Really good!　　Pretty good.　　So-So.　　I need to try again.

Why did I circle this? _____

_____

Skillstreaming

From *Skillstreaming Children and Youth with High-Functioning Autism: A Guide for Teaching Prosocial Skills,* © 2016 by E. McGinnis and R. L. Simpson. Champaign, IL: Research Press (www.researchpress.com, 800-519-2707).

Skill 3: Responding to a Greeting

Name_____Date_____

SKILL STEPS

1. Look at the person and smile.

2. Say "hi or "hello" and the person's name (if known).

3. Walk on.

	How did I do? *(circle the number)*			
When did I practice?	Really Good!	Pretty good.	So-So.	I need to try again.
1. _____	4	3	2	1
2. _____	4	3	2	1
3. _____	4	3	2	1

SUPPORTS

	Practice Situation *(circle)*		
With prompting	1	2	3
With coaching	1	2	3
With supportive peer	1	2	3
Other support *(specify)* _____	1	2	3
None	1	2	3

From *Skillstreaming Children and Youth with High-Functioning Autism: A Guide for Teaching Prosocial Skills,* © 2016 by E. McGinnis and R. L. Simpson. Champaign, IL: Research Press (www.researchpress.com, 800-519-2707).

Skill 4: Asking a Question About the Topic

SKILL STEPS

1. **Listen.**

   Review the steps to Listening Without Interrupting (Skill 1).

2. **What is the topic?**

   You may need to coach learners in identifying main topics. During classes, it's also helpful for teachers to identify the topic of the lesson or discussion to assist in skill use.

3. **Is there something I want to know about the topic?**

   Learners will likely need practice in asking questions about various topics. You may list several topics on the board and ask supportive peers to ask questions about the topics while you assist the learner in identifying the topics and point out how the questions were stated.

4. **Is this a good time?**

   Discuss various situations when asking a question would be a good time (e.g., class discussion of the topic, when working on an assignment related to the topic, when you are having a conversation with a peer) and when it would not be appropriate (e.g., when the bell rings, when the teacher direction is to put work away, when a peer needs to get to class).

5. **Ask in a respectful way.**

   Review the skill of Using a Respectful Voice (Skill 26) as needed.

SUGGESTED MODELING SITUATIONS

School: Your class is having a group discussion about a topic.

Home: Your parent is talking about the day at work.

Peer group: Your friend is telling you about her weekend.

Community: A neighbor is asking you to help with yard work.

COMMENTS

List topics that are typical for discussion in school, home, peer group, and community. Help the learner practice asking questions about these topics.

This skill may be used in social situations with peers and adults or during school-related activities. It is important that modeling, role-playing, and coaching situations include this variety.

Skillstreaming

From *Skillstreaming Children and Youth with High-Functioning Autism: A Guide for Teaching Prosocial Skills,* © 2016 by E. McGinnis and R. L. Simpson. Champaign, IL: Research Press (www.researchpress.com, 800-519-2707).

Skill 4: Asking a Question About the Topic

Name_____Date_____

SKILL STEPS

1. Listen.

2. What is the topic?

3. Is there something I want to know about the topic?

4. Is this a good time?

5. Ask in a respectful way.

FILL IN NOW

With whom will I try this? _____

When? _____

_____

SUPPORTS

☐ Coaching with *(name)* _____

☐ With supportive peer *(name)* _____

☐ Other *(specify)* _____

☐ None

FILL IN AFTER YOU PRACTICE THE SKILL

What happened? _____

_____

How did I do? *(circle the number)* 4 3 2 1

Really good! Pretty good. So-So. I need to try again.

Why did I circle this? _____

_____

From *Skillstreaming Children and Youth with High-Functioning Autism: A Guide for Teaching Prosocial Skills,* © 2016 by E. McGinnis and R. L. Simpson. Champaign, IL: Research Press (www.researchpress.com, 800-519-2707).

Skill 4: Asking a Question About the Topic

Name_____Date_____

SKILL STEPS

1. Listen.

2. What is the topic?

3. Is there something I want to know about the topic?

4. Is this a good time?

5. Ask in a respectful way.

When did I practice?	How did I do? (circle the number)			
	Really Good!	Pretty good.	So-So.	I need to try again.
1. _____	4	3	2	1
2. _____	4	3	2	1
3. _____	4	3	2	1

SUPPORTS

	Practice Situation (circle)		
With prompting	1	2	3
With coaching	1	2	3
With supportive peer	1	2	3
Other support (specify)_____	1	2	3
_____			
None	1	2	3

Skillstreaming From *Skillstreaming Children and Youth with High-Functioning Autism: A Guide for Teaching Prosocial Skills,* © 2016 by E. McGinnis and R. L. Simpson. Champaign, IL: Research Press (www.researchpress.com, 800-519-2707).

Skill 5: Staying on Topic

SKILL STEPS

1. **Decide on the topic.**

   If learners have difficulty identifying the topic, you may guide activities on identifying topics (e.g., during class activities, ask learners to identify the topic).

2. **Decide if you have something you want to say.**

   Learners may need a self-statement to allow them time to think, such as "I want to talk, but I can wait. I need to think first."

3. **Ask yourself, "Is this on the topic?"**

4. **If yes, make your comment.**

   Point out that the learner must wait until an appropriate time (e.g., when someone else isn't talking, when there is a pause in the discussion).

SUGGESTED MODELING SITUATIONS

School: The teacher is presenting a lesson on a school subject.

Home: Your parent is talking about a problem he has; your brother or sister is talking about what he/she did at school.

Peer group: A peer or group of peers are talking about the game or a favorite hobby.

Community: The coach is talking about a strategy at practice.

COMMENTS

Discuss what to do if the comment learners want to make is not on the topic (e.g., refrain from making the comment and continue listening; think of something else you want to say that is on the topic; say something like "I don't know much about this"). Learners may find a self-statement such as "It's not on the topic, so I won't say it" helpful and may need practice saying this to themselves.

Skill 5: Staying on Topic

Name_____Date_____

SKILL STEPS

1. Decide on the topic.
2. Decide if you have something you want to say.
3. Ask yourself, "Is this on the topic?"
4. If yes, make your comment.

FILL IN NOW

With whom will I try this? _____

When? _____

_____

SUPPORTS

☐ Coaching with *(name)* _____

☐ With supportive peer *(name)* _____

☐ Other *(specify)* _____

☐ None

FILL IN AFTER YOU PRACTICE THE SKILL

What happened? _____

_____

How did I do? *(circle the number)*   4   3   2   1

                          Really good!   Pretty good.   So-So.   I need to try again.

Why did I circle this? _____

_____

Skillstreaming

Skill 5: Staying on Topic

Name_____Date_____

SKILL STEPS

1. Decide on the topic.
2. Decide if you have something you want to say.
3. Ask yourself, "Is this on the topic?"
4. If yes, make your comment.

When did I practice?	How did I do? *(circle the number)*			
	Really Good!	Pretty good.	So-So.	I need to try again.
1. _____	4	3	2	1
2. _____	4	3	2	1
3. _____	4	3	2	1

SUPPORTS

	Practice Situation *(circle)*		
With prompting	1	2	3
With coaching	1	2	3
With supportive peer	1	2	3
Other support *(specify)* _____	1	2	3
None	1	2	3

From *Skillstreaming Children and Youth with High-Functioning Autism: A Guide for Teaching Prosocial Skills,* © 2016
by E. McGinnis and R. L. Simpson. Champaign, IL: Research Press (www.researchpress.com, 800-519-2707).

Skill 6: Responding to Questions

SKILL STEPS

1. **Stop. Think about what you are being asked.**

   Encourage learners to take a moment to consider the question and its meaning. Explain that some questions are simple ones (e.g., "Did you do your homework?"), while others will require more thought (e.g., "Do you want to go to the movie?").

2. **Think about options.**

   For simple questions, a brief answer is acceptable. For others, comments such as "I'll need to think about this. I'll let you know" give the learner some time to check with a parent or consider possible consequences.

3. **Answer the question or make a statement.**

   Explain that a short response, beyond "yes" or "no," is most acceptable.

SUGGESTED MODELING SITUATIONS

School: The teacher asks a question about a subject, and you know the answer.

Home: Your parent asks you what you did in school.

Peer group: A peer asks you to help her with her homework; a peer asks you to go to the game.

Community: A clerk at the store asks if you are looking for something.

COMMENTS

Learners will need practice responding to various types of questions. You may want to list headings such as "Factual," "Inference," and "Social" and generate from the group types of questions that are likely to be asked, writing these under each heading. You can then use these questions for modeling displays and subsequent role-plays as appropriate. It is important to point out which questions need a brief response, a delay statement, or a more in-depth response.

Skillstreaming

From *Skillstreaming Children and Youth with High-Functioning Autism: A Guide for Teaching Prosocial Skills,* © 2016 by E. McGinnis and R. L. Simpson. Champaign, IL: Research Press (www.researchpress.com, 800-519-2707).

Skill 6: Responding to Questions

Name_____Date_____

SKILL STEPS

1. Stop. Think about what you are being asked.

2. Think about options.

3. Answer the question or make a statement.

FILL IN NOW

With whom will I try this? _____

When? _____

_____

SUPPORTS

☐ Coaching with *(name)* _____

☐ With supportive peer *(name)* _____

☐ Other *(specify)* _____

☐ None

FILL IN AFTER YOU PRACTICE THE SKILL

What happened? _____

_____

How did I do? *(circle the number)*   4   3   2   1

Really good!   Pretty good.   So-So.   I need to try again.

Why did I circle this? _____

_____

From *Skillstreaming Children and Youth with High-Functioning Autism: A Guide for Teaching Prosocial Skills,* © 2016 by E. McGinnis and R. L. Simpson. Champaign, IL: Research Press (www.researchpress.com, 800-519-2707).

Skill 6: Responding to Questions

Name_____Date_____

SKILL STEPS

1. Stop. Think about what you are being asked.

2. Think about options.

3. Answer the question or make a statement.

When did I practice?	How did I do? *(circle the number)*			
	Really Good!	Pretty good.	So-So.	I need to try again.
1. _____	4	3	2	1
2. _____	4	3	2	1
3. _____	4	3	2	1

SUPPORTS

	Practice Situation *(circle)*		
With prompting	1	2	3
With coaching	1	2	3
With supportive peer	1	2	3
Other support *(specify)* _____	1	2	3
_____			
None	1	2	3

Skillstreaming

From *Skillstreaming Children and Youth with High-Functioning Autism: A Guide for Teaching Prosocial Skills,* © 2016 by E. McGinnis and R. L. Simpson. Champaign, IL: Research Press (www.researchpress.com, 800-519-2707).

Skill 7: Taking Turns

SKILL STEPS

1. **Say to yourself, "I know I can wait."**

   Suggest to learners that they may need to say this more than once. Explain that they must learn to wait quietly.

2. **Think about what to do while waiting.**

   Encourage learners to choose age-appropriate and acceptable activities, such as doodling or using a stress ball.

3. **Do it until it is your turn.**

SUGGESTED MODELING SITUATIONS

School: Someone else is using the art supplies you need to do your project.

Home: You are playing a video game with your brother or sister.

Peer group: You are playing a board game with a friend.

Community: You are shooting baskets with friends at the park.

COMMENTS

It is often helpful to have a basket of stress balls or other manipulatives that learners can use to help them wait their turn.

Skill 7: Taking Turns

Name_____Date_____

SKILL STEPS

1. Say to yourself, "I know I can wait."
2. Think about what to do while waiting.
3. Do it until it is your turn.

FILL IN NOW

With whom will I try this? _____

When? _____

_____

SUPPORTS

☐ Coaching with *(name)* _____

☐ With supportive peer *(name)* _____

☐ Other *(specify)* _____

☐ None

FILL IN AFTER YOU PRACTICE THE SKILL

What happened? _____

_____

How did I do? *(circle the number)*   4   3   2   1

                                       Really good!   Pretty good.   So-So.   I need to try again.

Why did I circle this? _____

_____

Skillstreaming

From *Skillstreaming Children and Youth with High-Functioning Autism: A Guide for Teaching Prosocial Skills,* © 2016
by E. McGinnis and R. L. Simpson. Champaign, IL: Research Press (www.researchpress.com, 800-519-2707).

Skill 7: Taking Turns

Name_____Date_____

SKILL STEPS

1. Say to yourself, "I know I can wait."
2. Think about what to do while waiting.
3. Do it until it is your turn.

	How did I do? *(circle the number)*			
When did I practice?	Really Good!	Pretty good.	So-So.	I need to try again.
1. _____	4	3	2	1
2. _____	4	3	2	1
3. _____	4	3	2	1

SUPPORTS

	Practice Situation *(circle)*		
With prompting	1	2	3
With coaching	1	2	3
With supportive peer	1	2	3
Other support *(specify)* _____	1	2	3
None	1	2	3

From *Skillstreaming Children and Youth with High-Functioning Autism: A Guide for Teaching Prosocial Skills,* © 2016 by E. McGinnis and R. L. Simpson. Champaign, IL: Research Press (www.researchpress.com, 800-519-2707).

Skill 8: Complimenting Others

SKILL STEPS

1. **Decide what you like about the person or what the person did.**

   Discuss the types of things to compliment someone on: the way they look (e.g., a new haircut, clothing) or something they did (e.g., playing sports or music, schoolwork).

2. **Plan what to say.**

   Examples of what to say to the person include "I like…" and "I think you did a good job with…"

3. **Choose a good time and place.**

   Discuss when would be a good time (e.g., when the person isn't with someone else, when you aren't supposed to be doing something else).

4. **Give your compliment.**

SUGGESTED MODELING SITUATIONS

School: Your teacher planned an interesting project for the class.

Home: Your sister or brother earned a good grade in a class.

Peer group: A classmate has a new haircut that you think looks good.

Community: A friend played a good game.

COMMENTS

When learners first begin using this skill, their use may seem mechanical and insincere. Additional practice will help this skill become more natural.

This is also a good time to discuss empathy: how the person might feel when given a compliment. Also discuss how the learner feels about saying something nice to someone else.

Skillstreaming

From *Skillstreaming Children and Youth with High-Functioning Autism: A Guide for Teaching Prosocial Skills,* © 2016 by E. McGinnis and R. L. Simpson. Champaign, IL: Research Press (www.researchpress.com, 800-519-2707).

Skill 8: Complimenting Others

Name_____Date_____

SKILL STEPS

1. Decide what you like about the person or what the person did.

2. Plan what to say.

3. Choose a good time and place.

4. Give your compliment.

FILL IN NOW

With whom will I try this? _____

When? _____

_____

SUPPORTS

☐ Coaching with *(name)* _____

☐ With supportive peer *(name)* _____

☐ Other *(specify)* _____

☐ None

FILL IN AFTER YOU PRACTICE THE SKILL

What happened? _____

_____

How did I do? *(circle the number)*   4   3   2   1

                         Really good!   Pretty good.   So-So.   I need to try again.

Why did I circle this? _____

_____

From *Skillstreaming Children and Youth with High-Functioning Autism: A Guide for Teaching Prosocial Skills,* © 2016 by E. McGinnis and R. L. Simpson. Champaign, IL: Research Press (www.researchpress.com, 800-519-2707).

Skill 8: Complimenting Others

Name_____Date_____

SKILL STEPS

1. Decide what you like about the person or what the person did.

2. Plan what to say.

3. Choose a good time and place.

4. Give your compliment.

When did I practice?	How did I do? (circle the number)			
	Really Good!	Pretty good.	So-So.	I need to try again.
1. _____	4	3	2	1
2. _____	4	3	2	1
3. _____	4	3	2	1

SUPPORTS

	Practice Situation (circle)		
With prompting	1	2	3
With coaching	1	2	3
With supportive peer	1	2	3
Other support (specify)_____	1	2	3
_____			
None	1	2	3

Skillstreaming

Skill 9: Helping Others

SKILL STEPS

1. **Decide if the person wants or needs help.**

   Talk about how to determine if another person needs help. How does the person look? What is he or she doing or saying? (If needed, refer to or teach Skill 23, Reading Others.)

2. **Think of ways you can help.**

   Point out that you could ask the person whether you could help or say "Let me help."

3. **Choose a way to help.**

   Choose one of the ways.

4. **Plan what to say or do.**

   Decide how you will offer help.

5. **Follow your plan.**

SUGGESTED MODELING SITUATIONS

School: Your teacher has dropped a pile of papers.

Home: A brother or sister is having trouble with a computer game.

Peer group: A classmate is struggling with an assignment.

Community: A neighbor is carrying groceries in from the car.

COMMENTS

After practicing this skill in role-play and coaching situations, learners will need to practice what to do if help is refused (e.g., walk away, do something else, say to themselves, "I did a good job asking"). This skill helps learners show interest in others.

Skill 9: Helping Others

Name_____Date_____

SKILL STEPS

1. Decide if the person wants or needs help.

2. Think of ways you can help.

3. Choose a way to help.

4. Plan what to say or do.

5. Follow your plan.

FILL IN NOW

With whom will I try this? _____

When? _____

_____

SUPPORTS

☐ Coaching with *(name)* _____

☐ With supportive peer *(name)* _____

☐ Other *(specify)* _____

☐ None

FILL IN AFTER YOU PRACTICE THE SKILL

What happened? _____

_____

How did I do? *(circle the number)*	4	3	2	1
	Really good!	Pretty good.	So-So.	I need to try again.

Why did I circle this? _____

_____

Skillstreaming

From *Skillstreaming Children and Youth with High-Functioning Autism: A Guide for Teaching Prosocial Skills,* © 2016
by E. McGinnis and R. L. Simpson. Champaign, IL: Research Press (www.researchpress.com, 800-519-2707).

Skill 9: Helping Others

Name_____Date_____

SKILL STEPS

1. Decide if the person wants or needs help.
2. Think of ways you can help.
3. Choose a way to help.
4. Plan what to say or do.
5. Follow your plan.

	How did I do? *(circle the number)*			
When did I practice?	Really Good!	Pretty good.	So-So.	I need to try again.
1. _____	4	3	2	1
2. _____	4	3	2	1
3. _____	4	3	2	1

SUPPORTS

	Practice Situation *(circle)*		
With prompting	1	2	3
With coaching	1	2	3
With supportive peer	1	2	3
Other support *(specify)*_____	1	2	3
None	1	2	3

Skill 10: Encouraging Others

SKILL STEPS

1. **Decide if the person needs encouragement.**

   Discuss ways of deciding if the person feels frustrated or teach Skill 23 (Reading Others) and Skill 30 (Showing Interest in Others), as needed.

2. **Decide what to do.**

   Explore ways of offering encouragement, such as saying something (e.g., "You can do it" or "You're almost done"), writing a note, drawing a picture, helping the person.

3. **Choose a good time.**

   Discuss times that would be good (e.g., when you aren't supposed to be doing something else, when lots of people aren't around and will notice). Discuss why these would not be good times to offer encouragement.

4. **Do it in a friendly way.**

   Review or teach Skill 25 (Using a Friendly Voice), as needed. Explain that smiling, even though this shows a friendly manner, could be interpreted as making fun of the person when he or she is frustrated.

SUGGESTED MODELING SITUATIONS

School: A classmate is frustrated with a school project or assignment.

Home: A parent is frustrated that she has too much work to do.

Peer group: A friend is frustrated that his best friend won't talk with him.

Community: A salesclerk is frustrated because the store is busy and there is no one else to help.

COMMENTS

Learners will likely need to practice recognizing frustration in someone else. This skill differs from Helping Others (Skill 9) and should be used when there isn't help the learner could offer.

Skillstreaming

From *Skillstreaming Children and Youth with High-Functioning Autism: A Guide for Teaching Prosocial Skills,* © 2016 by E. McGinnis and R. L. Simpson. Champaign, IL: Research Press (www.researchpress.com, 800-519-2707).

Skill 10: Encouraging Others

Name_____Date_____

SKILL STEPS

1. Decide if the person needs encouragement.
2. Decide what to do.
3. Choose a good time.
4. Do it in a friendly way.

FILL IN NOW

With whom will I try this? _____

When? _____

_____

SUPPORTS

☐ Coaching with *(name)* _____

☐ With supportive peer *(name)* _____

☐ Other *(specify)* _____

☐ None

FILL IN AFTER YOU PRACTICE THE SKILL

What happened? _____

_____

How did I do? *(circle the number)*   4   3   2   1

                                    Really good!   Pretty good.   So-So.   I need to try again.

Why did I circle this? _____

_____

From *Skillstreaming Children and Youth with High-Functioning Autism: A Guide for Teaching Prosocial Skills,* © 2016 by E. McGinnis and R. L. Simpson. Champaign, IL: Research Press (www.researchpress.com, 800-519-2707).

Skill 10: Encouraging Others

Name_____Date_____

SKILL STEPS

1. Decide if the person needs encouragement.
2. Decide what to do.
3. Choose a good time.
4. Do it in a friendly way.

	How did I do? *(circle the number)*			
When did I practice?	Really Good!	Pretty good.	So-So.	I need to try again.
1. _____	4	3	2	1
2. _____	4	3	2	1
3. _____	4	3	2	1

SUPPORTS

	Practice Situation *(circle)*		
With prompting	1	2	3
With coaching	1	2	3
With supportive peer	1	2	3
Other support *(specify)* _____	1	2	3
_____			
None	1	2	3

Skillstreaming

Skill 11: Cooperating with Others

SKILL STEPS

1. **Say to yourself, "I can work with others."**

   Depending on the learner, additional self-statements could be added, such as "I don't have to have control" or "It doesn't have to be my way."

2. **Listen to the directions.**

   Think about what you are being asked to do. Repeating the directions to yourself if needed. Ask questions about anything you don't understand.

3. **Wait your turn.**

   Wait for the other person to take a turn. Say to yourself, "I know I can wait. I know I can wait." Respect what the other person is doing.

4. **When it's your turn, do it.**

   Follow the direction. As appropriate, tell others you are finished.

5. **Wait and listen until your turn again.**

SUGGESTED MODELING SITUATIONS

School: The teacher gives directions for a group activity.

Home: You are playing a board game with your family.

Peer group: You are bowling with a group of friends.

Community: You are working on a group project at church or the community center.

COMMENTS

This skill helps deal with learners' desire to dominate an activity, and additional practice on some skill steps may be needed to fit different types of situations. For example, many times group activities do not take a round-robin approach (e.g., each person takes a turn) but instead are less structured. In such cases, learners will need to practice participating when there is a pause in the activity.

From *Skillstreaming Children and Youth with High-Functioning Autism: A Guide for Teaching Prosocial Skills,* © 2016 by E. McGinnis and R. L. Simpson. Champaign, IL: Research Press (www.researchpress.com, 800-519-2707).

Skill 11: Cooperating with Others

Name_____Date_____

SKILL STEPS

1. Say to yourself, "I can work with others."

2. Listen to the directions.

3. Wait your turn.

4. When it's your turn, do it.

5. Wait and listen until your turn again.

FILL IN NOW

With whom will I try this? _____

When? _____

_____

SUPPORTS

☐ Coaching with *(name)* _____

☐ With supportive peer *(name)* _____

☐ Other *(specify)* _____

☐ None

FILL IN AFTER YOU PRACTICE THE SKILL

What happened? _____

_____

How did I do? *(circle the number)*   4   3   2   1

                                  Really good!   Pretty good.   So-So.   I need to try again.

Why did I circle this? _____

_____

Skillstreaming

From *Skillstreaming Children and Youth with High-Functioning Autism: A Guide for Teaching Prosocial Skills,* © 2016 by E. McGinnis and R. L. Simpson. Champaign, IL: Research Press (www.researchpress.com, 800-519-2707).

Skill 11: Cooperating with Others

Name_____Date_____

SKILL STEPS

1. Say to yourself, "I can work with others."
2. Listen to the directions.
3. Wait your turn.
4. When it's your turn, do it.
5. Wait and listen until your turn again.

When did I practice?	Really Good!	Pretty good.	So-So.	I need to try again.
	How did I do? *(circle the number)*			
1. _____	4	3	2	1
2. _____	4	3	2	1
3. _____	4	3	2	1

SUPPORTS

	Practice Situation *(circle)*		
With prompting	1	2	3
With coaching	1	2	3
With supportive peer	1	2	3
Other support *(specify)* _____	1	2	3
None	1	2	3

Skill 12: Sharing

SKILL STEPS

1. **Decide if you want to share something.**

   Think about what it is you want to share. Decide if this is a reasonable item to share. If not, choose something else to share.

2. **Decide on the person with whom you would like to share.**

   Think about whether the person may want you to share with him/her.

3. **Choose a good time.**

   Think about when it would be a good time (e.g., make sure the person isn't supposed to be doing something else; when others aren't around if you can't share with them, too).

4. **Offer to share in a friendly way.**

   The learner may need to plan how to offer to share ahead of time. Emphasize friendly body language and voice tone. Skill 25 (Using a Friendly Voice) may be taught or reviewed.

SUGGESTED MODELING SITUATIONS

School: You want to share school materials (e.g., pencil, pen, markers) with someone who doesn't have them.

Home: You want to share some of your popcorn with a brother or sister.

Peer group: You want to share a music CD with a friend.

Community: You want to share your basketball with a friend at the park.

COMMENTS

It is helpful to talk about how learners feel when someone does and doesn't share with them, then discuss how the other person might feel in these circumstances.

Skillstreaming

From *Skillstreaming Children and Youth with High-Functioning Autism: A Guide for Teaching Prosocial Skills,* © 2016 by E. McGinnis and R. L. Simpson. Champaign, IL: Research Press (www.researchpress.com, 800-519-2707).

Skill 12: Sharing

Name_____Date_____

SKILL STEPS

1. Decide if you want to share something.

2. Decide on the person with whom you would like to share.

3. Choose a good time.

4. Offer to share in a friendly way.

FILL IN NOW

With whom will I try this? _____

When? _____

_____

SUPPORTS

☐ Coaching with *(name)* _____

☐ With supportive peer *(name)* _____

☐ Other *(specify)* _____

☐ None

FILL IN AFTER YOU PRACTICE THE SKILL

What happened? _____

_____

How did I do? *(circle the number)*   4   3   2   1

                                   Really good!   Pretty good.   So-So.   I need to try again.

Why did I circle this? _____

_____

From *Skillstreaming Children and Youth with High-Functioning Autism: A Guide for Teaching Prosocial Skills,* © 2016 by E. McGinnis and R. L. Simpson. Champaign, IL: Research Press (www.researchpress.com, 800-519-2707).

Skill 12: Sharing

Name_____Date_____

SKILL STEPS

1. Decide if you want to share something.
2. Decide on the person with whom you would like to share.
3. Choose a good time.
4. Offer to share in a friendly way.

	How did I do? *(circle the number)*			
When did I practice?	Really Good!	Pretty good.	So-So.	I need to try again.
1. _____	4	3	2	1
2. _____	4	3	2	1
3. _____	4	3	2	1

SUPPORTS

	Practice Situation *(circle)*		
With prompting	1	2	3
With coaching	1	2	3
With supportive peer	1	2	3
Other support *(specify)*_____	1	2	3
_____			
None	1	2	3

Skill 13: Asking a Favor

SKILL STEPS

1. **Do I want or need a favor?**

   Decide if you want or need someone to do something for you. Discuss with learners whether it is "fair" to ask this. Discuss favors that might be fair or unfair.

2. **Whom should I ask?**

   Decide on a person to ask the favor of. Decide whether you think the person will be receptive; if not, choose someone else. Review or teach Skill 23 (Reading Others), if needed.

3. **Is this a good time?**

   Decide whether this is a good time to ask (e.g., the person isn't busy with something else).

4. **Ask in a friendly way.**

   Learners may need to plan how they will ask and distinguish between asking in a friendly way and asking in a demanding or angry way. Explain that it is also sometimes helpful to give a reason for needing or wanting the favor.

SUGGESTED MODELING SITUATIONS

School: You need to borrow some materials to do a school project.

Home: The television is too loud for you.

Peer group: You would like to borrow a friend's computer game.

Community: You need help finding a book or movie in the library.

COMMENTS

When learners are successful in performing this skill in role-play and coaching situations, it will be important for them also to practice what to do when the favor is granted (e.g., say, "Thank you") and what to do when it is not (e.g., say, "Thanks anyway").

Skill 13: Asking a Favor

Name_____Date_____

SKILL STEPS

1. Do I want or need a favor?

2. Whom should I ask?

3. Is this a good time?

4. Ask in a friendly way.

FILL IN NOW

With whom will I try this? _____

When? _____

_____

SUPPORTS

☐ Coaching with *(name)* _____

☐ With supportive peer *(name)* _____

☐ Other *(specify)* _____

☐ None

FILL IN AFTER YOU PRACTICE THE SKILL

What happened? _____

_____

How did I do? *(circle the number)*　　　4　　　　　　3　　　　　　2　　　　　　1

　　　　　　　　　　　　　　Really good!　　Pretty good.　　So-So.　　I need to try again.

Why did I circle this? _____

_____

Skillstreaming

From *Skillstreaming Children and Youth with High-Functioning Autism: A Guide for Teaching Prosocial Skills,* © 2016
by E. McGinnis and R. L. Simpson. Champaign, IL: Research Press (www.researchpress.com, 800-519-2707).

Skill 13: Asking a Favor

Name_____Date_____

SKILL STEPS

1. Do I want or need a favor?

2. Whom should I ask?

3. Is this a good time?

4. Ask in a friendly way.

	How did I do? (circle the number)			
When did I practice?	Really Good!	Pretty good.	So-So.	I need to try again.
1. _____	4	3	2	1
2. _____	4	3	2	1
3. _____	4	3	2	1

SUPPORTS

	Practice Situation (circle)		
With prompting	1	2	3
With coaching	1	2	3
With supportive peer	1	2	3
Other support (specify)_____	1	2	3
None	1	2	3

From *Skillstreaming Children and Youth with High-Functioning Autism: A Guide for Teaching Prosocial Skills,* © 2016 by E. McGinnis and R. L. Simpson. Champaign, IL: Research Press (www.researchpress.com, 800-519-2707).

Skill 14: Starting a Conversation

SKILL STEPS

1. **Decide what you want to talk about and with whom.**

   Suggest topics like something the learner did during the weekend, a hobby, or a class project. Discuss the nonverbal behaviors that suggest the person is interested in having a conversation with you.

2. **Choose a good time.**

   Make sure the person isn't busy with something else, talking with someone else, or you are supposed to be doing something else.

3. **Stand at an appropriate distance.**

   Use cues, such as an arm's length away from the person. Explain that it is important to do this to respect a person's space.

4. **Look at the person.**

   Explain that looking at the person shows your interest in having the conversation and also lets you know if the person is interested in having a conversation.

5. **Give an opening statement.**

   These statements will vary with the person. Statements might include "Do you have a minute to talk?" and "I noticed you like (a hobby or activity) also."

SUGGESTED MODELING SITUATIONS

School: Before school starts, you see a classmate you'd like to know better.

Home: A relative comes over to visit.

Peer group: You see a classmate at the ballgame.

Community: You see a neighbor in the grocery store.

COMMENTS

It is important to discuss the various people the learner would like to get to know better. Explain that having a conversation with others is an important way to get to know someone better.

Learners should role-play this skill with both adults and peers to determine language and nonverbal behaviors appropriate for those in different roles—for example, teachers, parents, classmates, friends.

Skillstreaming From *Skillstreaming Children and Youth with High-Functioning Autism: A Guide for Teaching Prosocial Skills,* © 2016 by E. McGinnis and R. L. Simpson. Champaign, IL: Research Press (www.researchpress.com, 800-519-2707).

Skill 14: Starting a Conversation

Name_____Date_____

SKILL STEPS

1. Decide what you want to talk about and with whom.
2. Choose a good time.
3. Stand at an appropriate distance.
4. Look at the person.
5. Give an opening statement.

FILL IN NOW

With whom will I try this? _____

When? _____

_____

SUPPORTS

☐ Coaching with *(name)* _____

☐ With supportive peer *(name)* _____

☐ Other *(specify)* _____

☐ None

FILL IN AFTER YOU PRACTICE THE SKILL

What happened? _____

_____

How did I do? *(circle the number)*   4   3   2   1

                            Really good!   Pretty good.   So-So.   I need to try again.

Why did I circle this? _____

_____

Skill 14: Starting a Conversation

Name_____Date_____

SKILL STEPS

1. Decide what you want to talk about and with whom.
2. Choose a good time.
3. Stand at an appropriate distance.
4. Look at the person.
5. Give an opening statement.

	How did I do? *(circle the number)*			
When did I practice?	Really Good!	Pretty good.	So-So.	I need to try again.
1. _____	4	3	2	1
2. _____	4	3	2	1
3. _____	4	3	2	1

SUPPORTS

	Practice Situation *(circle)*		
With prompting	1	2	3
With coaching	1	2	3
With supportive peer	1	2	3
Other support *(specify)* _____	1	2	3
_____			
None	1	2	3

Skillstreaming

From *Skillstreaming Children and Youth with High-Functioning Autism: A Guide for Teaching Prosocial Skills,* © 2016 by E. McGinnis and R. L. Simpson. Champaign, IL: Research Press (www.researchpress.com, 800-519-2707).

Skill 15: Continuing a Conversation

SKILL STEPS

1. **Say what you want to say about a topic.**

   Stress not talking too long (two or three sentences) or the listener will become bored.

2. **Pause or ask a question.**

   Explain that pausing gives the other person a chance to talk. If the other person doesn't say anything, ask question (e.g., "What do you think?" or "What is your favorite hobby?").

3. **Listen to the other person.**

   Review or teach Skill 1 (Listening Without Interrupting).

4. **When there is a pause or a question, take your turn to talk.**

   Again, stress the importance of not talking too long.

SUGGESTED MODELING SITUATIONS

School: You have started a conversation with a peer before school; you have started a conversation with a teacher after school.

Home: You have started a conversation with your brother or sister; your parent has started a conversation with you.

Peer group: You have started a conversation with a peer at practice or at church.

Community: A neighbor has started a conversation with you about a hobby you enjoy.

COMMENTS

This skill may be used whether the learner begins a conversation or someone starts a conversation with the learner and should be modeled and role-played within both contexts.

Skill 15: Continuing a Conversation

Name_____Date_____

SKILL STEPS

1. Say what you want to say about a topic.

2. Pause or ask a question.

3. Listen to the other person.

4. When there is a pause or a question, take your turn to talk.

FILL IN NOW

With whom will I try this? _____

When? _____

_____

SUPPORTS

☐ Coaching with *(name)* _____

☐ With supportive peer *(name)* _____

☐ Other *(specify)* _____

☐ None

FILL IN AFTER YOU PRACTICE THE SKILL

What happened? _____

_____

How did I do? *(circle the number)*   4   3   2   1

Really good!   Pretty good.   So-So.   I need to try again.

Why did I circle this? _____

_____

Skillstreaming

From *Skillstreaming Children and Youth with High-Functioning Autism: A Guide for Teaching Prosocial Skills,* © 2016
by E. McGinnis and R. L. Simpson. Champaign, IL: Research Press (www.researchpress.com, 800-519-2707).

Skill 15: Continuing a Conversation

Name_____Date_____

SKILL STEPS

1. Say what you want to say about a topic.

2. Pause or ask a question.

3. Listen to the other person.

4. When there is a pause or a question, take your turn to talk.

When did I practice?	How did I do? *(circle the number)*			
	Really Good!	Pretty good.	So-So.	I need to try again.
1. _____	4	3	2	1
2. _____	4	3	2	1
3. _____	4	3	2	1

SUPPORTS

	Practice Situation *(circle)*		
With prompting	1	2	3
With coaching	1	2	3
With supportive peer	1	2	3
Other support *(specify)* _____	1	2	3
None	1	2	3

 From *Skillstreaming Children and Youth with High-Functioning Autism: A Guide for Teaching Prosocial Skills,* © 2016 by E. McGinnis and R. L. Simpson. Champaign, IL: Research Press (www.researchpress.com, 800-519-2707).

Skill 16: When to Introduce a New Topic

SKILL STEPS

1. **Watch the other person.**

   Is she listening? Is she talking about the topic? Watch her nonverbal behaviors. Does she seem bored or uninterested?

2. **Decide if there is more on this topic to talk about.**

   Is there something else you want to say? Are there other questions about the topic you want to ask?

3. **If not, suggest a new topic.**

   Stress the importance of choosing a good time to change the topic (e.g., when there is a pause in the conversation). Discuss choosing a topic the learner thinks the other person will be interested in as well.

4. **Continue the conversation.**

   Review or teach Skill 15 (Continuing a Conversation).

SUGGESTED MODELING SITUATIONS

School: You have been having a conversation with a peer about a school subject.

Home: You have been having a conversation with your parent or brother or sister.

Peer group: You have been talking with a peer at church.

Community: You have been talking with your favorite neighbor.

COMMENTS

Explain that some people become bored when talking about a topic for a while or about something in which they have no interest. Particular attention should be given to attending to the other person's nonverbal behaviors. When role-playing, explore topics in which both individuals may have interest.

Skillstreaming

From *Skillstreaming Children and Youth with High-Functioning Autism: A Guide for Teaching Prosocial Skills,* © 2016 by E. McGinnis and R. L. Simpson. Champaign, IL: Research Press (www.researchpress.com, 800-519-2707).

Skill 16: When to Introduce a New Topic

Name_____Date_____

SKILL STEPS

1. Watch the other person.

2. Decide if there is more on this topic to talk about.

3. If not, suggest a new topic.

4. Continue the conversation.

FILL IN NOW

With whom will I try this? _____

When? _____

_____

SUPPORTS

☐ Coaching with *(name)* _____

☐ With supportive peer *(name)* _____

☐ Other *(specify)* _____

☐ None

FILL IN AFTER YOU PRACTICE THE SKILL

What happened? _____

_____

How did I do? *(circle the number)*   4   3   2   1

Really good!   Pretty good.   So-So.   I need to try again.

Why did I circle this? _____

_____

From *Skillstreaming Children and Youth with High-Functioning Autism: A Guide for Teaching Prosocial Skills,* © 2016 by E. McGinnis and R. L. Simpson. Champaign, IL: Research Press (www.researchpress.com, 800-519-2707).

Skill 16: When to Introduce a New Topic

Name_____Date_____

SKILL STEPS

1. Watch the other person.

2. Decide if there is more on this topic to talk about.

3. If not, suggest a new topic.

4. Continue the conversation.

	How did I do? (circle the number)			
When did I practice?	Really Good!	Pretty good.	So-So.	I need to try again.
1. _____	4	3	2	1
2. _____	4	3	2	1
3. _____	4	3	2	1

SUPPORTS

	Practice Situation (circle)		
With prompting	1	2	3
With coaching	1	2	3
With supportive peer	1	2	3
Other support (specify)_____	1	2	3
_____			
None	1	2	3

Skillstreaming

Skill 17: Accepting a Topic Change

SKILL STEPS

1. **Decide if the topic has changed.**

    Explain that it is normal in the course of a conversation for the topic to change. Explain that topics that may be of great interest to one person are not always of great interest to another.

2. **Say to yourself, "I'm okay with this."**

    Explain that there will be other times when the learner can talk more about the topic he or she wants to discuss. Explain that this is a good time to learn about other topics.

3. **Think about what you know or want to know about the new topic.**

    Think of what you know or questions you might like to know about the new topic.

4. **Ask a question or make a comment about the new topic.**

    Emphasize making a comment about what is of interest to the learner about the topic or asking a question about the topic. Explain that it is also okay just to listen. Teach or review Skill 1 (Listening Without Interrupting) and Skill 4 (Asking a Question About the Topic).

SUGGESTED MODELING SITUATIONS

School: Your teacher is having a discussion about something that interests you, but then she states that it's time to work on something else.

Home: You are talking with your family about a school project, and your brother changes the subject.

Peer group: You are having a conversation with a friend about your hobby and he starts talking about the ball game.

Community: You are talking with a neighbor about your hobby and she changes the topic.

COMMENTS

If this is a difficult skill for learners, using a cue card (e.g., a red piece of construction paper) to signal a topic change will give them more time to prepare for the change. Using such a cue in role-play or coaching situations should gradually be faded as the learner demonstrates increased competence.

Skill 17: Accepting a Topic Change

Name_____Date_____

SKILL STEPS

1. Decide if the topic has changed.

2. Say to yourself, "I'm okay with this."

3. Think about what you know or want to know about the new topic.

4. Ask a question or make a comment about the new topic.

FILL IN NOW

With whom will I try this? _____

When? _____

_____

SUPPORTS

☐ Coaching with *(name)* _____

☐ With supportive peer *(name)* _____

☐ Other *(specify)* _____

☐ None

FILL IN AFTER YOU PRACTICE THE SKILL

What happened? _____

_____

How did I do? *(circle the number)*   4   3   2   1

                      Really good!   Pretty good.   So-So.   I need to try again.

Why did I circle this? _____

_____

Skillstreaming

Skill 17: Accepting a Topic Change

Name_____Date_____

SKILL STEPS

1. Decide if the topic has changed.

2. Say to yourself, "I'm okay with this."

3. Think about what you know or want to know about the new topic.

4. Ask a question or make a comment about the new topic.

	How did I do? *(circle the number)*			
When did I practice?	Really Good!	Pretty good.	So-So.	I need to try again.
1. _____	4	3	2	1
2. _____	4	3	2	1
3. _____	4	3	2	1

SUPPORTS

	Practice Situation *(circle)*		
With prompting	1	2	3
With coaching	1	2	3
With supportive peer	1	2	3
Other support *(specify)* _____	1	2	3
None	1	2	3

Skill 18: Ending a Conversation

SKILL STEPS

1. **Decide if you need or want to end the conversation.**

   Discuss times when ending a conversation is appropriate (e.g., you have somewhere else to be, you are bored with the discussion, the other person needs to leave).

2. **Decide what to say.**

   Explain that it is important to say something to the person rather than just walking away. Explain that it is helpful to give the person a reason (e.g., "I have to go to class now"). Then the person will know why the conversation is ending. A standard response such as "I need to go now—thanks for talking with me" or "I need to go now—talk to you later" is acceptable as well, especially if you are just bored with the discussion.

3. **Wait until the other person stops talking.**

   Discuss the importance of not interrupting and choosing a pause in the conversation. Because the learner may be bored or anxious, a self-statement such as "I know I can wait" may assist.

4. **Say it in a friendly way.**

   The learner may need to practice Skill 25 (Using a Friendly Voice).

SUGGESTED MODELING SITUATIONS

School: You are talking with a friend before school, but it's time for class.

Home: You are talking on the phone, and it's time for dinner.

Peer group: You are with a group of classmates, and you are bored with the conversation.

Community: You have been talking with a friend at the store, and your parent has finished shopping.

COMMENTS

Learning how to end a conversation reduces the awkwardness of ending a social interaction. After participants have learned Skills 14 through 18, teaching the skills as a skill sequence will help conversations become more natural.

Skillstreaming

From *Skillstreaming Children and Youth with High-Functioning Autism: A Guide for Teaching Prosocial Skills,* © 2016 by E. McGinnis and R. L. Simpson. Champaign, IL: Research Press (www.researchpress.com, 800-519-2707).

Skill 18: Ending a Conversation

Name_____Date_____

SKILL STEPS

1. Decide if you need or want to end the conversation.

2. Decide what to say.

3. Wait until the other person stops talking.

4. Say it in a friendly way.

FILL IN NOW

With whom will I try this? _____

When? _____

_____

SUPPORTS

☐ Coaching with *(name)* _____

☐ With supportive peer *(name)* _____

☐ Other *(specify)* _____

☐ None

FILL IN AFTER YOU PRACTICE THE SKILL

What happened? _____

_____

How did I do? *(circle the number)*   4   3   2   1

                                              Really good!   Pretty good.   So-So.   I need to try again.

Why did I circle this? _____

_____

Skill 18: Ending a Conversation

Name_____Date_____

SKILL STEPS

1. Decide if you need or want to end the conversation.

2. Decide what to say.

3. Wait until the other person stops talking.

4. Say it in a friendly way.

When did I practice?	How did I do? *(circle the number)*			
	Really Good!	Pretty good.	So-So.	I need to try again.
1. _____	4	3	2	1
2. _____	4	3	2	1
3. _____	4	3	2	1

SUPPORTS

	Practice Situation *(circle)*		
With prompting	1	2	3
With coaching	1	2	3
With supportive peer	1	2	3
Other support *(specify)* _____	1	2	3
_____			
None	1	2	3

Skillstreaming
From *Skillstreaming Children and Youth with High-Functioning Autism: A Guide for Teaching Prosocial Skills,* © 2016 by E. McGinnis and R. L. Simpson. Champaign, IL: Research Press (www.researchpress.com, 800-519-2707).

Skill 19: Responding to Offers to Join In

SKILL STEPS

1. **Decide if you want to join in.**

   Encourage the learner to try an activity that may be unfamiliar or seemingly uninteresting.

2. **If yes, ask about anything you don't understand.**

   The learner may need information about the rules of the game or directions to the activity.

3. **If no, give a reason.**

   Explain that giving a reason helps others understand and feel less offended. Remind learners to decline in a friendly manner (teach or review Skill 25, Using a Friendly Voice, as needed).

4. **Make your choice.**

SUGGESTED MODELING SITUATIONS

School: A peer asks you to read with him; a peer asks you to play a game.

Home: Your brother or sister asks you to play a board game.

Peer group: A friend asks you to play a game of basketball.

Community: A teacher asks you to join an activity at the community center.

COMMENTS

Both fine motor and gross motor activities (e.g., many sports) will likely be challenging for these learners. Listing activities and sports that "I Like," "I Want to Learn," and "I Don't Like" may help learners decide the activities they most want to join in.

Skill 19: Responding to Offers to Join In

Name_____Date_____

SKILL STEPS

1. Decide if you want to join in.

2. If yes, ask about anything you don't understand.

3. If no, give a reason.

4. Make your choice.

FILL IN NOW

With whom will I try this? _____

When? _____

_____

SUPPORTS

☐ Coaching with *(name)* _____

☐ With supportive peer *(name)* _____

☐ Other *(specify)* _____

☐ None

FILL IN AFTER YOU PRACTICE THE SKILL

What happened? _____

_____

How did I do? *(circle the number)*   4   3   2   1

            Really good!   Pretty good.   So-So.   I need to try again.

Why did I circle this? _____

_____

Skillstreaming

From *Skillstreaming Children and Youth with High-Functioning Autism: A Guide for Teaching Prosocial Skills,* © 2016 by E. McGinnis and R. L. Simpson. Champaign, IL: Research Press (www.researchpress.com, 800-519-2707).

Skill 19: Responding to Offers to Join In

Name_____Date_____

SKILL STEPS

1. Decide if you want to join in.

2. If yes, ask about anything you don't understand.

3. If no, give a reason.

4. Make your choice.

	How did I do? *(circle the number)*			
When did I practice?	Really Good!	Pretty good.	So-So.	I need to try again.
1. _____	4	3	2	1
2. _____	4	3	2	1
3. _____	4	3	2	1

SUPPORTS

	Practice Situation *(circle)*		
With prompting	1	2	3
With coaching	1	2	3
With supportive peer	1	2	3
Other support *(specify)* _____	1	2	3
None	1	2	3

From *Skillstreaming Children and Youth with High-Functioning Autism: A Guide for Teaching Prosocial Skills,* © 2016 by E. McGinnis and R. L. Simpson. Champaign, IL: Research Press (www.researchpress.com, 800-519-2707).

Skill 20: Asking to Join In

SKILL STEPS

1. **Decide if you want to join in.**

   Discuss with learners that they may want to watch the activity for a bit to see if this is something they would like to do.

2. **Ask, "Is this a good activity to ask to join?"**

   Talk about different activities that would be appropriate, such as group games or activities where another person joining in would not be a problem.

3. **Ask, "Is this a good time?"**

   Decide if this is a good time. Discuss a variety of games and activities the learner would like to join in and how to decide if it is a good time (e.g., when there is a break, when a person leaves the activity).

4. **Ask in a friendly way or do something else.**

   Discuss the body language and nonverbal behaviors that show a friendly way (review or teach Skill 25, Using a Friendly Voice, as needed).

SUGGESTED MODELING SITUATIONS

School: Ask to join in a group to complete a school project.

Home: Ask to join in an activity with your brother or sister.

Peer group: Ask to join in a group game at recess or after school.

Community: Ask to join in a group activity in the neighborhood.

COMMENTS

Discuss joining in a group that would likely welcome the learner, especially in the initial stages of learning this skill. Discuss how to assess the receptivity of the other person or group.

Skillstreaming

From *Skillstreaming Children and Youth with High-Functioning Autism: A Guide for Teaching Prosocial Skills,* © 2016 by E. McGinnis and R. L. Simpson. Champaign, IL: Research Press (www.researchpress.com, 800-519-2707).

Skill 20: Asking to Join In

Name_____Date_____

SKILL STEPS

1. Decide if you want to join in.

2. Ask, "Is this a good activity to ask to join?"

3. Ask, "Is this a good time?"

4. Ask in a friendly way or do something else.

FILL IN NOW

With whom will I try this? _____

When? _____

_____

SUPPORTS

☐ Coaching with *(name)* _____

☐ With supportive peer *(name)* _____

☐ Other *(specify)* _____

☐ None

FILL IN AFTER YOU PRACTICE THE SKILL

What happened? _____

_____

How did I do? *(circle the number)*   4   3   2   1

                                           Really good!   Pretty good.   So-So.   I need to try again.

Why did I circle this? _____

_____

Skill 20: Asking to Join In

Name_____Date_____

SKILL STEPS

1. Decide if you want to join in.
2. Ask, "Is this a good activity to ask to join?"
3. Ask, "Is this a good time?"
4. Ask in a friendly way or do something else.

| When did I practice? | How did I do? *(circle the number)* | | | |
	Really Good!	Pretty good.	So-So.	I need to try again.
1. _____	4	3	2	1
2. _____	4	3	2	1
3. _____	4	3	2	1

SUPPORTS

	Practice Situation *(circle)*		
With prompting	1	2	3
With coaching	1	2	3
With supportive peer	1	2	3
Other support *(specify)* _____	1	2	3
_____			
None	1	2	3

Skillstreaming

From *Skillstreaming Children and Youth with High-Functioning Autism: A Guide for Teaching Prosocial Skills,* © 2016 by E. McGinnis and R. L. Simpson. Champaign, IL: Research Press (www.researchpress.com, 800-519-2707).

Skill 21: Communicating Preferences

SKILL STEPS

1. **Think about what you like to do.**

   Make a list of the individual learner's preferences in a variety of situations and settings (school, home, community).

2. **Think of how to say this.**

   The learner should plan what to say and how to say it.

3. **Say your preference in a respectful way.**

   Explain to the learner that sometimes it may not be possible to honor a preference—for instance, in a school-related situation. The learner should use a skill such as Using Self-Control (Skill 39) in such cases.

SUGGESTED MODELING SITUATIONS

School: Your teacher asks you to write a paragraph using pencil and paper, but you would prefer to do the assignment on the computer.

Home: On the weekend, your parent asks you what you would like to do.

Peer group: A friend comes over to your house to play.

Community: A friend's parent wants to take your friend and you to the park.

COMMENTS

Encourage learners to list both quiet activities (those in which they could engage when others are still working on their assignments) and less quiet activities (those they can do at home or during a free period).

It will be helpful to teach a sentence stem, such as "I would like to _____; is this okay?"

Skill 21: Communicating Preferences

Name_____Date_____

SKILL STEPS

1. Think about what you like to do.

2. Think of how to say this.

3. Say your preference in a respectful way.

FILL IN NOW

With whom will I try this? _____

When? _____

_____

SUPPORTS

☐ Coaching with *(name)* _____

☐ With supportive peer *(name)* _____

☐ Other *(specify)* _____

☐ None

FILL IN AFTER YOU PRACTICE THE SKILL

What happened? _____

_____

How did I do? *(circle the number)*   4   3   2   1

                       Really good!   Pretty good.   So-So.   I need to try again.

Why did I circle this? _____

_____

Skill 21: Communicating Preferences

Name_____Date_____

SKILL STEPS

1. Think about what you like to do.

2. Think of how to say this.

3. Say your preference in a respectful way.

	How did I do? (circle the number)			
When did I practice?	Really Good!	Pretty good.	So-So.	I need to try again.
1. _____	4	3	2	1
2. _____	4	3	2	1
3. _____	4	3	2	1

SUPPORTS

	Practice Situation (circle)		
With prompting	1	2	3
With coaching	1	2	3
With supportive peer	1	2	3
Other support (specify)_____	1	2	3
None	1	2	3

From *Skillstreaming Children and Youth with High-Functioning Autism: A Guide for Teaching Prosocial Skills,* © 2016 by E. McGinnis and R. L. Simpson. Champaign, IL: Research Press (www.researchpress.com, 800-519-2707).

Skill 22: Accepting Another's Opinion

SKILL STEPS

1. **Listen without interrupting**

   Explain that it's important to get a good understanding of what the other person means and therefore it's important to listen carefully to what the person says. Review or teach Skill 1 (Listening Without Interrupting).

2. **Think about what is said.**

   Think about whether you agree with the other person's opinion. Explain it is important to stay calm or use another skill, such as Skill 39 (Using Self-Control) or Skill 43 (Checking Your Behavior).

3. **Say to yourself, "Everyone can have a different opinion. It's okay."**

4. **Answer or comment in a respectful way.**

   Explain that because it's okay for others to have different opinions, it's important to respond respectfully. Review or teach Skill 3 (Using a Respectful Voice) as needed.

SUGGESTED MODELING SITUATIONS

School: Your teacher says something about the lesson that you don't agree with.

Home: Your parent is telling you about weekend plans, and you don't think this will be fun.

Peer group: Your friend is talking about how much she likes a hobby, but you think it's boring.

Community: A neighbor is telling you how to help with the yard work, but you don't want to do it that way.

COMMENTS

Discuss comments and questions that are respectful (e.g., "That's interesting"; "I'll need to think about that"; "I'm not sure I agree, but I'll think about it more"; "Tell me more about what you are thinking"; "Why is this important to you?").

Skillstreaming

From *Skillstreaming Children and Youth with High-Functioning Autism: A Guide for Teaching Prosocial Skills,* © 2016 by E. McGinnis and R. L. Simpson. Champaign, IL: Research Press (www.researchpress.com, 800-519-2707).

Skill 22: Accepting Another's Opinion

Name_____Date_____

SKILL STEPS

1. Listen without interrupting

2. Think about what is said.

3. Say to yourself, "Everyone can have a different opinion. It's okay."

4. Answer or comment in a respectful way.

FILL IN NOW

With whom will I try this? _____

When? _____

_____

SUPPORTS

☐ Coaching with *(name)* _____

☐ With supportive peer *(name)* _____

☐ Other *(specify)* _____

☐ None

FILL IN AFTER YOU PRACTICE THE SKILL

What happened? _____

_____

How did I do? *(circle the number)*   4   3   2   1

Really good!   Pretty good.   So-So.   I need to try again.

Why did I circle this? _____

_____

From *Skillstreaming Children and Youth with High-Functioning Autism: A Guide for Teaching Prosocial Skills,* © 2016 by E. McGinnis and R. L. Simpson. Champaign, IL: Research Press (www.researchpress.com, 800-519-2707).

Skill 22: Accepting Another's Opinion

Name_____Date_____

SKILL STEPS

1. Listen without interrupting

2. Think about what is said.

3. Say to yourself, "Everyone can have a different opinion. It's okay."

4. Answer or comment in a respectful way.

	How did I do? *(circle the number)*			
When did I practice?	Really Good!	Pretty good.	So-So.	I need to try again.
1. _____	4	3	2	1
2. _____	4	3	2	1
3. _____	4	3	2	1

SUPPORTS

	Practice Situation *(circle)*		
With prompting	1	2	3
With coaching	1	2	3
With supportive peer	1	2	3
Other support *(specify)* _____	1	2	3
_____			
None	1	2	3

Skillstreaming

Group II: Social Comprehension
(Skills 23–32)

Skill 23: Reading Others

SKILL STEPS

1. **Look at the person's face.**

   Point out different facial expressions (smiling, frowning, angry look, etc.) and what these might mean. Explain that the person doesn't have to talk for the face to communicate.

2. **Look at the person's body.**

   Ask the learner how the person is standing (close, far away, leaning forward, a fighting stance, etc.).

3. **Look at the person's gestures.**

   Discuss what different gestures might mean (hands quietly by one's side, hands in fists, arms flailing, etc.).

4. **Decide.**

   Is the person welcoming to you? Does the person want you to stay away? Does the person seem neutral?

SUGGESTED MODELING SITUATIONS

School: A teacher is frustrated that the class is not listening; between classes, you approach a girl you like.

Home: A parent is hurrying to get dinner ready; you want to ask a brother or sister to play a game with you.

Peer group: A classmate has dropped all her books in the hallway; a classmate earned a good grade on his project; you want to join in a group after school; a friend keeps turning away from you and doesn't answer you when you say hi.

Community: A classmate scored in the big game; you need help from a salesperson at the store.

COMMENTS

It is helpful to show the learner pictures of different facial expressions, body posture, and gestures and to discuss the feelings the persons depicted may have. These expressions should be named.

This skill should precede the skill of Recognizing Another's Feelings (Skill 64). Learners first need to be able to attend to another's facial expressions, body posture, and gestures and describe these before they will be able to name the feelings someone may have.

Skill 23: Reading Others

Name_____Date_____

SKILL STEPS

1. Look at the person's face.

2. Look at the person's body.

3. Look at the person's gestures.

4. Decide.

FILL IN NOW

With whom will I try this? _____

When? _____

_____

SUPPORTS

☐ Coaching with *(name)* _____

☐ With supportive peer *(name)* _____

☐ Other *(specify)* _____

☐ None

FILL IN AFTER YOU PRACTICE THE SKILL

What happened? _____

_____

How did I do? *(circle the number)*   4   3   2   1

                           Really good!   Pretty good.   So-So.   I need to try again.

Why did I circle this? _____

_____

Skill 23: Reading Others

Name_____Date_____

SKILL STEPS

1. Look at the person's face.

2. Look at the person's body.

3. Look at the person's gestures.

4. Decide.

When did I practice?	How did I do? *(circle the number)*			
	Really Good!	Pretty good.	So-So.	I need to try again.
1. _____	4	3	2	1
2. _____	4	3	2	1
3. _____	4	3	2	1

SUPPORTS

	Practice Situation *(circle)*		
With prompting	1	2	3
With coaching	1	2	3
With supportive peer	1	2	3
Other support *(specify)* _____	1	2	3
None	1	2	3

Skill 24: Reading the Environment

SKILL STEPS

1. **Think about the setting.**

   Discuss different environments in which the learner interacts, such as school (classroom, hallway, cafeteria, gym), home, and community (places in the community the learner visits).

2. **Ask, "What are the clues about how to act?"**

   Is it a quiet or noisy place? Are there lots of people there? How are other people behaving?

3. **Decide on a plan.**

   Given these clues, talk through a plan of how to act in this setting.

4. **Follow your plan.**

SUGGESTED MODELING SITUATIONS

School: The weather is bad, so everyone is gathered in the gym.

Home: Your brother or sister is having a birthday party and there is a lot of noise and activity.

Peer group: You are having a conversation with a friend in the hallway, and suddenly the hallways become crowded.

Community: You and your family are waiting for a table at a restaurant.

COMMENTS

If environments are high activity and seem to create high stress for the learner, it may be helpful to think about quieter areas in the setting that may provide some relief. For example, if there are a lot of people gathered together after a community event, the learner may look for a quiet place to sit if the activity becomes too stressful. In addition, if there is a lot of noise and activity (e.g., during passing periods), the learner may wish to pass to the next class earlier than the crowd.

Skill 24: Reading the Environment

Name_____Date_____

SKILL STEPS

1. Think about the setting.

2. Ask, "What are the clues about how to act?"

3. Decide on a plan.

4. Follow your plan.

FILL IN NOW

With whom will I try this? _____

When? _____

_____

SUPPORTS

☐ Coaching with *(name)* _____

☐ With supportive peer *(name)* _____

☐ Other *(specify)* _____

☐ None

FILL IN AFTER YOU PRACTICE THE SKILL

What happened? _____

_____

How did I do? *(circle the number)*   4   3   2   1

                        Really good!   Pretty good.   So-So.   I need to try again.

Why did I circle this? _____

_____

From *Skillstreaming Children and Youth with High-Functioning Autism: A Guide for Teaching Prosocial Skills,* © 2016 by E. McGinnis and R. L. Simpson. Champaign, IL: Research Press (www.researchpress.com, 800-519-2707).

Skill 24: Reading the Environment

Name_____Date_____

SKILL STEPS

1. Think about the setting.
2. Ask, "What are the clues about how to act?"
3. Decide on a plan.
4. Follow your plan.

When did I practice?	How did I do? (circle the number)			
	Really Good!	Pretty good.	So-So.	I need to try again.
1. _____	4	3	2	1
2. _____	4	3	2	1
3. _____	4	3	2	1

SUPPORTS

	Practice Situation (circle)		
With prompting	1	2	3
With coaching	1	2	3
With supportive peer	1	2	3
Other support (specify) _____	1	2	3
_____			
None	1	2	3

Skillstreaming

From *Skillstreaming Children and Youth with High-Functioning Autism: A Guide for Teaching Prosocial Skills,* © 2016 by E. McGinnis and R. L. Simpson. Champaign, IL: Research Press (www.researchpress.com, 800-519-2707).

Skill 25: Using a Friendly Voice

SKILL STEPS

1. **Look at the person in a friendly way.**

   Discuss friendly facial expressions (e.g., a small smile), body posture (e.g., standing straight or leaning forward a bit), and gestures (e.g., waving "hi" or having arms hanging gently by the body). It is important to include a variety of ways a person might give a friendly look so learners do not learn only one "correct" response. You may want to act out different facial expressions and body postures to help learners identify what is friendly.

2. **Use a friendly voice.**

   Explain that a friendly voice is talking in a soft voice (not loud, angry, or in a whisper) and talking at a medium speed so the other person can think about what you are saying. Again, you may wish to act out different voice volumes and speed and have the learner identify which are friendly.

SUGGESTED MODELING SITUATIONS

School: A classmate starts talking with you in the hallway.

Home: A brother or sister asks you a question.

Peer group: A classmate who lives next door asks if you want to shoot baskets.

Community: You want to buy a soda at the concession stand.

COMMENTS

It will be helpful to use verbal cues for a friendly look (face, body posture, gestures) and a friendly voice (speed and volume) when learners are role-playing. Using these same verbal cues will further assist learners in using this skill in real-life situations. Writing these cues on a note card or using a picture of the cues will help learners remember the cues when a Skillstreaming coach is not present.

Explain that a friendly voice is typically used with people who are the same age as the learner or younger.

From *Skillstreaming Children and Youth with High-Functioning Autism: A Guide for Teaching Prosocial Skills,* © 2016 by E. McGinnis and R. L. Simpson. Champaign, IL: Research Press (www.researchpress.com, 800-519-2707).

Skill 25: Using a Friendly Voice

Name_____Date_____

SKILL STEPS

1. Look at the person in a friendly way.
2. Use a friendly voice.

FILL IN NOW

With whom will I try this? _____

When? _____

_____

SUPPORTS

☐ Coaching with *(name)* _____

☐ With supportive peer *(name)* _____

☐ Other *(specify)* _____

☐ None

FILL IN AFTER YOU PRACTICE THE SKILL

What happened? _____

_____

How did I do? *(circle the number)*   4   3   2   1

Really good!   Pretty good.   So-So.   I need to try again.

Why did I circle this? _____

_____

Skillstreaming

From *Skillstreaming Children and Youth with High-Functioning Autism: A Guide for Teaching Prosocial Skills,* © 2016 by E. McGinnis and R. L. Simpson. Champaign, IL: Research Press (www.researchpress.com, 800-519-2707).

Skill 25: Using a Friendly Voice

Name_____Date_____

SKILL STEPS

1. Look at the person in a friendly way.

2. Use a friendly voice.

When did I practice?	How did I do? *(circle the number)*			
	Really Good!	Pretty good.	So-So.	I need to try again.
1. _____	4	3	2	1
2. _____	4	3	2	1
3. _____	4	3	2	1

SUPPORTS

	Practice Situation *(circle)*		
With prompting	1	2	3
With coaching	1	2	3
With supportive peer	1	2	3
Other support *(specify)* _____	1	2	3
None	1	2	3

From *Skillstreaming Children and Youth with High-Functioning Autism: A Guide for Teaching Prosocial Skills,* © 2016 by E. McGinnis and R. L. Simpson. Champaign, IL: Research Press (www.researchpress.com, 800-519-2707).

Skill 26: Using a Respectful Voice

SKILL STEPS

1. **Look at the person.**

   Discuss that looking at the person means making eye contact, looking away briefly, and looking back at the person's face.

2. **Use respectful words.**

   Explain that using respectful words means using words appropriate for people in authority, such as adults. Discuss the people who are typically in authority positions, such as teachers, parents, and other adults in school and in the community. List examples of words that show respect, such as *please*; discuss asking instead of demanding and using the person's title, such as Mr. or Ms.

3. **Use a respectful voice.**

   Discuss what a respectful voice sounds like. For example, using an adult voice (not whiny or demanding).

SUGGESTED MODELING SITUATIONS

School: The principal wants to talk with you about a problem.

Home: Your parent tells you that you must do your chores.

Peer group: You are meeting a friend's parents.

Community: You want to apply for a job at the grocery store.

COMMENTS

Have learners practice different voice tones and vocabulary that demonstrate respectful, friendly, angry, demanding, and whiny voices so they have a better understanding of the differences.

Skillstreaming

From *Skillstreaming Children and Youth with High-Functioning Autism: A Guide for Teaching Prosocial Skills,* © 2016 by E. McGinnis and R. L. Simpson. Champaign, IL: Research Press (www.researchpress.com, 800-519-2707).

Skill 26: Using a Respectful Voice

Name_____Date_____

SKILL STEPS

1. Look at the person.

2. Use respectful words.

3. Use a respectful voice.

FILL IN NOW

With whom will I try this? _____

When? _____

_____

SUPPORTS

☐ Coaching with *(name)* _____

☐ With supportive peer *(name)* _____

☐ Other *(specify)* _____

☐ None

FILL IN AFTER YOU PRACTICE THE SKILL

What happened? _____

_____

How did I do? *(circle the number)*   4   3   2   1

Really good!   Pretty good.   So-So.   I need to try again.

Why did I circle this? _____

_____

Skill 26: Using a Respectful Voice

Name_____Date_____

SKILL STEPS

1. Look at the person.
2. Use respectful words.
3. Use a respectful voice.

When did I practice?	How did I do? (circle the number)			
	Really Good!	Pretty good.	So-So.	I need to try again.
1. _____	4	3	2	1
2. _____	4	3	2	1
3. _____	4	3	2	1

SUPPORTS

	Practice Situation (circle)		
With prompting	1	2	3
With coaching	1	2	3
With supportive peer	1	2	3
Other support (specify) _____	1	2	3
_____			
None	1	2	3

Skillstreaming From *Skillstreaming Children and Youth with High-Functioning Autism: A Guide for Teaching Prosocial Skills,* © 2016 by E. McGinnis and R. L. Simpson. Champaign, IL: Research Press (www.researchpress.com, 800-519-2707).

Skill 27: Giving Information Nonverbally

SKILL STEPS

1. **Check your face.**

   Point out different facial expressions (smiling, frowning, angry look, etc.) and what these might mean. Explain that someone doesn't have to talk for facial expressions to communicate meaning.

2. **Check your body.**

   Point out that how someone stands (close, far away, leaning forward, a fighting stance, etc.) communicates. Discuss what each of these actions may convey.

3. **Check your gestures.**

   Discuss what different gestures might mean (hands quietly by one's side, hands in fists, arms flailing, walking away, looking down, etc.).

4. **Decide what you are communicating.**

   Discuss various feelings, such as relaxed, angry, annoyed, frustrated, etc.

SUGGESTED MODELING DISPLAYS

School: You feel anxious about a project you don't want to do.

Home: You feel glad that your grandparent is coming to visit.

Peer group: You feel excited about going to a friend's party.

Community: You feel angry that a kid at the park teased you.

COMMENTS

Engaging supportive peers to model different feelings only by using body language, then pointing out facial expressions, body posture, and gestures, will assist learners in recognizing these differences. Then role-playing different feelings in different situations, with feedback from peers, will help learners understand how their body feels when they are showing different expressions.

This skill could be paired with Skill 23 (Reading Others).

Skill 27: Giving Information Nonverbally

Name_____Date_____

SKILL STEPS

1. Check your face.

2. Check your body.

3. Check your gestures.

4. Decide what you are communicating.

FILL IN NOW

With whom will I try this? _____

When? _____

_____

SUPPORTS

☐ Coaching with *(name)* _____

☐ With supportive peer *(name)* _____

☐ Other *(specify)* _____

☐ None

FILL IN AFTER YOU PRACTICE THE SKILL

What happened? _____

_____

How did I do? *(circle the number)*   4   3   2   1

Really good!   Pretty good.   So-So.   I need to try again.

Why did I circle this? _____

_____

Skillstreaming

From *Skillstreaming Children and Youth with High-Functioning Autism: A Guide for Teaching Prosocial Skills,* © 2016 by E. McGinnis and R. L. Simpson. Champaign, IL: Research Press (www.researchpress.com, 800-519-2707).

Skill 27: Giving Information Nonverbally

Name_____Date_____

SKILL STEPS

1. Check your face.
2. Check your body.
3. Check your gestures.
4. Decide what you are communicating.

How did I do? *(circle the number)*

When did I practice?	Really Good!	Pretty good.	So-So.	I need to try again.
1. _____	4	3	2	1
2. _____	4	3	2	1
3. _____	4	3	2	1

SUPPORTS

	Practice Situation *(circle)*		
With prompting	1	2	3
With coaching	1	2	3
With supportive peer	1	2	3
Other support *(specify)* _____	1	2	3
None	1	2	3

From *Skillstreaming Children and Youth with High-Functioning Autism: A Guide for Teaching Prosocial Skills,* © 2016 by E. McGinnis and R. L. Simpson. Champaign, IL: Research Press (www.researchpress.com, 800-519-2707).

Skill 28: Attending to a Model

SKILL STEPS

1. **Watch.**

   Direct learners to visually attend to the person modeling. Point out the skill steps as they are being modeled. Draw particular attention to the nonverbal actions of the model, as well as to each skill step.

2. **Listen.**

   Direct learners to think about what the model is saying and how he/she is saying it.

3. **Think, "What did the model do?"**

   What specific behaviors (skill steps) were followed?

4. **Think, "What did the model say?"**

   And how did he/she say it?

SUGGESTED MODELING SITUATIONS

School: You are participating in the Skillstreaming group; a supportive peer is dealing with a problem in a helpful way.

Home: Your brother or sister is greeting a friend; your parent is asking you a question.

Peer group: A peer is asking to join in a game that you would like to play, too.

Community: Your neighbor is having a conversation with another neighbor.

COMMENTS

This skill is useful if group participants have difficulty attending to the modeling displays. This is also good practice for learners to attend to others and to learn from modeling in natural environments.

.Skillstreaming

From *Skillstreaming Children and Youth with High-Functioning Autism: A Guide for Teaching Prosocial Skills,* © 2016 by E. McGinnis and R. L. Simpson. Champaign, IL: Research Press (www.researchpress.com, 800-519-2707).

Skill 28: Attending to a Model

Name_____Date_____

SKILL STEPS

1. Watch.

2. Listen.

3. Think, "What did the model do?"

4. Think, "What did the model say?"

FILL IN NOW

With whom will I try this? _____

When? _____

_____

SUPPORTS

☐ Coaching with *(name)* _____

☐ With supportive peer *(name)* _____

☐ Other *(specify)* _____

☐ None

FILL IN AFTER YOU PRACTICE THE SKILL

What happened? _____

_____

How did I do? *(circle the number)*   4   3   2   1

                  Really good!   Pretty good.   So-So.   I need to try again.

Why did I circle this? _____

_____

From *Skillstreaming Children and Youth with High-Functioning Autism: A Guide for Teaching Prosocial Skills,* © 2016
by E. McGinnis and R. L. Simpson. Champaign, IL: Research Press (www.researchpress.com, 800-519-2707).

Skill 28: Attending to a Model

Name_____Date_____

SKILL STEPS

1. Watch.

2. Listen.

3. Think, "What did the model do?"

4. Think, "What did the model say?"

When did I practice?	How did I do? *(circle the number)*			
	Really Good!	Pretty good.	So-So.	I need to try again.
1. _____	4	3	2	1
2. _____	4	3	2	1
3. _____	4	3	2	1

SUPPORTS

	Practice Situation *(circle)*		
With prompting	1	2	3
With coaching	1	2	3
With supportive peer	1	2	3
Other support *(specify)* _____	1	2	3
_____			
None	1	2	3

Skillstreaming From *Skillstreaming Children and Youth with High-Functioning Autism: A Guide for Teaching Prosocial Skills,* © 2016 by E. McGinnis and R. L. Simpson. Champaign, IL: Research Press (www.researchpress.com, 800-519-2707).

Skill 29: Respecting Another's Boundaries

SKILL STEPS

1. **Decide how far away.**

   Explain that distance depends on how well you know the person. For example, you may stand closer to a parent than to someone you do not know. Typically, it's most helpful to stand an arm's length away.

2. **Ask, "Do I touch the person?"**

   Explain appropriate touch (e.g., hugs, handshake, high-fives). List different people the learner encounters and decide which type of touch is appropriate for each. Explain that unless the learner knows the person well, it is best not to touch the person.

3. **Decide what to do instead.**

   Discuss other options that show friendship or respect that do not include touch.

SUGGESTED MODELING SITUATIONS

School: A group of classmates are in the library and you want to see the book they are looking at.

Home: Your sister is watching TV and you want to sit next to her.

Peer group: There is a girl or boy you would like to date and you see this person in the cafeteria.

Community: You see someone you don't know at a store but want to feel the fabric of his jacket.

COMMENTS

When the learner is familiar with a variety of relationship skills, these should be included as choices under Step 3.

Skill 29: Respecting Another's Boundaries

Name_____Date_____

SKILL STEPS

1. Decide how far away.

2. Ask, "Do I touch the person?"

3. Decide what to do instead.

FILL IN NOW

With whom will I try this? _____

When? _____

_____

SUPPORTS

☐ Coaching with *(name)* _____

☐ With supportive peer *(name)* _____

☐ Other *(specify)* _____

☐ None

FILL IN AFTER YOU PRACTICE THE SKILL

What happened? _____

_____

How did I do? *(circle the number)*   4   3   2   1

　　　　　　　　　　　　Really good!   Pretty good.   So-So.   I need to try again.

Why did I circle this? _____

_____

From *Skillstreaming Children and Youth with High-Functioning Autism: A Guide for Teaching Prosocial Skills,* © 2016 by E. McGinnis and R. L. Simpson. Champaign, IL: Research Press (www.researchpress.com, 800-519-2707).

Skill 29: Respecting Another's Boundaries

Name_____Date_____

SKILL STEPS

1. Decide how far away.

2. Ask, "Do I touch the person?"

3. Decide what to do instead.

When did I practice?	How did I do? (*circle the number*)			
	Really Good!	Pretty good.	So-So.	I need to try again.
1. _____	4	3	2	1
2. _____	4	3	2	1
3. _____	4	3	2	1

SUPPORTS

	Practice Situation (*circle*)		
With prompting	1	2	3
With coaching	1	2	3
With supportive peer	1	2	3
Other support (*specify*)_____	1	2	3
None	1	2	3

From *Skillstreaming Children and Youth with High-Functioning Autism: A Guide for Teaching Prosocial Skills,* © 2016 by E. McGinnis and R. L. Simpson. Champaign, IL: Research Press (www.researchpress.com, 800-519-2707).

Skill 30: Showing Interest in Others

SKILL STEPS

1. **Look at the person or group.**

   Explain or review appropriate eye gaze (looking occasionally at the person).

2. **Describe what the person or the group is doing.**

   During role-plays, this description should be stated aloud. In a real-life situation, this description should be said silently.

3. **Decide what to do next.**

   The learner may choose to ask to join in, move a bit closer to get more information, start a conversation, or go back to what he/she was doing.

SUGGESTED MODELING SITUATIONS

School: There are peers in your class that you haven't paid attention to.

Home: Your brother or sister is talking with a parent or neighbor; a brother or sister is in the bedroom crying.

Peer group: Classmates are walking home together after school.

Community: You are taking a walk and see someone you know.

COMMENTS

The goal of this skill is to teach learners to be aware of what is going on around them and to be less self-absorbed and isolated. This skill may be a prerequisite to other skills, such as Helping Others (Skill 9) and Encouraging Others (Skill 10).

Skillstreaming

From *Skillstreaming Children and Youth with High-Functioning Autism: A Guide for Teaching Prosocial Skills,* © 2016 by E. McGinnis and R. L. Simpson. Champaign, IL: Research Press (www.researchpress.com, 800-519-2707).

Skill 30: Showing Interest in Others

Name_____Date_____

SKILL STEPS

1. Look at the person or group.

2. Describe what the person or the group is doing.

3. Decide what to do next.

FILL IN NOW

With whom will I try this? _____

When?_____

_____

SUPPORTS

☐ Coaching with *(name)* _____

☐ With supportive peer *(name)* _____

☐ Other *(specify)* _____

☐ None

FILL IN AFTER YOU PRACTICE THE SKILL

What happened? _____

_____

How did I do? *(circle the number)*   4   3   2   1

Really good!   Pretty good.   So-So.   I need to try again.

Why did I circle this? _____

_____

Skill 30: Showing Interest in Others

Name_____Date_____

SKILL STEPS

1. Look at the person or group.

2. Describe what the person or the group is doing.

3. Decide what to do next.

	How did I do? (circle the number)			
When did I practice?	Really Good!	Pretty good.	So-So.	I need to try again.
1. _____	4	3	2	1
2. _____	4	3	2	1
3. _____	4	3	2	1

SUPPORTS

	Practice Situation (circle)		
With prompting	1	2	3
With coaching	1	2	3
With supportive peer	1	2	3
Other support (specify) _____	1	2	3
_____			
None	1	2	3

Skillstreaming

From *Skillstreaming Children and Youth with High-Functioning Autism: A Guide for Teaching Prosocial Skills,* © 2016 by E. McGinnis and R. L. Simpson. Champaign, IL: Research Press (www.researchpress.com, 800-519-2707).

Skill 31: Understanding Differences

SKILL STEPS

1. **Say to yourself, "Not everyone is the same."**

   Explain that people are different in the way they look and things they like.

2. **Say to yourself, "It's okay that people are different."**

   Explain that it's okay if other people aren't interested in what you like and that it's okay if you don't want to do what they want to do.

3. **Say to yourself, "I can handle this."**

   Learners may find it useful to repeat this statement several times to themselves.

4. **Decide.**

   Options include going back to the activity, giving your opinion, or doing something else. Explain that it is okay sometimes to give in to the way someone else wants to do something.

SUGGESTED MODELING SITUATIONS

School: Your work partner wants to do the project differently than you want to.

Home: Your brother or sister wants to watch a movie that you don't want to see.

Peer group: You are visiting a friend and you want to do something different than your friend does.

Community: You are at a restaurant with your family, but you don't like the type of food they have chosen.

COMMENTS

Discuss what *compromise* means—for example, sometimes doing what one person wants and then taking turns and doing what the other wants to do. Discuss situations in which compromise is appropriate.

Skill 31: Understanding Differences

Name_____Date_____

SKILL STEPS

1. Say to yourself, "Not everyone is the same."

2. Say to yourself, "It's okay that people are different."

3. Say to yourself, "I can handle this."

4. Decide.

FILL IN NOW

With whom will I try this?_____

When?_____

_____

SUPPORTS

☐ Coaching with *(name)* _____

☐ With supportive peer *(name)* _____

☐ Other *(specify)* _____

☐ None

FILL IN AFTER YOU PRACTICE THE SKILL

What happened? _____

_____

How did I do? *(circle the number)*   4   3   2   1

                                   Really good!   Pretty good.   So-So.   I need to try again.

Why did I circle this? _____

_____

Skillstreaming

Skill 31: Understanding Differences

Name_____Date_____

SKILL STEPS

1. Say to yourself, "Not everyone is the same."

2. Say to yourself, "It's okay that people are different."

3. Say to yourself, "I can handle this."

4. Decide.

	How did I do? *(circle the number)*			
When did I practice?	Really Good!	Pretty good.	So-So.	I need to try again.
1. _____	4	3	2	1
2. _____	4	3	2	1
3. _____	4	3	2	1

SUPPORTS

	Practice Situation *(circle)*		
With prompting	1	2	3
With coaching	1	2	3
With supportive peer	1	2	3
Other support *(specify)* _____	1	2	3
None	1	2	3

Skill 32: Taking Another's Perspective

SKILL STEPS

1. **Think about what happened.**

   Help the learner describe the event.

2. **Think about how the person might feel.**

   Display, teach, or review the feelings words from Skill 59 (Knowing Your Feelings).

3. **Think about how you might feel.**

   Encourage learners to pretend that this has happened and to think about how they would feel in the situation.

4. **Say to yourself, "If this happened to me, I would feel _____."**

SUGGESTED MODELING SITUATIONS

School: A classmate gives the wrong answer and the rest of the class laughs.

Home: A brother or sister isn't invited to a friend's party.

Peer group: A friend trips, falls down, and drops his school books and papers.

Community: A person is asked to leave the library for being too loud.

COMMENTS

Reading a variety of stories, then discussing how the characters might feel, will help to reinforce this concept.

When situations arise in the classroom that prompt perspective taking, guide learners through the steps of this skill.

Skillstreaming

From *Skillstreaming Children and Youth with High-Functioning Autism: A Guide for Teaching Prosocial Skills,* © 2016 by E. McGinnis and R. L. Simpson. Champaign, IL: Research Press (www.researchpress.com, 800-519-2707).

Skill 32: Taking Another's Perspective

Name_____Date_____

SKILL STEPS

1. Think about what happened.

2. Think about how the person might feel.

3. Think about how you might feel.

4. Say to yourself, "If this happened to me, I would feel _____."

FILL IN NOW

With whom will I try this? _____

When? _____

_____

SUPPORTS

☐ Coaching with *(name)* _____

☐ With supportive peer *(name)* _____

☐ Other *(specify)* _____

☐ None

FILL IN AFTER YOU PRACTICE THE SKILL

What happened? _____

_____

How did I do? *(circle the number)*	4	3	2	1
	Really good!	Pretty good.	So-So.	I need to try again.

Why did I circle this? _____

_____

From *Skillstreaming Children and Youth with High-Functioning Autism: A Guide for Teaching Prosocial Skills,* © 2016 by E. McGinnis and R. L. Simpson. Champaign, IL: Research Press (www.researchpress.com, 800-519-2707).

Skill 32: Taking Another's Perspective

Name_____Date_____

SKILL STEPS

1. Think about what happened.

2. Think about how the person might feel.

3. Think about how you might feel.

4. Say to yourself, "If this happened to me, I would feel _____."

When did I practice?	Really Good!	Pretty good.	So-So.	I need to try again.
	How did I do? *(circle the number)*			
1. _____	4	3	2	1
2. _____	4	3	2	1
3. _____	4	3	2	1

SUPPORTS

	Practice Situation *(circle)*		
With prompting	1	2	3
With coaching	1	2	3
With supportive peer	1	2	3
Other support *(specify)* _____	1	2	3
_____			
None	1	2	3

Skillstreaming

From *Skillstreaming Children and Youth with High-Functioning Autism: A Guide for Teaching Prosocial Skills,* © 2016
by E. McGinnis and R. L. Simpson. Champaign, IL: Research Press (www.researchpress.com, 800-519-2707).

Group III: Self-Regulation
(Skills 33–44)

Skill 33: Regulating Your Attention

SKILL STEPS

1. **Ask, "Am I doing what I should be?"**

   Ask learners if they are looking, listening, and doing what they should be.

2. **If yes, say, "Good for me. I'm staying on track."**

3. **If no, say, "I need to get back on track."**

   Explain that "back on track" means to get back to the task they should be doing. If needed, use the analogy of a train that is off the track. Have learners practice this self-statement. Ask learners what will help them get back on track. Develop a second self-statement for each individual that will be useful in paying attention. Have them practice their self-statements.

SUGGESTED MODELING SITUATIONS

School: It is a bit noisy in class and you are doing your assignment.

Home: You are supposed to be doing your homework, but you want to watch TV.

Peer group: You are playing a game with a peer and others are playing different games.

Community: You are attending a community event with your family and it's difficult to stay focused.

COMMENTS

This skill can be useful as an impulse control strategy when noise or other distractions exist. The classroom teacher can also prompt learners to use this skill if their attention is wandering in class.

Skill 33: Regulating Your Attention

Name_____Date_____

SKILL STEPS

1. Ask, "Am I doing what I should be?"

2. If yes, say, "Good for me. I'm staying on track."

3. If no, say, "I need to get back on track."

FILL IN NOW

With whom will I try this?_____

When?_____

_____

SUPPORTS

☐ Coaching with *(name)* _____

☐ With supportive peer *(name)* _____

☐ Other *(specify)* _____

☐ None

FILL IN AFTER YOU PRACTICE THE SKILL

What happened? _____

_____

How did I do? *(circle the number)*   4   3   2   1

                       Really good!   Pretty good.   So-So.   I need to try again.

Why did I circle this? _____

_____

Skillstreaming

From *Skillstreaming Children and Youth with High-Functioning Autism: A Guide for Teaching Prosocial Skills,* © 2016 by E. McGinnis and R. L. Simpson. Champaign, IL: Research Press (www.researchpress.com, 800-519-2707).

Skill 33: Regulating Your Attention

Name_____Date_____

SKILL STEPS

1. Ask, "Am I doing what I should be?"

2. If yes, say, "Good for me. I'm staying on track."

3. If no, say, "I need to get back on track."

When did I practice?	Really Good!	Pretty good.	So-So.	I need to try again.
1. _____	4	3	2	1
2. _____	4	3	2	1
3. _____	4	3	2	1

How did I do? (circle the number)

SUPPORTS

	Practice Situation *(circle)*		
With prompting	1	2	3
With coaching	1	2	3
With supportive peer	1	2	3
Other support *(specify)* _____	1	2	3
None	1	2	3

From *Skillstreaming Children and Youth with High-Functioning Autism: A Guide for Teaching Prosocial Skills,* © 2016 by E. McGinnis and R. L. Simpson. Champaign, IL: Research Press (www.researchpress.com, 800-519-2707).

Skill 34: Recognizing Anxiety

SKILL STEPS

1. **Think of how your body feels.**

   Discuss the cues the body gives, including feeling warm or hot, sweating, racing thoughts, feeling tight all over, feeling shaky, etc. Each learner may experience different cues.

2. **Say to yourself how your body shows anxiety.**

   Have each learner make a list of the symptoms of anxiety he/she experiences. For example, "I feel shaky."

3. **Decide if this is anxiety.**

   If yes, say, "I feel anxious." If no, it might be another feeling.

SUGGESTED MODELING SITUATIONS

School: There is an unannounced fire drill.

Home: A relative who hasn't seen you in a long time gives you a big hug.

Peer group: A classmate bumps into you in the hallway.

Community: You are on an outing to the store, but it's too noisy.

COMMENTS

Learners must first recognize that they are experiencing anxiety before learning how to deal effectively with it.

Skillstreaming

From *Skillstreaming Children and Youth with High-Functioning Autism: A Guide for Teaching Prosocial Skills,* © 2016 by E. McGinnis and R. L. Simpson. Champaign, IL: Research Press (www.researchpress.com, 800-519-2707).

Skill 34: Recognizing Anxiety

Name_____Date_____

SKILL STEPS

1. Think of how your body feels.
2. Say to yourself how your body shows anxiety.
3. Decide if this is anxiety.

FILL IN NOW

With whom will I try this? _____

When? _____

_____

SUPPORTS

☐ Coaching with *(name)* _____

☐ With supportive peer *(name)* _____

☐ Other *(specify)* _____

☐ None

FILL IN AFTER YOU PRACTICE THE SKILL

What happened? _____

_____

How did I do? *(circle the number)*	4	3	2	1
	Really good!	Pretty good.	So-So.	I need to try again.

Why did I circle this? _____

_____

Skill 34: Recognizing Anxiety

Name_____Date_____

SKILL STEPS

1. Think of how your body feels.

2. Say to yourself how your body shows anxiety.

3. Decide if this is anxiety.

	How did I do? *(circle the number)*			
When did I practice?	Really Good!	Pretty good.	So-So.	I need to try again.
1. _____	4	3	2	1
2. _____	4	3	2	1
3. _____	4	3	2	1

SUPPORTS

	Practice Situation *(circle)*		
With prompting	1	2	3
With coaching	1	2	3
With supportive peer	1	2	3
Other support *(specify)* _____	1	2	3
_____			
None	1	2	3

Skillstreaming

From *Skillstreaming Children and Youth with High-Functioning Autism: A Guide for Teaching Prosocial Skills,* © 2016 by E. McGinnis and R. L. Simpson. Champaign, IL: Research Press (www.researchpress.com, 800-519-2707).

Skill 35: Deciding What Causes Your Anxiety

SKILL STEPS

1. **Think about what creates anxiety for you.**

    List specific situations for each learner, both that he/she has identified and that teachers or parents note. These situations may be used for role-plays.

2. **Decide what has made you uncomfortable now.**

    Refer to the list of situations to help decide.

3. **Say to yourself, "I feel uncomfortable when _____."**

SUGGESTED MODELING SITUATIONS

School: Your class is in the gym and it's very noisy.

Home: You need to dress up for an event, but you aren't comfortable in what you are wearing.

Peer group: A classmate bumps into you in the hallway.

Community: A person you don't know touches you to move you away; you want to touch a person's coat, but she screams at you.

COMMENTS

Anxiety-producing situations for these learners may relate to sound (e.g., loud noises), smell (e.g., certain foods), touch (e.g., unanticipated touch), taste (e.g., certain textures of food), or vision (e.g., seeing a large group of people).

From *Skillstreaming Children and Youth with High-Functioning Autism: A Guide for Teaching Prosocial Skills,* © 2016 by E. McGinnis and R. L. Simpson. Champaign, IL: Research Press (www.researchpress.com, 800-519-2707).

Skill 35: Deciding What Causes Your Anxiety

Name_____Date_____

SKILL STEPS

1. Think about what creates anxiety for you.

2. Decide what has made you uncomfortable now.

3. Say to yourself, "I feel uncomfortable when _____."

FILL IN NOW

With whom will I try this? _____

When? _____

_____

SUPPORTS

☐ Coaching with *(name)* _____

☐ With supportive peer *(name)* _____

☐ Other *(specify)* _____

☐ None

FILL IN AFTER YOU PRACTICE THE SKILL

What happened? _____

_____

How did I do? *(circle the number)*   4   3   2   1

                               Really good!   Pretty good.   So-So.   I need to try again.

Why did I circle this? _____

_____

Skillstreaming

From *Skillstreaming Children and Youth with High-Functioning Autism: A Guide for Teaching Prosocial Skills,* © 2016 by E. McGinnis and R. L. Simpson. Champaign, IL: Research Press (www.researchpress.com, 800-519-2707).

Skill 35: Deciding What Causes Your Anxiety

Name_____Date_____

SKILL STEPS

1. Think about what creates anxiety for you.

2. Decide what has made you uncomfortable now.

3. Say to yourself, "I feel uncomfortable when _____."

	How did I do? (circle the number)			
When did I practice?	Really Good!	Pretty good.	So-So.	I need to try again.
1. _____	4	3	2	1
2. _____	4	3	2	1
3. _____	4	3	2	1

SUPPORTS

	Practice Situation (circle)		
With prompting	1	2	3
With coaching	1	2	3
With supportive peer	1	2	3
Other support (specify)_____	1	2	3
None	1	2	3

From *Skillstreaming Children and Youth with High-Functioning Autism: A Guide for Teaching Prosocial Skills,* © 2016 by E. McGinnis and R. L. Simpson. Champaign, IL: Research Press (www.researchpress.com, 800-519-2707).

Skill 36: Dealing with Anxiety

SKILL STEPS

1. **Think of your choices.**

   Choices will vary depending on the type of event. Create a list of positive ways learners could deal with the stress (e.g., say, "I don't like to be touched," use headphones or move to a quiet area, ask to leave the setting or sit in a quiet place).

2. **Make a plan.**

   It is helpful if this plan is in writing to help prompt the learner.

3. **Say, "I can follow my plan."**

4. **Follow your plan.**

SUGGESTED MODELING SITUATIONS

School: There is an unannounced fire drill.

Home: A relative who hasn't seen you in a long time gives you a big hug.

Peer group: A classmate bumps into you in the hallway.

Community: You are on an outing to the store, but it's too noisy.

COMMENTS

It is important to let others in the school setting and family members know about these triggers for learners. While teachers and parents may work to minimize these events, it is also important for the individual learner to deal independently with these experiences in a way that is helpful to him or her.

Skill 36: Dealing with Anxiety

Name_____Date_____

SKILL STEPS

1. Think of your choices.

2. Make a plan.

3. Say, "I can follow my plan."

4. Follow your plan.

FILL IN NOW

With whom will I try this? _____

When? _____

_____

SUPPORTS

☐ Coaching with *(name)* _____

☐ With supportive peer *(name)* _____

☐ Other *(specify)* _____

☐ None

FILL IN AFTER YOU PRACTICE THE SKILL

What happened? _____

_____

How did I do? *(circle the number)*   4   3   2   1

Really good!   Pretty good.   So-So.   I need to try again.

Why did I circle this? _____

_____

Skill 36: Dealing with Anxiety

Name_____Date_____

SKILL STEPS

1. Think of your choices.
2. Make a plan.
3. Say, "I can follow my plan."
4. Follow your plan.

	How did I do? (circle the number)			
When did I practice?	Really Good!	Pretty good.	So-So.	I need to try again.
1. _____	4	3	2	1
2. _____	4	3	2	1
3. _____	4	3	2	1

SUPPORTS

	Practice Situation (circle)		
With prompting	1	2	3
With coaching	1	2	3
With supportive peer	1	2	3
Other support (specify)_____	1	2	3
_____			
None	1	2	3

Skillstreaming

From *Skillstreaming Children and Youth with High-Functioning Autism: A Guide for Teaching Prosocial Skills,* © 2016 by E. McGinnis and R. L. Simpson. Champaign, IL: Research Press (www.researchpress.com, 800-519-2707).

Skill 37: Checking Your Voice and Interests

SKILL STEPS

1. **Are you using a friendly or respectful voice?**

   Be sure learners have mastered Skill 25 (Using a Friendly Voice) and Skill 26 (Using a Respectful Voice). If not, reteach these skills.

2. **Is the person listening?**

   Explain that talking for more than three or four sentences can be boring for the listener. Discuss how to check if the person is listening. Prompt the learner to make a self-statement, such as "I can stop talking now. It's okay."

3. **Are you sticking too long with your interest?**

   Explain that the learner's interest may not be of great interest to others. If needed, set a timer for 2 minutes for the learner to stay with his/her interest, then prompt him/her to change interests. Again, a self-statement, such as "I can change my interest and do this later; it's okay" may help the learner transition to something else.

4. **If yes, stop and do something else.**

   Explore other options with the learners.

SUGGESTED MODELING SITUATIONS

School: Your teacher asks you to answer a question.

Home: You are playing in your room and your parent calls you for dinner; your parents have friends over and you are expected to play with their son/daughter.

Peer group: You are talking with a peer group at a ballgame.

Community: You are engaged with items at a store and your parent says it's time to leave.

COMMENTS

The goal of this skill is to deal with learners' verbal monologues and obsessive interests. Self-statements help the learners to lessen their anxiety about stopping these behaviors for the time being.

Skill 37: Checking Your Voice and Interests

Name_____Date_____

SKILL STEPS

1. Are you using a friendly or respectful voice?

2. Is the person listening?

3. Are you sticking too long with your interest?

4. If yes, stop and do something else.

FILL IN NOW

With whom will I try this? _____

When? _____

_____

SUPPORTS

☐ Coaching with *(name)* _____

☐ With supportive peer *(name)* _____

☐ Other *(specify)* _____

☐ None

FILL IN AFTER YOU PRACTICE THE SKILL

What happened? _____

_____

How did I do? *(circle the number)*   4   3   2   1

                                 Really good!   Pretty good.   So-So.   I need to try again.

Why did I circle this? _____

_____

Skillstreaming

From *Skillstreaming Children and Youth with High-Functioning Autism: A Guide for Teaching Prosocial Skills,* © 2016 by E. McGinnis and R. L. Simpson. Champaign, IL: Research Press (www.researchpress.com, 800-519-2707).

Skill 37: Checking Your Voice and Interests

Name_____Date_____

SKILL STEPS

1. Are you using a friendly or respectful voice?

2. Is the person listening?

3. Are you sticking too long with your interest?

4. If yes, stop and do something else.

When did I practice?	How did I do? (circle the number)			
	Really Good!	Pretty good.	So-So.	I need to try again.
1. _____	4	3	2	1
2. _____	4	3	2	1
3. _____	4	3	2	1

SUPPORTS

	Practice Situation (circle)		
With prompting	1	2	3
With coaching	1	2	3
With supportive peer	1	2	3
Other support (specify)_____	1	2	3
None	1	2	3

From *Skillstreaming Children and Youth with High-Functioning Autism: A Guide for Teaching Prosocial Skills,* © 2016 by E. McGinnis and R. L. Simpson. Champaign, IL: Research Press (www.researchpress.com, 800-519-2707).

Skill 38: No Means No

SKILL STEPS

1. **Stop and think about what you want to do.**

2. **Think, "Is this a no means no situation?"**

    Does the action invade someone's physical boundaries? Can what is said be interpreted as sexual? Is the action unsafe for me or someone else?

3. **Say to yourself, "In this situation, I can accept that no means no."**

    Learners may need to repeat this statement (or another self-statement) over and over until they are comfortable in moving to Step 4.

4. **Do something else.**

    Generate a list of acceptable alternatives.

SUGGESTED MODELING SITUATIONS

School: You see a girl/ boy you like in the hallway and want to touch her/him; you are standing too close to a classmate and he/she asks you to stop.

Home: You are angry with your brother/sister and want to say something sexual.

Peer group: You see a girl at the movies and want to play with her long hair.

Community: A customer at the store has a coat you want to touch.

COMMENTS

Explain that this skill is to be used when the learner feels the urge to invade someone else's physical boundary, to make comments that are sexual in nature, or when safety is a concern (either for the learner or for others). Learners in need of this skill will need to understand what is sexual talk and touch, even if they don't mean their actions in this way. They need to understand that the determination is made by the receiver of the touch or words.

Skillstreaming

From *Skillstreaming Children and Youth with High-Functioning Autism: A Guide for Teaching Prosocial Skills,* © 2016 by E. McGinnis and R. L. Simpson. Champaign, IL: Research Press (www.researchpress.com, 800-519-2707).

Skill 38: No Means No

Name_____Date_____

SKILL STEPS

1. Stop and think about what you want to do.

2. Think, "Is this a no means no situation?"

3. Say to yourself, "In this situation, I can accept that no means no."

4. Do something else.

FILL IN NOW

With whom will I try this? _____

When? _____

_____

SUPPORTS

☐ Coaching with *(name)* _____

☐ With supportive peer *(name)* _____

☐ Other *(specify)* _____

☐ None

FILL IN AFTER YOU PRACTICE THE SKILL

What happened? _____

_____

How did I do? *(circle the number)*	4	3	2	1
	Really good!	Pretty good.	So-So.	I need to try again.

Why did I circle this? _____

_____

From *Skillstreaming Children and Youth with High-Functioning Autism: A Guide for Teaching Prosocial Skills,* © 2016
by E. McGinnis and R. L. Simpson. Champaign, IL: Research Press (www.researchpress.com, 800-519-2707).

Skill 38: No Means No

Name_____Date_____

SKILL STEPS

1. Stop and think about what you want to do.

2. Think, "Is this a no means no situation?"

3. Say to yourself, "In this situation, I can accept that no means no."

4. Do something else.

When did I practice?	How did I do? *(circle the number)*			
	Really Good!	Pretty good.	So-So.	I need to try again.
1. _____	4	3	2	1
2. _____	4	3	2	1
3. _____	4	3	2	1

SUPPORTS

	Practice Situation *(circle)*		
With prompting	1	2	3
With coaching	1	2	3
With supportive peer	1	2	3
Other support *(specify)* _____	1	2	3
_____			
None	1	2	3

Skillstreaming

Skill 39: Using Self-Control

SKILL STEPS

1. **Say to yourself, "Stop and think."**

   Discuss the importance of allowing yourself time to cool off and think.

2. **Think of how your body feels.**

   Discuss how bodily cues may signal losing control (hands become sweaty, you feel hot or weak, you feel like there's a fire in your stomach).

3. **Ask, "If I lose control, what could happen?"**

   Discuss possible negative consequences of acting out with aggression.

4. **Stay in control by doing something else.**

   Discuss and practice choices such as walking away for now, doing a relaxation exercise, talking with someone, writing or drawing about how you feel, or asking to take a break.

SUGGESTED MODELING SITUATIONS

School: Your teacher has an activity planned that you do not want to do.

Home: A brother or sister has borrowed your art supplies without asking.

Peer group: A friend has taken something of yours and won't give it back.

Community: Someone accidently bumps into you at the ballgame.

COMMENTS

Learners should use this skill when they are too angry or upset to identify how they feel. Explain to them that this skill helps them gain control, but they may need to use another skill to solve the problem. Suggest that it is better to delay dealing with a problem than to lose control and get in trouble.

Skill 39: Using Self-Control

Name_____Date_____

SKILL STEPS

1. Say to yourself, "Stop and think."
2. Think of how your body feels.
3. Ask, "If I lose control, what could happen?"
4. Stay in control by doing something else.

FILL IN NOW

With whom will I try this? _____

When? _____

_____

SUPPORTS

☐ Coaching with *(name)* _____

☐ With supportive peer *(name)* _____

☐ Other *(specify)* _____

☐ None

FILL IN AFTER YOU PRACTICE THE SKILL

What happened? _____

_____

How did I do? *(circle the number)*   4   3   2   1

                              Really good!   Pretty good.   So-So.   I need to try again.

Why did I circle this? _____

_____

From *Skillstreaming Children and Youth with High-Functioning Autism: A Guide for Teaching Prosocial Skills,* © 2016 by E. McGinnis and R. L. Simpson. Champaign, IL: Research Press (www.researchpress.com, 800-519-2707).

Skill 39: Using Self-Control

Name_____Date_____

SKILL STEPS

1. Say to yourself, "Stop and think."

2. Think of how your body feels.

3. Ask, "If I lose control, what could happen?"

4. Stay in control by doing something else.

	How did I do? *(circle the number)*			
When did I practice?	Really Good!	Pretty good.	So-So.	I need to try again.
1. _____	4	3	2	1
2. _____	4	3	2	1
3. _____	4	3	2	1

SUPPORTS

	Practice Situation *(circle)*		
With prompting	1	2	3
With coaching	1	2	3
With supportive peer	1	2	3
Other support *(specify)*_____	1	2	3
None	1	2	3

Skill 40: Dealing with Change

SKILL STEPS

1. **Say to yourself, "This isn't what usually happens next."**

   It is important for learners to understand that a change in the routine has occurred and that this will likely be stressful.

2. **Say to yourself, "I know I can handle the change."**

3. **Stop and take three deep breaths.**

   Other self-control strategies may be added or substituted, depending on the learner's needs.

4. **Follow the direction.**

SUGGESTED MODELING SITUATIONS

School: You are going on a field trip, but you didn't know ahead of time.

Home: Your TV doesn't work and you usually watch a show after school.

Peer group: A friend usually walks home from school with you, but he was absent today.

Community: You go to the library, but the library is closed.

COMMENTS

Change in routine or schedule is very challenging for this population. While many times learners can be prepared in advance for a change, it isn't always possible to do so. Learners will therefore need practice with this skill in a variety of different situations and settings.

Skillstreaming

From *Skillstreaming Children and Youth with High-Functioning Autism: A Guide for Teaching Prosocial Skills,* © 2016 by E. McGinnis and R. L. Simpson. Champaign, IL: Research Press (www.researchpress.com, 800-519-2707).

Skill 40: Dealing with Change

Name_____Date_____

SKILL STEPS

1. Say to yourself, "This isn't what usually happens next."

2. Say to yourself, "I know I can handle the change."

3. Stop and take three deep breaths.

4. Follow the direction.

FILL IN NOW

With whom will I try this? _____

When? _____

_____

SUPPORTS

☐ Coaching with *(name)* _____

☐ With supportive peer *(name)* _____

☐ Other *(specify)* _____

☐ None

FILL IN AFTER YOU PRACTICE THE SKILL

What happened? _____

_____

How did I do? *(circle the number)*   4   3   2   1

                                 Really good!   Pretty good.   So-So.   I need to try again.

Why did I circle this? _____

_____

From *Skillstreaming Children and Youth with High-Functioning Autism: A Guide for Teaching Prosocial Skills,* © 2016 by E. McGinnis and R. L. Simpson. Champaign, IL: Research Press (www.researchpress.com, 800-519-2707).

Skill 40: Dealing with Change

Name_____Date_____

SKILL STEPS

1. Say to yourself, "This isn't what usually happens next."

2. Say to yourself, "I know I can handle the change."

3. Stop and take three deep breaths.

4. Follow the direction.

When did I practice?	How did I do? (circle the number)			
	Really Good!	Pretty good.	So-So.	I need to try again.
1. _____	4	3	2	1
2. _____	4	3	2	1
3. _____	4	3	2	1

SUPPORTS

	Practice Situation (circle)		
With prompting	1	2	3
With coaching	1	2	3
With supportive peer	1	2	3
Other support (specify)_____	1	2	3
None	1	2	3

Skillstreaming

From *Skillstreaming Children and Youth with High-Functioning Autism: A Guide for Teaching Prosocial Skills,* © 2016 by E. McGinnis and R. L. Simpson. Champaign, IL: Research Press (www.researchpress.com, 800-519-2707).

Skill 41: Dealing with Boredom

SKILL STEPS

1. **Decide if you are feeling bored.**

   Discuss how to recognize signs of boredom (e.g., you don't enjoy the activity you've been assigned).

2. **Think of your options.**

   a. **Ask if you can do something else.**

   b. **Ask to take a break.**

   c. **Say, "I'm bored, but I can do this anyway."**

   Other acceptable options may be added for particular learners.

3. **Do it.**

SUGGESTED MODELING SITUATIONS

School: You've been given an assignment you find boring.

Home: You feel bored with the conversation (or activity) with your family and you want to do something else.

Peer group: You have a friend over and you're tired of playing and want her to leave so you can watch TV.

Community: You are in a restaurant with your family and the wait for dinner is too long.

COMMENTS

It is not unusual for youth with these disorders to resist doing tasks they find boring. This skill is useful for addressing resistance in these situations.

Skill 41: Dealing with Boredom

Name_____Date_____

SKILL STEPS

1. Decide if you are feeling bored.

2. Think of your options.

    a. Ask if you can do something else.

    b. Ask to take a break.

    c. Say, "I'm bored, but I can do this anyway."

3. Do it.

FILL IN NOW

With whom will I try this? _____

When? _____

_____

SUPPORTS

☐ Coaching with *(name)* _____

☐ With supportive peer *(name)* _____

☐ Other *(specify)* _____

☐ None

FILL IN AFTER YOU PRACTICE THE SKILL

What happened? _____

_____

How did I do? *(circle the number)*	4	3	2	1
	Really good!	Pretty good.	So-So.	I need to try again.

Why did I circle this? _____

_____

Skillstreaming

Skill 41: Dealing with Boredom

Name_____Date_____

SKILL STEPS

1. Decide if you are feeling bored.
2. Think of your options.
   a. Ask if you can do something else.
   b. Ask to take a break.
   c. Say, "I'm bored, but I can do this anyway."
3. Do it.

When did I practice?	How did I do? *(circle the number)*			
	Really Good!	Pretty good.	So-So.	I need to try again.
1. _____	4	3	2	1
2. _____	4	3	2	1
3. _____	4	3	2	1

SUPPORTS

	Practice Situation *(circle)*		
With prompting	1	2	3
With coaching	1	2	3
With supportive peer	1	2	3
Other support *(specify)* _____	1	2	3
None	1	2	3

From *Skillstreaming Children and Youth with High-Functioning Autism: A Guide for Teaching Prosocial Skills,* © 2016 by E. McGinnis and R. L. Simpson. Champaign, IL: Research Press (www.researchpress.com, 800-519-2707).

Skill 42: Responding to Authority

SKILL STEPS

1. **Think about the person's role.**

   Discuss the roles of adults in the school, home, and community. Explain which people are in an authority role.

2. **Ask, "What are the rules?"**

   Review the rules or expectations for a variety of settings. Think about why a person in authority would have these rules. Explore possible reasons (e.g., to keep you safe, help others learn).

3. **Say to yourself, "I don't like this, but I can handle it."**

   The learner may need to repeat this more than once before responding.

4. **Follow the expectation.**

   Learners may also state to the person in authority, "Okay, I can do this."

SUGGESTED MODELING SITUATIONS

School: You are expected to be in your seat when the bell rings, but you'd rather use the headphones and listen to music.

Home: Your parent tells you that it's time to get ready for bed.

Peer group: You and a friend are playing, but the break (or recess) is over.

Community: You are using the computer at the library, and the librarian tells you another person wants to use it.

COMMENTS

If learners make a statement in Step 4, it will be important to review Skill 26 (Using a Respectful Voice).

Skillstreaming

From *Skillstreaming Children and Youth with High-Functioning Autism: A Guide for Teaching Prosocial Skills,* © 2016 by E. McGinnis and R. L. Simpson. Champaign, IL: Research Press (www.researchpress.com, 800-519-2707).

Skill 42: Responding to Authority

Name_____Date_____

SKILL STEPS

1. Think about the person's role.

2. Ask, "What are the rules?"

3. Say to yourself, "I don't like this, but I can handle it."

4. Follow the expectation.

FILL IN NOW

With whom will I try this? _____

When? _____

_____

SUPPORTS

☐ Coaching with *(name)* _____

☐ With supportive peer *(name)* _____

☐ Other *(specify)* _____

☐ None

FILL IN AFTER YOU PRACTICE THE SKILL

What happened? _____

_____

How did I do? *(circle the number)*   4   3   2   1

                     Really good!   Pretty good.   So-So.   I need to try again.

Why did I circle this? _____

_____

Skill 42: Responding to Authority

Name_____Date_____

SKILL STEPS

1. Think about the person's role.

2. Ask, "What are the rules?"

3. Say to yourself, "I don't like this, but I can handle it."

4. Follow the expectation.

	How did I do? *(circle the number)*			
When did I practice?	Really Good!	Pretty good.	So-So.	I need to try again.
1. _____	4	3	2	1
2. _____	4	3	2	1
3. _____	4	3	2	1

SUPPORTS

	Practice Situation *(circle)*		
With prompting	1	2	3
With coaching	1	2	3
With supportive peer	1	2	3
Other support *(specify)*_____	1	2	3
None	1	2	3

Skillstreaming

From *Skillstreaming Children and Youth with High-Functioning Autism: A Guide for Teaching Prosocial Skills,* © 2016 by E. McGinnis and R. L. Simpson. Champaign, IL: Research Press (www.researchpress.com, 800-519-2707).

Skill 43: Checking Your Behavior

SKILL STEPS

1. **Check yourself.**

   How does your body feel? Are you calm or getting angry or frustrated? Teach or review Skill 34 (Recognizing Anxiety), as needed.

2. **Do I need to relax?**

   a. **Take three deep breaths (breathe in through the nose and out through the mouth).**

   b. **Tighten one part of your body, count to three, relax. Continue for each body part.**

   c. **Take a break.**

3. **Return to what you were doing.**

SUGGESTED MODELING SITUATIONS

School: You are frustrated with a school task and want to stop.

Home: You are picking up your room but don't want to do it.

Peer group: A peer is teasing you and you don't know if it's friendly or mean teasing.

Community: You are in the store with your parent and the lights bother you.

COMMENTS

The goal of this skill is for learners to recognize their stress before they lose control. After teaching this skill, it is useful to prompt learners to "Check your behavior" when you notice they are becoming agitated.

Skill 43: Checking Your Behavior

Name_____Date_____

SKILL STEPS

1. Check yourself.

2. Do I need to relax?

   a. Take three deep breaths (breathe in through the nose and out through the mouth).

   b. Tighten one part of your body, count to three, relax. Continue for each body part.

   c. Take a break.

3. Return to what you were doing.

FILL IN NOW

With whom will I try this? _____

When? _____

_____

SUPPORTS

☐ Coaching with *(name)* _____

☐ With supportive peer *(name)* _____

☐ Other *(specify)* _____

☐ None

FILL IN AFTER YOU PRACTICE THE SKILL

What happened? _____

_____

How did I do? *(circle the number)*   4   3   2   1

　　　　　　　　　　　　　Really good!   Pretty good.   So-So.   I need to try again.

Why did I circle this? _____

_____

.Skillstreaming
∎∎∎∎∎∎∎∎∎∎∎∎∎∎

Skill 43: Checking Your Behavior

Name_____Date_____

SKILL STEPS

1. Check yourself.

2. Do I need to relax?

    a. Take three deep breaths (breathe in through the nose and out through the mouth).

    b. Tighten one part of your body, count to three, relax. Continue for each body part.

    c. Take a break.

3. Return to what you were doing.

	How did I do? *(circle the number)*			
When did I practice?	Really Good!	Pretty good.	So-So.	I need to try again.
1. _____	4	3	2	1
2. _____	4	3	2	1
3. _____	4	3	2	1

SUPPORTS

	Practice Situation *(circle)*		
With prompting	1	2	3
With coaching	1	2	3
With supportive peer	1	2	3
Other support *(specify)*_____	1	2	3
None	1	2	3

From *Skillstreaming Children and Youth with High-Functioning Autism: A Guide for Teaching Prosocial Skills,* © 2016 by E. McGinnis and R. L. Simpson. Champaign, IL: Research Press (www.researchpress.com, 800-519-2707).

Skill 44: Affirming Yourself

SKILL STEPS

1. **Think about what you do well.**

   This could relate to a social behavior or academic task. Encourage learners to think about times when they completed something they didn't really want to do.

2. **Think about what you could say about yourself.**

   Say, "It was tough, but I did it! Good for me"; "I really tried hard and did it"; "I stayed on track and got it done!" Explain that making these affirmations helps learners recognize what they do well and will help them do challenging tasks. The self-statements can be modified to fit each learner.

3. **Write down your affirmation.**

   Affirmations could be written on a small index card or on an iPad to help them remember their plan.

4. **Say it. Repeat it.**

SUGGESTED MODELING SITUATIONS

School: You didn't want to work with the group, but you did it.

Home: You didn't want to make the trip with your parents, but you went.

Peer group: You took a chance to join in a new game and learn the rules.

Community: You helped a neighbor with yard work even though it was hard.

COMMENTS

Making positive affirmations will help learners realistically recognize things they do well and build their self-confidence.

Skillstreaming

From *Skillstreaming Children and Youth with High-Functioning Autism: A Guide for Teaching Prosocial Skills,* © 2016 by E. McGinnis and R. L. Simpson. Champaign, IL: Research Press (www.researchpress.com, 800-519-2707).

Skill 44: Affirming Yourself

Name_____Date_____

SKILL STEPS

1. Think about what you do well.
2. Think about what you could say about yourself.
3. Write down your affirmation.
4. Say it. Repeat it.

FILL IN NOW

With whom will I try this? _____

When? _____

_____

SUPPORTS

☐ Coaching with *(name)* _____

☐ With supportive peer *(name)* _____

☐ Other *(specify)* _____

☐ None

FILL IN AFTER YOU PRACTICE THE SKILL

What happened? _____

_____

How did I do? *(circle the number)*   4   3   2   1

Really good!   Pretty good.   So-So.   I need to try again.

Why did I circle this? _____

_____

From *Skillstreaming Children and Youth with High-Functioning Autism: A Guide for Teaching Prosocial Skills,* © 2016
by E. McGinnis and R. L. Simpson. Champaign, IL: Research Press (www.researchpress.com, 800-519-2707).

Skill 44: Affirming Yourself

Name_____Date_____

SKILL STEPS

1. Think about what you do well.
2. Think about what you could say about yourself.
3. Write down your affirmation.
4. Say it. Repeat it.

	How did I do? *(circle the number)*			
When did I practice?	Really Good!	Pretty good.	So-So.	I need to try again.
1. _____	4	3	2	1
2. _____	4	3	2	1
3. _____	4	3	2	1

SUPPORTS

	Practice Situation *(circle)*		
With prompting	1	2	3
With coaching	1	2	3
With supportive peer	1	2	3
Other support *(specify)* _____	1	2	3
_____			
None	1	2	3

From *Skillstreaming Children and Youth with High-Functioning Autism: A Guide for Teaching Prosocial Skills,* © 2016 by E. McGinnis and R. L. Simpson. Champaign, IL: Research Press (www.researchpress.com, 800-519-2707).

Group IV: Problem Solving
(Skills 45–58)

Skill 45: Determining Private Information

SKILL STEPS

1. **Think about the information before you share it.**

   Explain that some information or questions should be kept to themselves.

2. **Ask yourself, "Is this private information?"**

   Discuss types of private information (e.g., physical characteristics a person cannot change; personal information about family and friends). Generate a list of information that should be kept private. Discuss why others may not want the information shared (e.g., feelings of embarrassment.) Explain that if it is a safety concern (e.g., someone is being hurt), they should share the information.

3. **Say to yourself, "They can share it if they want, but I won't."**

4. **Think about or do something else.**

SUGGESTED MODELING SITUATIONS

School: You want to ask a teacher how old he is.

Home: You want to tell your neighbor what your parent said about her.

Peer group: You overheard a conversation and want to share the information.

Community: You want to tell someone you just met how much money your parents make.

COMMENTS

It may be difficult for learners to stop thinking about the information. If so, they may need additional self-statements, such as "I won't think about it anymore. I'll do _____ (something else)." Explain that private information could be shared with a counselor or a parent.

Skill 45: Determining Private Information

Name_____Date_____

SKILL STEPS

1. Think about the information before you share it.

2. Ask yourself, "Is this private information?"

3. Say to yourself, "They can share it if they want, but I won't."

4. Think about or do something else.

FILL IN NOW

With whom will I try this? _____

When? _____

_____

SUPPORTS

☐ Coaching with *(name)* _____

☐ With supportive peer *(name)* _____

☐ Other *(specify)* _____

☐ None

FILL IN AFTER YOU PRACTICE THE SKILL

What happened? _____

_____

How did I do? *(circle the number)*   4   3   2   1

              Really good!   Pretty good.   So-So.   I need to try again.

Why did I circle this? _____

_____

Skillstreaming

From *Skillstreaming Children and Youth with High-Functioning Autism: A Guide for Teaching Prosocial Skills,* © 2016 by E. McGinnis and R. L. Simpson. Champaign, IL: Research Press (www.researchpress.com, 800-519-2707).

Skill 45: Determining Private Information

Name_____Date_____

SKILL STEPS

1. Think about the information before you share it.

2. Ask yourself, "Is this private information?"

3. Say to yourself, "They can share it if they want, but I won't."

4. Think about or do something else.

When did I practice?	How did I do? *(circle the number)*			
	Really Good!	Pretty good.	So-So.	I need to try again.
1. _____	4	3	2	1
2. _____	4	3	2	1
3. _____	4	3	2	1

SUPPORTS

	Practice Situation *(circle)*		
With prompting	1	2	3
With coaching	1	2	3
With supportive peer	1	2	3
Other support *(specify)* _____	1	2	3
None	1	2	3

From *Skillstreaming Children and Youth with High-Functioning Autism: A Guide for Teaching Prosocial Skills,* © 2016 by E. McGinnis and R. L. Simpson. Champaign, IL: Research Press (www.researchpress.com, 800-519-2707).

Skill 46: Understanding Rules of Swearing

SKILL STEPS

1. **Stop and ask yourself, "Is it okay to swear?"**

   Discuss other ways to control the impulse to swear, if needed.

2. **Think about the setting.**

   Is the environment public or private?

3. **Think about the person who will hear it.**

   Will a person in authority hear it? Is it likely to offend someone? Discuss what offending someone means.

4. **Decide to say something else.**

   Teach other things learners could say, such as, "Oh, rats!"

SUGGESTED MODELING SITUATIONS

School: You drop your books in the hallway.

Home: You are in your room by yourself.

Peer group: You are playing a game at the park and little kids are around.

Community: You are bowling and miss a strike; you are in the library and can't find a book you want.

COMMENTS

Depending on the reason for swearing, learners may need to practice other skills to take the place of swearing inappropriately, such as Skill 55 (Seeking Attention) and Skill 62 (Calming Your Feelings).

Skillstreaming

From *Skillstreaming Children and Youth with High-Functioning Autism: A Guide for Teaching Prosocial Skills,* © 2016 by E. McGinnis and R. L. Simpson. Champaign, IL: Research Press (www.researchpress.com, 800-519-2707).

Skill 46: Understanding Rules of Swearing

Name_____Date_____

SKILL STEPS

1. Stop and ask yourself, "Is it okay to swear?"
2. Think about the setting.
3. Think about the person who will hear it.
4. Decide to say something else.

FILL IN NOW

With whom will I try this? _____

When? _____

_____

SUPPORTS

☐ Coaching with *(name)* _____

☐ With supportive peer *(name)* _____

☐ Other *(specify)* _____

☐ None

FILL IN AFTER YOU PRACTICE THE SKILL

What happened? _____

_____

How did I do? *(circle the number)*   4   3   2   1

Really good!   Pretty good.   So-So.   I need to try again.

Why did I circle this? _____

_____

Skill 46: Understanding Rules of Swearing

Name_____Date_____

SKILL STEPS

1. Stop and ask yourself, "Is it okay to swear?"
2. Think about the setting.
3. Think about the person who will hear it.
4. Decide to say something else.

When did I practice?	How did I do? (*circle the number*)			
	Really Good!	Pretty good.	So-So.	I need to try again.
1. _____	4	3	2	1
2. _____	4	3	2	1
3. _____	4	3	2	1

SUPPORTS

	Practice Situation (*circle*)		
With prompting	1	2	3
With coaching	1	2	3
With supportive peer	1	2	3
Other support (*specify*)_____	1	2	3
_____			
None	1	2	3

Skill 47: Understanding Rules of Touch

SKILL STEPS

1. **Say, "I can stop and think before I touch something or someone."**

2. **Think and decide if it is okay to touch this person or thing.**

   Discuss who and what is okay to touch and not okay. Develop a list for reference.

3. **If yes, decide where to touch.**

   With peers, explain it is okay to shake hands, high-five or fist bump, but learners must not touch anywhere else on the person's body without permission. With family members, it's okay to hug, snuggle, and hold hands. If someone is wearing something you want to touch, you must ask permission.

4. **If no, do not touch. Think of something else to do.**

SUGGESTED MODELING SITUATIONS

School: You want to touch a girl's hair.

Home: You want to touch your brother's/sister's friend, who is visiting, because you like her.

Peer group: You want to touch a teammate's new jacket, but you don't know the teammate well.

Community: You want to touch an item in the store, but a sign says "Do Not Touch."

COMMENTS

Additional strategies, such as self-statements/affirmations, may need to be taught to help learners stop thinking about wanting to touch something or someone.

Skill 47: Understanding Rules of Touch

Name_____Date_____

SKILL STEPS

1. Say, "I can stop and think before I touch something or someone."

2. Think and decide if it is okay to touch this person or thing.

3. If yes, decide where to touch.

4. If no, do not touch. Think of something else to do.

FILL IN NOW

With whom will I try this? _____

When? _____

_____

SUPPORTS

☐ Coaching with *(name)* _____

☐ With supportive peer *(name)* _____

☐ Other *(specify)* _____

☐ None

FILL IN AFTER YOU PRACTICE THE SKILL

What happened? _____

_____

How did I do? *(circle the number)*   4   3   2   1
                          Really good!   Pretty good.   So-So.   I need to try again.

Why did I circle this? _____

_____

Skillstreaming

From *Skillstreaming Children and Youth with High-Functioning Autism: A Guide for Teaching Prosocial Skills,* © 2016 by E. McGinnis and R. L. Simpson. Champaign, IL: Research Press (www.researchpress.com, 800-519-2707).

Skill 47: Understanding Rules of Touch

Name_____Date_____

SKILL STEPS

1. Say, "I can stop and think before I touch something or someone."
2. Think and decide if it is okay to touch this person or thing.
3. If yes, decide where to touch.
4. If no, do not touch. Think of something else to do.

When did I practice?	How did I do? *(circle the number)*			
	Really Good!	Pretty good.	So-So.	I need to try again.
1. _____	4	3	2	1
2. _____	4	3	2	1
3. _____	4	3	2	1

SUPPORTS

	Practice Situation *(circle)*		
With prompting	1	2	3
With coaching	1	2	3
With supportive peer	1	2	3
Other support *(specify)* _____	1	2	3
None	1	2	3

Skill 48: Planning for Stressful Situations

SKILL STEPS

1. **Decide why the situation is stressful.**

   Making this decision will help identify the most helpful calming strategy for Step 2.

2. **Think of ways to calm yourself to get through the situation.**

   Generate a list of calming strategies for each type of situation.

3. **Choose a strategy and make a plan.**

   Each learner may fill in the blanks to the plan: "When _____ (situation) happens, I will _____ (calming strategy)."

4. **Follow your plan.**

SUGGESTED MODELING SITUATIONS

School: You know there will be a different routine tomorrow.

Home: Your parents are having friends over and the noise bothers you.

Peer group: You are going to a birthday party and all the activity is stressful for you.

Community: You are going to a community event and are worried it will be crowded.

COMMENTS

Guide the group in making a list of stressful situations. Each participant should then identify the situations that are stressful for him/her. Use these situations for the modeling and role-playing.

Skillstreaming

From *Skillstreaming Children and Youth with High-Functioning Autism: A Guide for Teaching Prosocial Skills,* © 2016 by E. McGinnis and R. L. Simpson. Champaign, IL: Research Press (www.researchpress.com, 800-519-2707).

Skill 48: Planning for Stressful Situations

Name_____Date_____

SKILL STEPS

1. Decide why the situation is stressful.
2. Think of ways to calm yourself to get through the situation.
3. Choose a strategy and make a plan.
4. Follow your plan.

FILL IN NOW

With whom will I try this?_____

When?_____

_____

SUPPORTS

☐ Coaching with *(name)*_____

☐ With supportive peer *(name)*_____

☐ Other *(specify)*_____

☐ None

FILL IN AFTER YOU PRACTICE THE SKILL

What happened?_____

_____

How did I do? *(circle the number)*	4	3	2	1
	Really good!	Pretty good.	So-So.	I need to try again.

Why did I circle this?_____

_____

From *Skillstreaming Children and Youth with High-Functioning Autism: A Guide for Teaching Prosocial Skills,* © 2016 by E. McGinnis and R. L. Simpson. Champaign, IL: Research Press (www.researchpress.com, 800-519-2707).

Skill 48: Planning for Stressful Situations

Name_____Date_____

SKILL STEPS

1. Decide why the situation is stressful.
2. Think of ways to calm yourself to get through the situation.
3. Choose a strategy and make a plan.
4. Follow your plan.

	How did I do? *(circle the number)*			
When did I practice?	Really Good!	Pretty good.	So-So.	I need to try again.
1. _____	4	3	2	1
2. _____	4	3	2	1
3. _____	4	3	2	1

SUPPORTS

	Practice Situation *(circle)*		
With prompting	1	2	3
With coaching	1	2	3
With supportive peer	1	2	3
Other support *(specify)* _____	1	2	3
None	1	2	3

Skillstreaming

From *Skillstreaming Children and Youth with High-Functioning Autism: A Guide for Teaching Prosocial Skills,* © 2016 by E. McGinnis and R. L. Simpson. Champaign, IL: Research Press (www.researchpress.com, 800-519-2707).

Skill 49: Defining a Problem

SKILL STEPS

1. **Think about what happened.**

   Who was involved? What did other(s) do? What did you do?

2. **Decide on your part in the problem.**

   Explain that we can't necessarily change others' behavior; we can only change what we do or how we respond.

3. **Say, "The problem is _____."**

   Guide each learner in writing a brief definitive statement.

SUGGESTED MODELING SITUATIONS

School: A teacher seems angry with you.

Home: A brother or sister won't let you come in his/her room.

Peer group: A peer has left you out of the activity.

Community: The store manager tells you that you have to leave.

COMMENTS

Initially, learners will likely need to talk through this skill with the group leader, coach, or supportive peer. If it appears that bullying is involved, the teacher or school official must step in to stop the bullying.

Skill 49: Defining a Problem

Name_____Date_____

SKILL STEPS

1. Think about what happened.

2. Decide on your part in the problem.

3. Say, "The problem is _____."

FILL IN NOW

With whom will I try this? _____

When? _____

_____

SUPPORTS

☐ Coaching with *(name)* _____

☐ With supportive peer *(name)* _____

☐ Other *(specify)* _____

☐ None

FILL IN AFTER YOU PRACTICE THE SKILL

What happened? _____

_____

How did I do? *(circle the number)*   4   3   2   1

                               Really good!   Pretty good.   So-So.   I need to try again.

Why did I circle this? _____

_____

Skillstreaming

From *Skillstreaming Children and Youth with High-Functioning Autism: A Guide for Teaching Prosocial Skills,* © 2016
by E. McGinnis and R. L. Simpson. Champaign, IL: Research Press (www.researchpress.com, 800-519-2707).

Skill 49: Defining a Problem

Name_____Date_____

SKILL STEPS

1. Think about what happened.

2. Decide on your part in the problem.

3. Say, "The problem is _____."

	How did I do? *(circle the number)*			
When did I practice?	Really Good!	Pretty good.	So-So.	I need to try again.
1. _____	4	3	2	1
2. _____	4	3	2	1
3. _____	4	3	2	1

SUPPORTS

	Practice Situation *(circle)*		
With prompting	1	2	3
With coaching	1	2	3
With supportive peer	1	2	3
Other support *(specify)* _____	1	2	3
None	1	2	3

Skill 50: Considering Alternatives

SKILL STEPS

1. **Think of options to help resolve the problem.**

   Each learner should use his/her problem definition from Skill 49 (Defining a Problem). Lead the group in generating a list of options for the problems defined in the previous skill.

2. **Think of the consequences of each option.**

   Discuss what is likely to happen with each option, both positive and negative. Discuss why these consequences are likely.

3. **Decide whether the consequences are positive, negative, or neutral for you and others.**

   Make sure the group understands the meaning of each evaluative term. Depending on the maturity level of group members, short-term and long-term consequences of each option may also be discussed.

SUGGESTED MODELING SITUATIONS

School: You are thinking of alternatives to help you turn in your homework on time.

Home: You are thinking of alternatives to sharing a room with your little brother or sister.

Peer group: You are thinking of alternatives to get a girl/boy to like you.

Community: You are thinking of alternatives for how to get money so you can buy a video game you really want.

COMMENTS

This skill is a continuation of the problem-solving process; instruction should follow Skill 49 (Defining a Problem).

Skillstreaming

From *Skillstreaming Children and Youth with High-Functioning Autism: A Guide for Teaching Prosocial Skills,* © 2016 by E. McGinnis and R. L. Simpson. Champaign, IL: Research Press (www.researchpress.com, 800-519-2707).

Skill 50: Considering Alternatives

Name_____Date_____

SKILL STEPS

1. Think of options to help resolve the problem.

2. Think of the consequences of each option.

3. Decide whether the consequences are positive, negative, or neutral for you and others.

FILL IN NOW

With whom will I try this?_____

When?_____

_____

SUPPORTS

☐ Coaching with *(name)* _____

☐ With supportive peer *(name)* _____

☐ Other *(specify)* _____

☐ None

FILL IN AFTER YOU PRACTICE THE SKILL

What happened?_____

_____

How did I do? *(circle the number)*	4	3	2	1
	Really good!	Pretty good.	So-So.	I need to try again.

Why did I circle this? _____

_____

Skill 50: Considering Alternatives

Name_____Date_____

SKILL STEPS

1. Think of options to help resolve the problem.

2. Think of the consequences of each option.

3. Decide whether the consequences are positive, negative, or neutral for you and others.

When did I practice?	How did I do? *(circle the number)*			
	Really Good!	Pretty good.	So-So.	I need to try again.
1. _____	4	3	2	1
2. _____	4	3	2	1
3. _____	4	3	2	1

SUPPORTS

	Practice Situation *(circle)*		
With prompting	1	2	3
With coaching	1	2	3
With supportive peer	1	2	3
Other support *(specify)* _____	1	2	3
_____			
None	1	2	3

.Skillstreaming
. . . .

From *Skillstreaming Children and Youth with High-Functioning Autism: A Guide for Teaching Prosocial Skills,* © 2016 by E. McGinnis and R. L. Simpson. Champaign, IL: Research Press (www.researchpress.com, 800-519-2707).

Skill 51: Choosing an Alternative

SKILL STEPS

1. **Decide on one alternative.**

   Use the list generated in Skill 50 (Considering Alternatives). Selecting the alternative with the most positive and least negative likely consequences should guide the decision.

2. **Decide if you can do this.**

   Decisions should include a discussion of how comfortable each learner feels with the alternative he/she selected. If yes, continue to Step 3. If no, go back to Step 1 and decide on another alternative, using the same guidance.

3. **Make a plan to do this.**

   It is helpful if this plan is in writing. For example, "I will _____."

4. **Follow your plan.**

   Affirmations such as "I can follow my plan" may be helpful.

SUGGESTED MODELING SITUATIONS

School: You forget to turn in your homework.

Home: You get angry with your parent and say mean things.

Peer group: A peer teases you not in a mean way, but you still don't like it.

Community: You want to eat at one restaurant, but your parents want to go somewhere else.

COMMENTS

The learner must be aware of both the consequences of the alternative selected and his/her comfort in trying the plan. This skill follows Skill 50 (Considering Alternatives).

Skill 51: Choosing an Alternative

Name_____Date_____

SKILL STEPS

1 Decide on one alternative.

2. Decide if you can do this.

3. Make a plan to do this.

4. Follow your plan.

FILL IN NOW

With whom will I try this? _____

When? _____

_____

SUPPORTS

☐ Coaching with *(name)* _____

☐ With supportive peer *(name)* _____

☐ Other *(specify)* _____

☐ None

FILL IN AFTER YOU PRACTICE THE SKILL

What happened? _____

_____

How did I do? *(circle the number)*	4	3	2	1
	Really good!	Pretty good.	So-So.	I need to try again.

Why did I circle this? _____

_____

Skillstreaming

From *Skillstreaming Children and Youth with High-Functioning Autism: A Guide for Teaching Prosocial Skills,* © 2016 by E. McGinnis and R. L. Simpson. Champaign, IL: Research Press (www.researchpress.com, 800-519-2707).

Skill 51: Choosing an Alternative

Name_____Date_____

SKILL STEPS

1 Decide on one alternative.

2. Decide if you can do this.

3. Make a plan to do this.

4. Follow your plan.

	How did I do? *(circle the number)*			
When did I practice?	Really Good!	Pretty good.	So-So.	I need to try again.
1. _____	4	3	2	1
2. _____	4	3	2	1
3. _____	4	3	2	1

SUPPORTS

	Practice Situation *(circle)*		
With prompting	1	2	3
With coaching	1	2	3
With supportive peer	1	2	3
Other support *(specify)* _____	1	2	3
None	1	2	3

From *Skillstreaming Children and Youth with High-Functioning Autism: A Guide for Teaching Prosocial Skills,* © 2016 by E. McGinnis and R. L. Simpson. Champaign, IL: Research Press (www.researchpress.com, 800-519-2707).

Skill 52: When to Change Strategies

SKILL STEPS

1. **Decide if the alternative you tried solved the problem.**

   Did this solve the problem? It may be that the alternative helped with the problem but didn't solve it.

2. **Decide why it was successful (or not successful).**

   Discuss how to evaluate the success of the alternative: Did this help you get your needs met? Were others okay with the alternative? Were you comfortable in using the plan (from the previous skill) ?

3. **If yes, say "Good for me!" If no, go on to Step 4.**

4. **Choose a different alternative.**

   Provide the list of alternatives generated in Skill 50.

SUGGESTED MODELING SITUATIONS

School: You tried a plan for handing in your homework, but you still forgot.

Home: You tried a plan for handing your anger, but you said mean things to your family.

Peer group: You tried your plan for handling teasing, but the teasing didn't stop.

Community: You tried to join a busy activity, but you had a meltdown.

COMMENTS

The most helpful modeling and role-play scenarios will be those the group members planned from Skill 51 (Choosing an Alternative).

Skillstreaming

From *Skillstreaming Children and Youth with High-Functioning Autism: A Guide for Teaching Prosocial Skills,* © 2016 by E. McGinnis and R. L. Simpson. Champaign, IL: Research Press (www.researchpress.com, 800-519-2707).

Skill 52: When to Change Strategies

Name_____Date_____

SKILL STEPS

1. Decide if the alternative you tried solved the problem.

2. Decide why it was successful (or not successful).

3. If yes, say "Good for me!" If no, go on to Step 4.

4. Choose a different alternative.

FILL IN NOW

With whom will I try this? _____

When? _____

_____

SUPPORTS

☐ Coaching with *(name)* _____

☐ With supportive peer *(name)* _____

☐ Other *(specify)* _____

☐ None

FILL IN AFTER YOU PRACTICE THE SKILL

What happened? _____

_____

How did I do? *(circle the number)*   4   3   2   1

Really good!   Pretty good.   So-So.   I need to try again.

Why did I circle this? _____

_____

From *Skillstreaming Children and Youth with High-Functioning Autism: A Guide for Teaching Prosocial Skills,* © 2016 by E. McGinnis and R. L. Simpson. Champaign, IL: Research Press (www.researchpress.com, 800-519-2707).

Skill 52: When to Change Strategies

Name_____Date_____

SKILL STEPS

1. Decide if the alternative you tried solved the problem.

2. Decide why it was successful (or not successful).

3. If yes, say "Good for me!" If no, go on to Step 4.

4. Choose a different alternative.

	How did I do? *(circle the number)*			
When did I practice?	Really Good!	Pretty good.	So-So.	I need to try again.
1. _____	4	3	2	1
2. _____	4	3	2	1
3. _____	4	3	2	1

SUPPORTS

	Practice Situation *(circle)*		
With prompting	1	2	3
With coaching	1	2	3
With supportive peer	1	2	3
Other support *(specify)* _____	1	2	3
_____			
None	1	2	3

.Skillstreaming

From *Skillstreaming Children and Youth with High-Functioning Autism: A Guide for Teaching Prosocial Skills,* © 2016 by E. McGinnis and R. L. Simpson. Champaign, IL: Research Press (www.researchpress.com, 800-519-2707).

Skill 53: When a Rule Doesn't Work

SKILL STEPS

1. **Think about why.**

   Explain that rules must be followed in most situations, but there are exceptions. Learners may need to talk with someone to better understand why the rule doesn't apply in the situation.

2. **Say to yourself, "I can handle it. I'm okay with this."**

   Learners may need to repeat this affirmation multiple times.

3. **Do a calming activity if needed.**

   Review Skill 36 (Dealing with Anxiety), if necessary.

SUGGESTED MODELING SITUATIONS

School: Your class has to raise hands before talking, but the substitute isn't requiring this.

Home: You and your sister have the same regular bedtime, but on this night, she gets to stay up late.

Peer group: You understand everyone takes one turn in the game, but a peer gets two turns.

Community: You have been told you cannot use the library computer, but others are.

COMMENTS

Refer to participants' lists of calming activities, if generated in previous skills. If not, guide the group in listing a variety of calming activities appropriate to different situations.

Skill 53: When a Rule Doesn't Work

Name_____Date_____

SKILL STEPS

1. Think about why.

2. Say to yourself, "I can handle it. I'm okay with this."

3. Do a calming activity if needed.

FILL IN NOW

With whom will I try this? _____

When? _____

_____

SUPPORTS

☐ Coaching with *(name)* _____

☐ With supportive peer *(name)* _____

☐ Other *(specify)* _____

☐ None

FILL IN AFTER YOU PRACTICE THE SKILL

What happened? _____

_____

How did I do? *(circle the number)*   4   3   2   1

                                   Really good!   Pretty good.   So-So.   I need to try again.

Why did I circle this? _____

_____

From *Skillstreaming Children and Youth with High-Functioning Autism: A Guide for Teaching Prosocial Skills,* © 2016
by E. McGinnis and R. L. Simpson. Champaign, IL: Research Press (www.researchpress.com, 800-519-2707).

Skill 53: When a Rule Doesn't Work

Name_____Date_____

SKILL STEPS

1. Think about why.

2. Say to yourself, "I can handle it. I'm okay with this."

3. Do a calming activity if needed.

When did I practice?	How did I do? *(circle the number)*			
	Really Good!	Pretty good.	So-So.	I need to try again.
1. _____	4	3	2	1
2. _____	4	3	2	1
3. _____	4	3	2	1

SUPPORTS

	Practice Situation *(circle)*		
With prompting	1	2	3
With coaching	1	2	3
With supportive peer	1	2	3
Other support *(specify)* _____	1	2	3
None	1	2	3

Skill 54: Giving Feedback

SKILL STEPS

1. **Think about what was helpful.**

   Explain that it is important to tell people what they have done that is helpful to you or someone else. Encourage learners to focus on the behaviors, or what they saw or heard.

2. **Plan what to say.**

   Think about how you could tell the person (e.g., "You followed the directions" or "You talked in a friendly way"). Encourage learners to be specific and state the behavior.

3. **Say it in a friendly way.**

   Review or teach Skill 25 (Using a Friendly Voice), as needed.

SUGGESTED MODELING SITUATIONS

School: The group is watching the teacher model a skill.

Home: A parent helps you with your homework.

Peer group: A classmate is modeling a social skill for you.

Community: A coach is helping you with a sport.

COMMENTS

If group members are not giving appropriate feedback to others regarding their role-plays, this skill should be taught.

Skillstreaming

From *Skillstreaming Children and Youth with High-Functioning Autism: A Guide for Teaching Prosocial Skills,* © 2016 by E. McGinnis and R. L. Simpson. Champaign, IL: Research Press (www.researchpress.com, 800-519-2707).

Skill 54: Giving Feedback

Name_____Date_____

SKILL STEPS

1. Think about what was helpful.

2. Plan what to say.

3. Say it in a friendly way.

FILL IN NOW

With whom will I try this? _____

When? _____

_____

SUPPORTS

☐ Coaching with *(name)* _____

☐ With supportive peer *(name)* _____

☐ Other *(specify)* _____

☐ None

FILL IN AFTER YOU PRACTICE THE SKILL

What happened? _____

_____

How did I do? *(circle the number)*   4   3   2   1

Really good!   Pretty good.   So-So.   I need to try again.

Why did I circle this? _____

_____

Skill 54: Giving Feedback

Name_____Date_____

SKILL STEPS

1. Think about what was helpful.
2. Plan what to say.
3. Say it in a friendly way.

	How did I do? *(circle the number)*			
When did I practice?	Really Good!	Pretty good.	So-So.	I need to try again.
1. _____	4	3	2	1
2. _____	4	3	2	1
3. _____	4	3	2	1

SUPPORTS

	Practice Situation *(circle)*		
With prompting	1	2	3
With coaching	1	2	3
With supportive peer	1	2	3
Other support *(specify)* _____	1	2	3
_____			
None	1	2	3

Skillstreaming

Skill 55: Seeking Attention

SKILL STEPS

1. **Decide if you want attention.**

   Encourage learners to think about why they want attention.

2. **Ask, "From whom?"**

   Discuss whether it is attention from a peer, parent, teacher, or other.

3. **Think of how to get attention in a positive way.**

   Explain that a learner may get attention by acting out, shouting, or hitting someone, but that this isn't positive attention. Explain that others may avoid the learner in the future. Generate a list of ways to get positive attention, such as Skill 9 (Helping Others) or Skill 30 (Showing Interest in Others).

4. **Decide.**

   Make a decision on the best way to get attention in the situation.

5. **Do it.**

SUGGESTED MODELING SITUATIONS

School: You have finished your work and you want your teacher's attention.

Home: A parent has been busy and you want your parent's attention.

Peer group: Your friend is busy with another group of friends and you want to be with your friend.

Community: You are at the community center (or another location), but no one is paying any attention to you.

COMMENTS

It may be helpful for the learner to write down a plan for getting attention from others in particular situations or settings in which the learner acts out or inappropriately attempts to get attention from others. This plan could be written in the learner's school planner or on a note card that can be carried in a pocket for quick reference.

From *Skillstreaming Children and Youth with High-Functioning Autism: A Guide for Teaching Prosocial Skills,* © 2016 by E. McGinnis and R. L. Simpson. Champaign, IL: Research Press (www.researchpress.com, 800-519-2707).

Skill 55: Seeking Attention

Name_____Date_____

SKILL STEPS

1. Decide if you want attention.
2. Ask, "From whom?"
3. Think of how to get attention in a positive way.
4. Decide.
5. Do it.

FILL IN NOW

With whom will I try this? _____

When? _____

_____

SUPPORTS

☐ Coaching with *(name)* _____

☐ With supportive peer *(name)* _____

☐ Other *(specify)* _____

☐ None

FILL IN AFTER YOU PRACTICE THE SKILL

What happened? _____

_____

How did I do? *(circle the number)*   4   3   2   1

        Really good!   Pretty good.   So-So.   I need to try again.

Why did I circle this? _____

_____

Skillstreaming

Skill 55: Seeking Attention

Name_____Date_____

SKILL STEPS

1. Decide if you want attention.
2. Ask, "From whom?"
3. Think of how to get attention in a positive way.
4. Decide.
5. Do it.

| | How did I do? *(circle the number)* | | | |
When did I practice?	Really Good!	Pretty good.	So-So.	I need to try again.
1. _____	4	3	2	1
2. _____	4	3	2	1
3. _____	4	3	2	1

SUPPORTS

	Practice Situation *(circle)*		
With prompting	1	2	3
With coaching	1	2	3
With supportive peer	1	2	3
Other support *(specify)* _____	1	2	3
None	1	2	3

From *Skillstreaming Children and Youth with High-Functioning Autism: A Guide for Teaching Prosocial Skills,* © 2016 by E. McGinnis and R. L. Simpson. Champaign, IL: Research Press (www.researchpress.com, 800-519-2707).

Skill 56: Accepting Attention

SKILL STEPS

1. **Think about the attention you are given.**

   Encourage learners to describe what the other person is doing to get the learner's attention.

2. **Decide if you want this attention from this person.**

3. **If yes, accept the attention.**

   Accepting the attention may mean engaging in the game, conversation, or other activity. The learner may say something like "Okay, sounds good."

4. **If no, say no in a friendly way.**

   Review or teach Using a Friendly Voice (Skill 25) as needed. List different prosocial statements that could be made to the person giving the attention (e.g., "Thanks anyway, but I have to do something else").

SUGGESTED MODELING SITUATIONS

School: The teacher assigns you to a group to do an assignment.

Home: A brother or sister wants you to play with him/her.

Peer group: A classmate approaches you to play a game on the computer.

Community: A store clerk starts a conversation with you.

COMMENTS

Practice in Understanding Another's Intentions (Skill 66) may be useful.

Skillstreaming

From *Skillstreaming Children and Youth with High-Functioning Autism: A Guide for Teaching Prosocial Skills,* © 2016 by E. McGinnis and R. L. Simpson. Champaign, IL: Research Press (www.researchpress.com, 800-519-2707).

Skill 56: Accepting Attention

Name_____Date_____

SKILL STEPS

1. Think about the attention you are given.

2. Decide if you want this attention from this person.

3. If yes, accept the attention.

4. If no, say no in a friendly way.

FILL IN NOW

With whom will I try this? _____

When? _____

_____

SUPPORTS

☐ Coaching with *(name)* _____

☐ With supportive peer *(name)* _____

☐ Other *(specify)* _____

☐ None

FILL IN AFTER YOU PRACTICE THE SKILL

What happened? _____

_____

How did I do? *(circle the number)*   4   3   2   1

Really good!   Pretty good.   So-So.   I need to try again.

Why did I circle this? _____

_____

From *Skillstreaming Children and Youth with High-Functioning Autism: A Guide for Teaching Prosocial Skills,* © 2016 by E. McGinnis and R. L. Simpson. Champaign, IL: Research Press (www.researchpress.com, 800-519-2707).

Skill 56: Accepting Attention

Name_____Date_____

SKILL STEPS

1. Think about the attention you are given.
2. Decide if you want this attention from this person.
3. If yes, accept the attention.
4. If no, say no in a friendly way.

	How did I do? *(circle the number)*			
When did I practice?	Really Good!	Pretty good.	So-So.	I need to try again.
1. _____	4	3	2	1
2. _____	4	3	2	1
3. _____	4	3	2	1

SUPPORTS

	Practice Situation *(circle)*		
With prompting	1	2	3
With coaching	1	2	3
With supportive peer	1	2	3
Other support *(specify)* _____	1	2	3
_____			
None	1	2	3

.Skillstreaming

From *Skillstreaming Children and Youth with High-Functioning Autism: A Guide for Teaching Prosocial Skills,* © 2016 by E. McGinnis and R. L. Simpson. Champaign, IL: Research Press (www.researchpress.com, 800-519-2707).

Skill 57: Making a Complaint

SKILL STEPS

1. **Decide on the problem.**

   Encourage learners to state facts instead of opinion. Review the skill of Understanding Another's Intentions (Skill 66), if needed.

2. **Decide whom to tell.**

   Explain that it is most helpful to tell someone who can either help with the problem or give you helpful advice.

3. **Choose a good time.**

   Discuss times that would be appropriate to make the complaint.

4. **State your complaint.**

   Point out the importance of making the complaint in a respectful, not angry, way.

SUGGESTED MODELING SITUATIONS

School: Your teacher tells you that you have to write the answers instead of using the computer.

Home: Your parent said you could go to a movie, but now he/she is too busy to take you.

Peer group: A friend invited you over, but now he/she isn't home.

Community: Someone has taken your seat at the game.

COMMENTS

Learners may need instruction on what is a fact and what is opinion. Understanding Another's Intentions (Skill 66) may also help in deciding if the complaint is justified.

Skill 57: Making a Complaint

Name_____Date_____

SKILL STEPS

1. Decide on the problem.

2. Decide whom to tell.

3. Choose a good time.

4. State your complaint.

FILL IN NOW

With whom will I try this?_____

When?_____

_____

SUPPORTS

☐ Coaching with *(name)*_____

☐ With supportive peer *(name)*_____

☐ Other *(specify)*_____

☐ None

FILL IN AFTER YOU PRACTICE THE SKILL

What happened?_____

_____

How did I do? *(circle the number)*   4   3   2   1

Really good!   Pretty good.   So-So.   I need to try again.

Why did I circle this?_____

_____

.Skillstreaming

From *Skillstreaming Children and Youth with High-Functioning Autism: A Guide for Teaching Prosocial Skills,* © 2016 by E. McGinnis and R. L. Simpson. Champaign, IL: Research Press (www.researchpress.com, 800-519-2707).

Skill 57: Making a Complaint

Name_____Date_____

SKILL STEPS

1. Decide on the problem.
2. Decide whom to tell.
3. Choose a good time.
4. State your complaint.

	How did I do? *(circle the number)*			
When did I practice?	Really Good!	Pretty good.	So-So.	I need to try again.
1. _____	4	3	2	1
2. _____	4	3	2	1
3. _____	4	3	2	1

SUPPORTS

	Practice Situation *(circle)*		
With prompting	1	2	3
With coaching	1	2	3
With supportive peer	1	2	3
Other support *(specify)* _____	1	2	3
None	1	2	3

From *Skillstreaming Children and Youth with High-Functioning Autism: A Guide for Teaching Prosocial Skills,* © 2016 by E. McGinnis and R. L. Simpson. Champaign, IL: Research Press (www.researchpress.com, 800-519-2707).

Skill 58: When You Don't Understand

SKILL STEPS

1. **Think about what you don't understand.**

   A sentence starter such as "I don't understand _____" may be helpful.

2. **Decide whom to talk with.**

   Think about who is most likely to have the information.

3. **Choose a good time.**

   Discuss times that would be appropriate (e.g., when the person isn't working with someone else, when the person doesn't seem busy).

4. **Ask to talk in a respectful/friendly way.**

   Learners may need to practice how to ask (e.g., using the question "Can you help me understand something?").

SUGGESTED MODELING SITUATIONS

School: You don't understand why you can't go to gym with the rest of your class.

Home: You don't understand why you can't go to a friend's house by yourself.

Peer group: You don't understand why a peer didn't get in trouble for swearing, even though he swore quietly.

Community: You don't understand why you have to wait so long for your food at a restaurant.

COMMENTS

This skill focuses on giving learners an option of what to do when something doesn't seem fair or when a situation is handled in a way the learner doesn't feel is appropriate.

Skillstreaming

From *Skillstreaming Children and Youth with High-Functioning Autism: A Guide for Teaching Prosocial Skills,* © 2016 by E. McGinnis and R. L. Simpson. Champaign, IL: Research Press (www.researchpress.com, 800-519-2707).

Skill 58: When You Don't Understand

Name_____Date_____

SKILL STEPS

1. Think about what you don't understand.

2. Decide whom to talk with.

3. Choose a good time.

4. Ask to talk in a respectful/friendly way.

FILL IN NOW

With whom will I try this? _____

When? _____

_____

SUPPORTS

☐ Coaching with *(name)* _____

☐ With supportive peer *(name)* _____

☐ Other *(specify)* _____

☐ None

FILL IN AFTER YOU PRACTICE THE SKILL

What happened? _____

_____

How did I do? *(circle the number)*   4   3   2   1

Really good!   Pretty good.   So-So.   I need to try again.

Why did I circle this? _____

_____

From *Skillstreaming Children and Youth with High-Functioning Autism: A Guide for Teaching Prosocial Skills,* © 2016
by E. McGinnis and R. L. Simpson. Champaign, IL: Research Press (www.researchpress.com, 800-519-2707).

Skill 58: When You Don't Understand

Name_____Date_____

SKILL STEPS

1. Think about what you don't understand.

2. Decide whom to talk with.

3. Choose a good time.

4. Ask to talk in a respectful/friendly way.

	How did I do? *(circle the number)*			
When did I practice?	Really Good!	Pretty good.	So-So.	I need to try again.
1. _____	4	3	2	1
2. _____	4	3	2	1
3. _____	4	3	2	1

SUPPORTS

	Practice Situation *(circle)*		
With prompting	1	2	3
With coaching	1	2	3
With supportive peer	1	2	3
Other support *(specify)*_____	1	2	3
_____			
None	1	2	3

Skillstreaming

From *Skillstreaming Children and Youth with High-Functioning Autism: A Guide for Teaching Prosocial Skills,* © 2016 by E. McGinnis and R. L. Simpson. Champaign, IL: Research Press (www.researchpress.com, 800-519-2707).

Group V: Understanding Emotions
(Skill 59-67)

Skill 59: Knowing Your Feelings

SKILL STEPS

1. **Think of how your body feels.**

   Discuss cues for each part of the body (head, face, hands, stomach, breathing, etc.).

2. **Decide what you would call the feeling.**

   Display a list of feelings words and pictures (as available). It is helpful for the leader or a supportive peer to model a variety of feelings. Pictures of the models may be taken and displayed along with the words for each feeling. Ask learners to show each feeling following the modeling.

3. **Say, "I feel _____."**

SUGGESTED MODELING SITUATIONS

School: Your school routine changes without notice.

Home: You find out that your computer doesn't work.

Peer group: You weren't included in an activity with a friend.

Community: The movie you wanted to see isn't playing at the movie theater anymore.

COMMENTS

Additional activities specific to identifying and labeling feelings will be needed. Such activities might include generating a list of feelings words to be displayed in the classroom, discussing different situations and how people might feel, and having participants enact different feelings, with the rest of the group guessing the emotion.

Skill 59: Knowing Your Feelings

Name_____Date_____

SKILL STEPS

1. Think of how your body feels.

2. Decide what you would call the feeling.

3. Say, "I feel _____."

FILL IN NOW

With whom will I try this? _____

When? _____

_____

SUPPORTS

☐ Coaching with *(name)* _____

☐ With supportive peer *(name)* _____

☐ Other *(specify)* _____

☐ None

FILL IN AFTER YOU PRACTICE THE SKILL

What happened? _____

_____

How did I do? *(circle the number)*   4   3   2   1

                                Really good!   Pretty good.   So-So.   I need to try again.

Why did I circle this? _____

_____

From *Skillstreaming Children and Youth with High-Functioning Autism: A Guide for Teaching Prosocial Skills,* © 2016 by E. McGinnis and R. L. Simpson. Champaign, IL: Research Press (www.researchpress.com, 800-519-2707).

Skill 59: Knowing Your Feelings

Name_____Date_____

SKILL STEPS

1. Think of how your body feels.

2. Decide what you would call the feeling.

3. Say, "I feel _____."

	How did I do? *(circle the number)*			
When did I practice?	Really Good!	Pretty good.	So-So.	I need to try again.
1. _____	4	3	2	1
2. _____	4	3	2	1
3. _____	4	3	2	1

SUPPORTS

	Practice Situation *(circle)*		
With prompting	1	2	3
With coaching	1	2	3
With supportive peer	1	2	3
Other support *(specify)* _____	1	2	3
None	1	2	3

Skill 60: Feeling Different

SKILL STEPS

1. **Decide if you feel different from others.**

2. **Decide why you feel this way.**

   This will vary from person to person. Examples may include "Some learning seems more difficult," "Sometimes I don't understand the way others do," and "I don't like to do some things others like."

3. **Say, "Everyone is different and it's okay."**

   Additional self-statements may be helpful (e.g., listing individual strengths). Supportive peers may also share their strengths and weaknesses with the group.

SUGGESTED MODELING SITUATIONS

School: You realize some things in school, like gym class, are hard for you.

Home: You don't like to do many of the things your family likes to do.

Peer group: Sometimes you just want to be alone.

Community: Sometimes you would rather just be on your computer than go out.

COMMENTS

Many learners with high-functioning autism disorders feel that they are different from others and need to understand how to cope with this. A review of Skill 31 (Understanding Differences) my be helpful.

.Skillstreaming

From *Skillstreaming Children and Youth with High-Functioning Autism: A Guide for Teaching Prosocial Skills,* © 2016 by E. McGinnis and R. L. Simpson. Champaign, IL: Research Press (www.researchpress.com, 800-519-2707).

Skill 60: Feeling Different

Name_____Date_____

SKILL STEPS

1. Decide if you feel different from others.

2. Decide why you feel this way.

3. Say, "Everyone is different and it's okay."

FILL IN NOW

With whom will I try this? _____

When?_____

_____

SUPPORTS

☐ Coaching with *(name)* _____

☐ With supportive peer *(name)* _____

☐ Other *(specify)* _____

☐ None

FILL IN AFTER YOU PRACTICE THE SKILL

What happened? _____

_____

How did I do? *(circle the number)*   4   3   2   1

Really good!   Pretty good.   So-So.   I need to try again.

Why did I circle this? _____

_____

From *Skillstreaming Children and Youth with High-Functioning Autism: A Guide for Teaching Prosocial Skills,* © 2016 by E. McGinnis and R. L. Simpson. Champaign, IL: Research Press (www.researchpress.com, 800-519-2707).

Skill 60: Feeling Different

Name_____Date_____

SKILL STEPS

1. Decide if you feel different from others.

2. Decide why you feel this way.

3. Say, "Everyone is different and it's okay."

When did I practice?	How did I do? *(circle the number)*			
	Really Good!	Pretty good.	So-So.	I need to try again.
1. _____	4	3	2	1
2. _____	4	3	2	1
3. _____	4	3	2	1

SUPPORTS

	Practice Situation *(circle)*		
With prompting	1	2	3
With coaching	1	2	3
With supportive peer	1	2	3
Other support *(specify)*_____	1	2	3
_____			
None	1	2	3

Skillstreaming

From *Skillstreaming Children and Youth with High-Functioning Autism: A Guide for Teaching Prosocial Skills,* © 2016 by E. McGinnis and R. L. Simpson. Champaign, IL: Research Press (www.researchpress.com, 800-519-2707).

Skill 61: Expressing Your Feelings

SKILL STEPS

1. **Say to yourself, "I feel _____."**

   Reference the list of feelings words from Skill 59 (Knowing Your Feelings).

2. **Think of choices you have for dealing with the feeling.**

   Include choices from the learner's list of preferences (Skill 21, Communicating Preferences): talk about it with someone, say how you feel, and so forth. Discuss potential positive and negative consequences connected with each choice.

3. **Ask yourself, "Is this a good choice?"**

   Ask the learner whether this choice would likely bring about a positive consequence. If not, he/she should consider a different choice.

4. **If okay, do it.**

SUGGESTED MODELING SITUATIONS

School: You give an answer in class, but the teacher says the answer is incorrect.

Home: A parent is angry with you for not doing your chores.

Peer group: You are supposed to go to a club meeting, but your parent can't drive you.

Community: You were looking forward to going to the pet store, but it's closed.

COMMENTS

Instruction in this skill should follow Skill 59 (Knowing Your Feelings). The list of feelings words generated previously can be used to practice alternative ways to deal with these feelings.

Skill 61: Expressing Your Feelings

Name_____Date_____

SKILL STEPS

1. Say to yourself, "I feel _____."

2. Think of choices you have for dealing with the feeling.

3. Ask yourself, "Is this a good choice?"

4. If okay, do it.

FILL IN NOW

With whom will I try this?_____

When?_____

_____

SUPPORTS

☐ Coaching with *(name)* _____

☐ With supportive peer *(name)* _____

☐ Other *(specify)* _____

☐ None

FILL IN AFTER YOU PRACTICE THE SKILL

What happened?_____

_____

How did I do? *(circle the number)*   4   3   2   1

Really good!   Pretty good.   So-So.   I need to try again.

Why did I circle this?_____

_____

Skillstreaming

From *Skillstreaming Children and Youth with High-Functioning Autism: A Guide for Teaching Prosocial Skills,* © 2016 by E. McGinnis and R. L. Simpson. Champaign, IL: Research Press (www.researchpress.com, 800-519-2707).

Skill 61: Expressing Your Feelings

Name_____Date_____

SKILL STEPS

1. Say to yourself, "I feel _____."

2. Think of choices you have for dealing with the feeling.

3. Ask yourself, "Is this a good choice?"

4. If okay, do it.

When did I practice?	How did I do? *(circle the number)*			
	Really Good!	Pretty good.	So-So.	I need to try again.
1. _____	4	3	2	1
2. _____	4	3	2	1
3. _____	4	3	2	1

SUPPORTS

	Practice Situation *(circle)*		
With prompting	1	2	3
With coaching	1	2	3
With supportive peer	1	2	3
Other support *(specify)* _____	1	2	3
None	1	2	3

Skill 62: Calming Your Feelings

SKILL STEPS

1. **Decide what is calming to you.**

   Guide learners in making a list of activities that calm them in school, at home, with peers, and in the community. Ask learners to select the ones that work for them and keep a personal list for future reference.

2. **Choose one activity that is appropriate to the setting.**

   Guide the group in selecting an activity that is appropriate to the situation/setting.

3. **Do it.**

4. **Decide if your choice calmed your feelings.**

   If yes, return to your task. If not, make another choice.

SUGGESTED MODELING SITUATIONS

School: You are angry (or having another emotion) when a peer is mean to you.

Home: You are frustrated that your parents won't let you stay home.

Peer group: You feel sad because you feel like you don't have any friends.

Community: A clerk is yelling at you in the store and you feel scared.

COMMENTS

Learners should select a variety of choices appropriate to each setting; when one strategy doesn't work, they should try another one.

Skill 62: Calming Your Feelings

Name_____Date_____

SKILL STEPS

1. Decide what is calming to you.
2. Choose one activity that is appropriate to the setting.
3. Do it.
4. Decide if your choice calmed your feelings.

FILL IN NOW

With whom will I try this? _____

When? _____

_____

SUPPORTS

☐ Coaching with *(name)* _____

☐ With supportive peer *(name)* _____

☐ Other *(specify)* _____

☐ None

FILL IN AFTER YOU PRACTICE THE SKILL

What happened? _____

_____

How did I do? *(circle the number)*   4   3   2   1

                                  Really good!   Pretty good.   So-So.   I need to try again.

Why did I circle this? _____

_____

Skill 62: Calming Your Feelings

Name_____Date_____

SKILL STEPS

1. Decide what is calming to you.
2. Choose one activity that is appropriate to the setting.
3. Do it.
4. Decide if your choice calmed your feelings.

	How did I do? *(circle the number)*			
When did I practice?	Really Good!	Pretty good.	So-So.	I need to try again.
1. _____	4	3	2	1
2. _____	4	3	2	1
3. _____	4	3	2	1

SUPPORTS

	Practice Situation *(circle)*		
With prompting	1	2	3
With coaching	1	2	3
With supportive peer	1	2	3
Other support *(specify)*_____	1	2	3
_____			
None	1	2	3

Skillstreaming

From *Skillstreaming Children and Youth with High-Functioning Autism: A Guide for Teaching Prosocial Skills,* © 2016 by E. McGinnis and R. L. Simpson. Champaign, IL: Research Press (www.researchpress.com, 800-519-2707).

Skill 63: Showing Affection

SKILL STEPS

1. **Decide if you have nice feelings.**

   Discuss how to decide (e.g., you like the person, you want to spend time with the person, the person is helpful to you).

2. **Plan how to show affection.**

   Discuss the different ways of showing affection and explain that these ways depend upon the person you like.

3. **Choose a good time.**

   Decide when would be a good time (e.g., when others aren't around, when you aren't supposed to be doing something else).

4. **Do it, then do something else.**

   Explain to learners that after they show affection, it is appropriate to get involved in something else so the person doesn't feel embarrassed.

SUGGESTED MODELING SITUATIONS

School: You like a teacher who has helped you a lot.

Home: Your grandmother comes to visit.

Peer group: There is a girl/ boy you would like to get to know.

Community: A good friend asks you to a movie.

COMMENTS

Work with learners to determine the different ways to show affection depending on how well learners know the person. For example, you might show affection to a parent by hugging him or her, saying, "I love you," or doing something helpful. With good friends, you might tell them you like spending time with them. With teachers, you might tell them you really like them. With someone you don't know very well, you would probably use a different skill, such as Starting a Conversation (Skill 14) or Sharing (Skill 12) until you get to know the person better.

Skill 63: Showing Affection

Name_____Date_____

SKILL STEPS

1. Decide if you have nice feelings.

2. Plan how to show affection.

3. Choose a good time.

4. Do it, then do something else.

FILL IN NOW

With whom will I try this? _____

When? _____

_____

SUPPORTS

☐ Coaching with *(name)* _____

☐ With supportive peer *(name)* _____

☐ Other *(specify)* _____

☐ None

FILL IN AFTER YOU PRACTICE THE SKILL

What happened? _____

_____

How did I do? *(circle the number)*   4   3   2   1

Really good! Pretty good. So-So. I need to try again.

Why did I circle this? _____

_____

Skillstreaming

From *Skillstreaming Children and Youth with High-Functioning Autism: A Guide for Teaching Prosocial Skills,* © 2016 by E. McGinnis and R. L. Simpson. Champaign, IL: Research Press (www.researchpress.com, 800-519-2707).

Skill 63: Showing Affection

Name_____Date_____

SKILL STEPS

1. Decide if you have nice feelings.
2. Plan how to show affection.
3. Choose a good time.
4. Do it, then do something else.

	How did I do? *(circle the number)*			
When did I practice?	Really Good!	Pretty good.	So-So.	I need to try again.
1. _____	4	3	2	1
2. _____	4	3	2	1
3. _____	4	3	2	1

SUPPORTS

	Practice Situation *(circle)*		
With prompting	1	2	3
With coaching	1	2	3
With supportive peer	1	2	3
Other support *(specify)* _____	1	2	3
None	1	2	3

From *Skillstreaming Children and Youth with High-Functioning Autism: A Guide for Teaching Prosocial Skills,* © 2016
by E. McGinnis and R. L. Simpson. Champaign, IL: Research Press (www.researchpress.com, 800-519-2707). **229**

Skill 64: Recognizing Another's Feelings

SKILL STEPS

1. **Watch the person.**

   Discuss attending to the way the person looks (posture, facial expression), what the person does, what the person says, and how the person says it. Review or teach Skill 23 (Reading Others).

2. **Name what you think the person is feeling.**

   Discuss a variety of feelings. Use the list of feelings words developed in the discussion of Skill 59 (Knowing Your Feelings) for discussion and review.

3. **Think about whether you have felt this way.**

   Encourage learners to feel what the other person is feeling for a moment.

SUGGESTED MODELING SITUATIONS

School: A classmate is crying.

Home: A brother or sister slams the door and yells.

Peer group: A friend is sitting down while everyone else is playing.

Community: Someone is talking on the phone and laughing.

COMMENTS

Following this skill, Skill 65 (Showing Concern for Another) should be taught.

Skillstreaming

From *Skillstreaming Children and Youth with High-Functioning Autism: A Guide for Teaching Prosocial Skills,* © 2016 by E. McGinnis and R. L. Simpson. Champaign, IL: Research Press (www.researchpress.com, 800-519-2707).

Skill 64: Recognizing Another's Feelings

Name_____Date_____

SKILL STEPS

1. Watch the person.

2. Name what you think the person is feeling.

3. Think about whether you have felt this way.

FILL IN NOW

With whom will I try this? _____

When? _____

_____

SUPPORTS

☐ Coaching with *(name)* _____

☐ With supportive peer *(name)* _____

☐ Other *(specify)* _____

☐ None

FILL IN AFTER YOU PRACTICE THE SKILL

What happened? _____

_____

How did I do? *(circle the number)*   4   3   2   1

Really good!   Pretty good.   So-So.   I need to try again.

Why did I circle this? _____

_____

From *Skillstreaming Children and Youth with High-Functioning Autism: A Guide for Teaching Prosocial Skills,* © 2016 by E. McGinnis and R. L. Simpson. Champaign, IL: Research Press (www.researchpress.com, 800-519-2707).

Skill 64: Recognizing Another's Feelings

Name_____Date_____

SKILL STEPS

1. Watch the person.

2. Name what you think the person is feeling.

3. Think about whether you have felt this way.

	How did I do? *(circle the number)*			
When did I practice?	Really Good!	Pretty good.	So-So.	I need to try again.
1. _____	4	3	2	1
2. _____	4	3	2	1
3. _____	4	3	2	1

SUPPORTS

	Practice Situation *(circle)*		
With prompting	1	2	3
With coaching	1	2	3
With supportive peer	1	2	3
Other support *(specify)* _____	1	2	3
_____			
None	1	2	3

Skillstreaming

From *Skillstreaming Children and Youth with High-Functioning Autism: A Guide for Teaching Prosocial Skills,* © 2016 by E. McGinnis and R. L. Simpson. Champaign, IL: Research Press (www.researchpress.com, 800-519-2707).

Skill 65: Showing Concern for Another

SKILL STEPS

1. **Decide if someone is having a problem or is feeling bad.**

   What is the person doing or saying? Review or teach Skill 23 (Reading Others).

2. **Say, "I want to be kind to the person."**

3. **Think of your choices.**

   a. **Offer to help.**

   Review or teach Skill 9 (Helping Others).

   b. **Ask if the person is feeling bad.**

   Explain that, if the person seems very angry, it might be best to wait until the person is calm.

   c. **Do something nice for the person.**

   Discuss options for a good friend, a classmate, a family member, and someone learners don't know well.

4. **Act out your best choice.**

SUGGESTED MODELING SITUATIONS

School: A student is pushed in the hallway and is now crying.

Home: A brother or sister is doing homework but now has his/her head down on the table.

Peer group: A friend tries to join in a game, but is told no.

Community: A neighbor is carrying in groceries, but the bags rip and groceries spill over the sidewalk.

COMMENTS

Explain to learners that the choices they think about in Step 3 should take into account how well they know the other person. How well they know the person will likely affect how receptive the other person will be to the attempt. For example, if the person is a good friend, he or she would likely be more receptive to the learner.

From *Skillstreaming Children and Youth with High-Functioning Autism: A Guide for Teaching Prosocial Skills,* © 2016 by E. McGinnis and R. L. Simpson. Champaign, IL: Research Press (www.researchpress.com, 800-519-2707).

Skill 65: Showing Concern for Another

Name_____Date_____

SKILL STEPS

1. Decide if someone is having a problem or is feeling bad.

2. Say, "I want to be kind to the person."

3. Think of your choices.

    a. Offer to help.

    b. Ask if the person is feeling bad.

    c. Do something nice for the person.

4. Act out your best choice.

FILL IN NOW

With whom will I try this? _____

When? _____

_____

SUPPORTS

☐ Coaching with *(name)* _____

☐ With supportive peer *(name)* _____

☐ Other *(specify)* _____

☐ None

FILL IN AFTER YOU PRACTICE THE SKILL

What happened? _____

_____

How did I do? *(circle the number)*   4   3   2   1

                       Really good!   Pretty good.   So-So.   I need to try again.

Why did I circle this? _____

_____

Skillstreaming

From *Skillstreaming Children and Youth with High-Functioning Autism: A Guide for Teaching Prosocial Skills,* © 2016 by E. McGinnis and R. L. Simpson. Champaign, IL: Research Press (www.researchpress.com, 800-519-2707).

Skill 65: Showing Concern for Another

Name_____Date_____

SKILL STEPS

1. Decide if someone is having a problem or is feeling bad.

2. Say, "I want to be kind to the person."

3. Think of your choices.

   a. Offer to help.

   b. Ask if the person is feeling bad.

   c. Do something nice for the person.

4. Act out your best choice.

	How did I do? *(circle the number)*			
When did I practice?	Really Good!	Pretty good.	So-So.	I need to try again.
1. _____	4	3	2	1
2. _____	4	3	2	1
3. _____	4	3	2	1

SUPPORTS

	Practice Situation *(circle)*		
With prompting	1	2	3
With coaching	1	2	3
With supportive peer	1	2	3
Other support *(specify)*_____	1	2	3
None	1	2	3

Skill 66: Understanding Another's Intentions

SKILL STEPS

1. **Think about what happened.**

   What did the person do or say? How was this said or done (in an angry way, in a friendly way)?

2. **Think about why the person may have done this.**

   Discuss possible options. Explain that a person's actions might mean different things.

3. **Think of other information you may need.**

   Explain that sometimes it's helpful to talk with someone (e.g., a teacher or parent) about a situation to get another's thoughts. It may also be helpful to talk to the person concerned.

4. **Make your best guess.**

SUGGESTED MODELING SITUATIONS

School: A classmate walks by your desk and knocks your books onto the floor. The classmate apologizes and helps you pick up the books.

Home: A sister or a brother borrows your iPad without asking.

Peer group: You like a girl or boy, but you don't know if the person wants to be a friend.

Community: A person at a restaurant seems to be staring at you.

COMMENTS

Clues to another person's intentions include answers to the following questions: Is this the first time an event has happened or is this a repeated event? What happened before the event occurred? What happened after the event? What is your relationship with the person?

Skill 67 (Dealing with Another's Anger) or Skill 65 (Showing Concern for Another) may follow this skill.

. Skillstreaming

From *Skillstreaming Children and Youth with High-Functioning Autism: A Guide for Teaching Prosocial Skills*, © 2016 by E. McGinnis and R. L. Simpson. Champaign, IL: Research Press (www.researchpress.com, 800-519-2707).

Skill 66: Understanding Another's Intentions

Name_____Date_____

SKILL STEPS

1. Think about what happened.

2. Think about why the person may have done this.

3. Think of other information you may need.

4. Make your best guess.

FILL IN NOW

With whom will I try this? _____

When?_____

_____

SUPPORTS

☐ Coaching with *(name)* _____

☐ With supportive peer *(name)* _____

☐ Other *(specify)* _____

☐ None

FILL IN AFTER YOU PRACTICE THE SKILL

What happened? _____

_____

How did I do? *(circle the number)*   4   3   2   1

Really good!   Pretty good.   So-So.   I need to try again.

Why did I circle this?_____

_____

From *Skillstreaming Children and Youth with High-Functioning Autism: A Guide for Teaching Prosocial Skills,* © 2016
by E. McGinnis and R. L. Simpson. Champaign, IL: Research Press (www.researchpress.com, 800-519-2707).

Skill 66: Understanding Another's Intentions

Name_____Date_____

SKILL STEPS

1. Think about what happened.

2. Think about why the person may have done this.

3. Think of other information you may need.

4. Make your best guess.

When did I practice?	How did I do? *(circle the number)*			
	Really Good!	Pretty good.	So-So.	I need to try again.
1. _____	4	3	2	1
2. _____	4	3	2	1
3. _____	4	3	2	1

SUPPORTS

	Practice Situation *(circle)*		
With prompting	1	2	3
With coaching	1	2	3
With supportive peer	1	2	3
Other support *(specify)* _____	1	2	3
_____			
None	1	2	3

Skill 67: Dealing with Another's Anger

1. **Say to yourself, "I can stay calm."**

   Explain the importance of not becoming angry also. Ask what could happen if this should occur. If needed, review or teach Skill 39 (Using Self-Control).

2. **Listen to what the person has to say.**

   Review or teach Skill 1 (Listening Without Interrupting).

3. **Think about the person's role.**

   Is this an adult in authority? A peer? Explain that the choice in Step 4 should be appropriate to the person's role.

4. **Think of your choices:**

   a. **Keep listening.**

   b. **Apologize if appropriate.**

      Explain that apologizing is appropriate only if the apology is sincere and if the learner did something wrong.

   c. **Suggest a way to fix the problem.**

   d. **Walk away for now and think of what to do.**

      Explain that learners may choose to talk with someone about this.

5. **Act out your best choice.**

SUGGESTED MODELING SITUATIONS

School: Your teacher seems angry with you for using the computer when you should have been working at your desk.

Home: Your parent seems angry with you for not coming home right after school.

Peer group: A peer seems angry with you because you didn't play well in the game.

Community: A clerk at the store seems angry with you for knocking down a display.

COMMENTS

Explain that it may be okay to delay discussing the situation when a peer is angry. If an adult is angry, delaying may only create more problems for the learner. Stress the importance of adjusting one's behavior according to the role of the person with whom the problem exists.

Skill 67: Dealing with Another's Anger

Name_____Date_____

SKILL STEPS

1. Say to yourself, "I can stay calm."

2. Listen to what the person has to say.

3. Think about the person's role.

4. Think of your choices:

   a. Keep listening.

   b. Apologize if appropriate.

   c. Suggest a way to fix the problem.

   d. Walk away for now and think of what to do.

5. Act out your best choice.

FILL IN NOW

With whom will I try this?_____

When?_____

_____

SUPPORTS

☐ Coaching with *(name)* _____

☐ With supportive peer *(name)* _____

☐ Other *(specify)* _____

☐ None

FILL IN AFTER YOU PRACTICE THE SKILL

What happened?_____

_____

How did I do? *(circle the number)*   4   3   2   1

Really good!   Pretty good.   So-So.   I need to try again.

Why did I circle this? _____

_____

.**Skillstreaming**
■ ■ ■ ■ ■ ■ ■ ■ ■ ■ ■ ■ ■

Skill 67: Dealing with Another's Anger

Name_____Date_____

SKILL STEPS

1. Say to yourself, "I can stay calm."
2. Listen to what the person has to say.
3. Think about the person's role.
4. Think of your choices:
    a. Keep listening.
    b. Apologize if appropriate.
    c. Suggest a way to fix the problem.
    d. Walk away for now and think of what to do.
5. Act out your best choice.

When did I practice?	How did I do? *(circle the number)*			
	Really Good!	Pretty good.	So-So.	I need to try again.
1. _____	4	3	2	1
2. _____	4	3	2	1
3. _____	4	3	2	1

SUPPORTS

	Practice Situation *(circle)*		
With prompting	1	2	3
With coaching	1	2	3
With supportive peer	1	2	3
Other support *(specify)* _____	1	2	3
None	1	2	3

Group VI: School-Related Skills
(Skills 68–80)

Skill 68: Asking for Help

SKILL STEPS

1. **Ask yourself, "Can I do this alone?"**

   Encourage learners to try the task on their own first.

2. **If not, raise your hand.**

   Discuss that this is appropriate in class but not at home or with friends.

3. **Wait. Say to yourself, "I know I can wait without getting upset."**

   It may be necessary for learners to repeat this statement until help is given.

4. **Ask for help in a friendly or respectful way.**

   Learners may need practice in deciding when to use a friendly or respectful voice. Review or teach Skill 25 (Using a Friendly Voice) and Skill 26 (Using a Respectful Voice).

SUGGESTED MODELING SITUATIONS

School: You are struggling with an assignment; you are struggling with an activity in gym class.

Home: You are struggling with your homework; you are struggling with a chore you have been asked to do.

Peer group: You don't understand the rules of a game you want to play.

Community: You need help with directions to your friend's house; you are looking for something in the store and don't know where to find it.

COMMENTS

Learners with high-functioning autism disorders may easily become upset when frustrated. If necessary, the skill of Using Self-Control (Skill 39) may be taught prior to this one.

Skill 68: Asking for Help

Name_____Date_____

SKILL STEPS

1. Ask yourself, "Can I do this alone?"

2. If not, raise your hand.

3. Wait. Say to yourself, "I know I can wait without getting upset."

4. Ask for help in a friendly or respectful way.

FILL IN NOW

With whom will I try this? _____

When? _____

_____

SUPPORTS

☐ Coaching with *(name)* _____

☐ With supportive peer *(name)* _____

☐ Other *(specify)* _____

☐ None

FILL IN AFTER YOU PRACTICE THE SKILL

What happened? _____

_____

How did I do? *(circle the number)*   4   3   2   1

                       Really good!   Pretty good.   So-So.   I need to try again.

Why did I circle this? _____

_____

Skillstreaming

From *Skillstreaming Children and Youth with High-Functioning Autism: A Guide for Teaching Prosocial Skills,* © 2016
by E. McGinnis and R. L. Simpson. Champaign, IL: Research Press (www.researchpress.com, 800-519-2707).

Skill 68: Asking for Help

Name_____Date_____

SKILL STEPS

1. Ask yourself, "Can I do this alone?"

2. If not, raise your hand.

3. Wait. Say to yourself, "I know I can wait without getting upset."

4. Ask for help in a friendly or respectful way.

When did I practice?	How did I do? *(circle the number)*			
	Really Good!	Pretty good.	So-So.	I need to try again.
1. _____	4	3	2	1
2. _____	4	3	2	1
3. _____	4	3	2	1

SUPPORTS

	Practice Situation *(circle)*		
With prompting	1	2	3
With coaching	1	2	3
With supportive peer	1	2	3
Other support *(specify)* _____	1	2	3
None	1	2	3

Skill 69: Ignoring Distractions

SKILL STEPS

1. **Stop and take three deep breaths.**

   Explain that doing this helps you calm down and gives you time to think instead of acting impulsively.

2. **Say to yourself, "I can ignore this."**

   Learners may need to repeat this statement more than once.

3. **Go back to your work.**

4. **Say to yourself, "Good for me. I did it!"**

SUGGESTED MODELING SITUATIONS

School: A classmate is acting silly in class while you are working on an assignment.

Home: A brother or sister is making noise playing while you are doing your homework.

Peer group: You are playing a game with friends and some younger kids are trying to distract the players.

Community: People are walking around in the library while you are reading.

COMMENTS

If the distraction is too bothersome or one learners are unable to ignore, direct them to choose another skill, such as Asking for Help (Skill 68) or Dealing with Anxiety (Skill 36).

.Skillstreaming

From *Skillstreaming Children and Youth with High-Functioning Autism: A Guide for Teaching Prosocial Skills,* © 2016 by E. McGinnis and R. L. Simpson. Champaign, IL: Research Press (www.researchpress.com, 800-519-2707).

Skill 69: Ignoring Distractions

Name_____Date_____

SKILL STEPS

1. Stop and take three deep breaths.

2. Say to yourself, "I can ignore this."

3. Go back to your work.

4. Say to yourself, "Good for me. I did it!"

FILL IN NOW

With whom will I try this? _____

When? _____

_____

SUPPORTS

☐ Coaching with *(name)* _____

☐ With supportive peer *(name)* _____

☐ Other *(specify)* _____

☐ None

FILL IN AFTER YOU PRACTICE THE SKILL

What happened? _____

_____

How did I do? *(circle the number)*	4	3	2	1
	Really good!	Pretty good.	So-So.	I need to try again.

Why did I circle this? _____

_____

From *Skillstreaming Children and Youth with High-Functioning Autism: A Guide for Teaching Prosocial Skills*, © 2016 by E. McGinnis and R. L. Simpson. Champaign, IL: Research Press (www.researchpress.com, 800-519-2707).

Skill 69: Ignoring Distractions

Name_____Date_____

SKILL STEPS

1. Stop and take three deep breaths.

2. Say to yourself, "I can ignore this."

3. Go back to your work.

4. Say to yourself, "Good for me. I did it!"

When did I practice?	How did I do? *(circle the number)*			
	Really Good!	Pretty good.	So-So.	I need to try again.
1. _____	4	3	2	1
2. _____	4	3	2	1
3. _____	4	3	2	1

SUPPORTS

	Practice Situation *(circle)*		
With prompting	1	2	3
With coaching	1	2	3
With supportive peer	1	2	3
Other support *(specify)* _____	1	2	3
_____			
None	1	2	3

Skillstreaming

From *Skillstreaming Children and Youth with High-Functioning Autism: A Guide for Teaching Prosocial Skills,* © 2016 by E. McGinnis and R. L. Simpson. Champaign, IL: Research Press (www.researchpress.com, 800-519-2707).

Skill 70: Contributing to Discussions

SKILL STEPS

1. **Decide if you have something you want to say.**

    Ask yourself whether you have something to say to contribute to the discussion.

2. **Ask yourself, "Is this about the topic?"**

    If yes, go on to the next step. If no, wait until another time when your comment will fit better.

3. **Decide what you want to say.**

    Explain that learners will need to raise their hands (if this is an expectation) to contribute to a school discussion.

4. **Wait until no one else is talking.**

5. **Say what you want to say.**

SUGGESTED MODELING SITUATIONS

School: The class is discussing one of your favorite subjects.

Home: At dinner, your family members are discussing their day.

Peer group: A group of friends is discussing the game last night.

Community: You are in a discussion at church or in another community setting.

COMMENTS

When providing opportunities for learners to practice this skill, choose familiar and interesting topics for discussion.

From *Skillstreaming Children and Youth with High-Functioning Autism: A Guide for Teaching Prosocial Skills,* © 2016 by E. McGinnis and R. L. Simpson. Champaign, IL: Research Press (www.researchpress.com, 800-519-2707).

Skill 70: Contributing to Discussions

Name_____Date_____

SKILL STEPS

1. Decide if you have something you want to say.

2. Ask yourself, "Is this about the topic?"

3. Decide what you want to say.

4. Wait until no one else is talking.

5. Say what you want to say.

FILL IN NOW

With whom will I try this? _____

When? _____

_____

SUPPORTS

☐ Coaching with *(name)* _____

☐ With supportive peer *(name)* _____

☐ Other *(specify)* _____

☐ None

FILL IN AFTER YOU PRACTICE THE SKILL

What happened? _____

_____

How did I do? *(circle the number)*　　　4　　　　　　3　　　　　　2　　　　　　1

　　　　　　　　　　　　　　Really good!　Pretty good.　　So-So.　I need to try again.

Why did I circle this? _____

_____

Skillstreaming

From *Skillstreaming Children and Youth with High-Functioning Autism: A Guide for Teaching Prosocial Skills,* © 2016 by E. McGinnis and R. L. Simpson. Champaign, IL: Research Press (www.researchpress.com, 800-519-2707).

Skill 70: Contributing to Discussions

Name_____Date_____

SKILL STEPS

1. Decide if you have something you want to say.

2. Ask yourself, "Is this about the topic?"

3. Decide what you want to say.

4. Wait until no one else is talking.

5. Say what you want to say.

When did I practice?	How did I do? *(circle the number)*			
	Really Good!	Pretty good.	So-So.	I need to try again.
1. _____	4	3	2	1
2. _____	4	3	2	1
3. _____	4	3	2	1

SUPPORTS

	Practice Situation *(circle)*		
With prompting	1	2	3
With coaching	1	2	3
With supportive peer	1	2	3
Other support *(specify)* _____	1	2	3
None	1	2	3

From *Skillstreaming Children and Youth with High-Functioning Autism: A Guide for Teaching Prosocial Skills,* © 2016
by E. McGinnis and R. L. Simpson. Champaign, IL: Research Press (www.researchpress.com, 800-519-2707).

Skill 71: Taking a Break

SKILL STEPS

1. **Decide if you need or want to take a break.**

   Explain that doing this can prevent a learner from becoming more upset.

2. **Decide the reason.**

   This may be because the learner is frustrated, anxious, or a bit tired. Explain that a break is not appropriate when people just don't want to do something. However, a break could be used to allow time to think of another social skill learners could use when they return to the task.

3. **Decide whom to ask.**

   Explain that the person to ask should be someone who has the authority to grant this permission.

4. **Ask in a respectful way.**

   Review or teach the skill of Using a Respectful Voice (Skill 26) as needed.

SUGGESTED MODELING SITUATIONS

School: It's noisy in the classroom and you are getting anxious.

Home: You have been helping your parents with chores and you are getting tired.

Peer group: You are playing with a friend and need some time to yourself.

Community: You are doing an activity at the community center and want some quiet time.

COMMENTS

Many classrooms for learners with high-functioning autism disorders have areas for youth to take a break that include a variety of materials that can be manipulated or used to provide comfort.

Teachers are sometimes concerned that learners ask for a break to avoid a task. Yet sometimes a break is needed before completing a challenging activity. It is preferable to allow a brief break than for a youth to have a meltdown.

From *Skillstreaming Children and Youth with High-Functioning Autism: A Guide for Teaching Prosocial Skills,* © 2016 by E. McGinnis and R. L. Simpson. Champaign, IL: Research Press (www.researchpress.com, 800-519-2707).

Skill 71: Taking a Break

Name_____Date_____

SKILL STEPS

1. Decide if you need or want to take a break.
2. Decide the reason.
3. Decide whom to ask.
4. Ask in a respectful way.

FILL IN NOW

With whom will I try this? _____

When? _____

_____

SUPPORTS

☐ Coaching with *(name)* _____

☐ With supportive peer *(name)* _____

☐ Other *(specify)* _____

☐ None

FILL IN AFTER YOU PRACTICE THE SKILL

What happened? _____

_____

How did I do? *(circle the number)*   4   3   2   1

                                 Really good!   Pretty good.   So-So.   I need to try again.

Why did I circle this? _____

_____

Skill 71: Taking a Break

Name_____Date_____

SKILL STEPS

1. Decide if you need or want to take a break.
2. Decide the reason.
3. Decide whom to ask.
4. Ask in a respectful way.

	How did I do? *(circle the number)*			
When did I practice?	Really Good!	Pretty good.	So-So.	I need to try again.
1. _____	4	3	2	1
2. _____	4	3	2	1
3. _____	4	3	2	1

SUPPORTS

	Practice Situation *(circle)*		
With prompting	1	2	3
With coaching	1	2	3
With supportive peer	1	2	3
Other support *(specify)*_____	1	2	3
None	1	2	3

Skill 72: Setting a Goal

SKILL STEPS

1. **Decide on a goal you want to reach.**

   Discuss choosing a realistic goal (e.g., consider content, time frame). Goals may be related to social skills, recreational skills, or academics.

2. **Decide on the steps to get there.**

   These should be written down and kept for future reference.

3. **Take each step, one at a time.**

   Encourage learners to mark off each step as it is achieved.

4. **Make an affirmation when your goal is reached.**

   Review or teach Skill 44 (Affirming Yourself) as needed.

SUGGESTED MODELING SITUATIONS

School: You want to turn in all of your homework on time for a week.

Home: You want to learn to bake cookies.

Peer group: You want to learn a new game to play with peers.

Community: You want to do chores for others to earn spending money.

COMMENTS

Depending on learners' age and maturity level, setting small goals that can be easily achieved in a relatively short period of time (e.g., within a week) is more beneficial than setting goals that will take longer, at least when first learning this skill.

Skill 72: Setting a Goal

Name_____Date_____

SKILL STEPS

1. Decide on a goal you want to reach.

2. Decide on the steps to get there.

3. Take each step, one at a time.

4. Make an affirmation when your goal is reached.

FILL IN NOW

With whom will I try this? _____

When? _____

_____

SUPPORTS

☐ Coaching with *(name)* _____

☐ With supportive peer *(name)* _____

☐ Other *(specify)* _____

☐ None

FILL IN AFTER YOU PRACTICE THE SKILL

What happened? _____

_____

How did I do? *(circle the number)*   4   3   2   1

Really good!   Pretty good.   So-So.   I need to try again.

Why did I circle this? _____

_____

Skillstreaming

Skill 72: Setting a Goal

Name_____Date_____

SKILL STEPS

1. Decide on a goal you want to reach.
2. Decide on the steps to get there.
3. Take each step, one at a time.
4. Make an affirmation when your goal is reached.

	How did I do? *(circle the number)*			
When did I practice?	Really Good!	Pretty good.	So-So.	I need to try again.
1. _____	4	3	2	1
2. _____	4	3	2	1
3. _____	4	3	2	1

SUPPORTS

	Practice Situation *(circle)*		
With prompting	1	2	3
With coaching	1	2	3
With supportive peer	1	2	3
Other support *(specify)* _____	1	2	3
None	1	2	3

From *Skillstreaming Children and Youth with High-Functioning Autism: A Guide for Teaching Prosocial Skills,* © 2016 by E. McGinnis and R. L. Simpson. Champaign, IL: Research Press (www.researchpress.com, 800-519-2707). **259**

Skill 73: Completing Assignments

SKILL STEPS

1. **Listen for instructions.**

   Discuss that the learner should look at the teacher, listen with both eyes and ears, and think about what the teacher is saying. It may be helpful for learners to repeat the instructions (covertly, if possible) or take notes on the expectations.

2. **Ask about anything you don't understand.**

   Review or teach Skill 4 (Asking a Question About the Topic) or Skill 75 (Asking for Information). Remind learners to make sure the teacher has finished giving directions before asking for additional information.

3. **Work on the assignment.**

   Do what the teacher has asked you to do.

4. **Turn in the assignment on time.**

   Discuss making sure you know when the assignment is due, writing that date down in a planner, and looking over the assignment before turning it in to be sure you have finished.

SUGGESTED MODELING SITUATIONS

The following situations focus on school only.

Your teacher gives you a math assignment that is difficult for you.

Your teacher gives you a project that is due in two weeks.

Your teacher gives you an assignment that you think is boring.

COMMENTS

For assignments due in a week or two, discuss the need to plan strategies for working on the assignment throughout this time period. If learners do not have an assignment book or planner, you can provide one.

Many times, learners complete an assignment but fail to turn it in to the teacher. Be sure learners understand where the assignment should be placed (e.g., on the teacher's desk, in a specified basket).

Skill 73: Completing Assignments

Name_____Date_____

SKILL STEPS

1. Listen for instructions.

2. Ask about anything you don't understand.

3. Work on the assignment.

4. Turn in the assignment on time.

FILL IN NOW

With whom will I try this? _____

When? _____

_____

SUPPORTS

☐ Coaching with *(name)* _____

☐ With supportive peer *(name)* _____

☐ Other *(specify)* _____

☐ None

FILL IN AFTER YOU PRACTICE THE SKILL

What happened? _____

_____

How did I do? *(circle the number)*   4   3   2   1

                            Really good!   Pretty good.   So-So.   I need to try again.

Why did I circle this? _____

_____

From *Skillstreaming Children and Youth with High-Functioning Autism: A Guide for Teaching Prosocial Skills,* © 2016
by E. McGinnis and R. L. Simpson. Champaign, IL: Research Press (www.researchpress.com, 800-519-2707).

Skill 73: Completing Assignments

Name_____Date_____

SKILL STEPS

1. Listen for instructions.

2. Ask about anything you don't understand.

3. Work on the assignment.

4. Turn in the assignment on time.

	How did I do? (circle the number)			
When did I practice?	Really Good!	Pretty good.	So-So.	I need to try again.
1. _____	4	3	2	1
2. _____	4	3	2	1
3. _____	4	3	2	1

SUPPORTS

	Practice Situation (circle)		
With prompting	1	2	3
With coaching	1	2	3
With supportive peer	1	2	3
Other support (specify)_____	1	2	3
_____			
None	1	2	3

.Skillstreaming From *Skillstreaming Children and Youth with High-Functioning Autism: A Guide for Teaching Prosocial Skills,* © 2016 by E. McGinnis and R. L. Simpson. Champaign, IL: Research Press (www.researchpress.com, 800-519-2707).

Skill 74: Following Adult Directions

SKILL STEPS

1. **Listen to the direction.**

   Review or teach the skill of Listening Without Interrupting (Skill 1) as needed.

2. **Make sure you understand what is said.**

   Encourage learners to make sure they understand what the adult is telling them to do. If not, they may need to ask for additional information (Skill 75).

3. **Follow the direction.**

4. **Say to yourself, "Good for me. I followed the direction."**

SUGGESTED MODELING SITUATIONS

School: A teacher tells you to go to class.

Home: A parent tells you to turn off your computer.

Community: The store clerk tells you to stop playing with an item that belongs to the store.

COMMENTS

Make sure that learners understand that if an adult, especially one they do not know, gives them a direction to do something unsafe or inappropriate, they should immediately find an adult they know and report the situation.

 From *Skillstreaming Children and Youth with High-Functioning Autism: A Guide for Teaching Prosocial Skills,* © 2016 by E. McGinnis and R. L. Simpson. Champaign, IL: Research Press (www.researchpress.com, 800-519-2707). **263**

Skill 74: Following Adult Directions

Name_____Date_____

SKILL STEPS

1. Listen to the direction.

2. Make sure you understand what is said.

3. Follow the direction.

4. Say to yourself, "Good for me. I followed the direction."

FILL IN NOW

With whom will I try this? _____

When? _____

_____

SUPPORTS

☐ Coaching with *(name)* _____

☐ With supportive peer *(name)* _____

☐ Other *(specify)* _____

☐ None

FILL IN AFTER YOU PRACTICE THE SKILL

What happened? _____

_____

How did I do? *(circle the number)*   4   3   2   1

     Really good!   Pretty good.   So-So.   I need to try again.

Why did I circle this? _____

_____

.Skillstreaming

From *Skillstreaming Children and Youth with High-Functioning Autism: A Guide for Teaching Prosocial Skills,* © 2016 by E. McGinnis and R. L. Simpson. Champaign, IL: Research Press (www.researchpress.com, 800-519-2707).

Skill 74: Following Adult Directions

Name_____Date_____

SKILL STEPS

1. Listen to the direction.

2. Make sure you understand what is said.

3. Follow the direction.

4. Say to yourself, "Good for me. I followed the direction."

When did I practice?	How did I do? *(circle the number)*			
	Really Good!	Pretty good.	So-So.	I need to try again.
1. _____	4	3	2	1
2. _____	4	3	2	1
3. _____	4	3	2	1

SUPPORTS

	Practice Situation *(circle)*		
With prompting	1	2	3
With coaching	1	2	3
With supportive peer	1	2	3
Other support *(specify)*_____	1	2	3
None	1	2	3

Skill 75: Asking for Information

SKILL STEPS

1. **What relevant information do I want or need?**

   Think about what information is important to what the learner wants or needs to do. Decide whether the information needed is appropriate to the situation or topic. If no, write down the question and ask later.

2. **Is this a good time?**

   Decide whether this is an appropriate time. (Is the other person busy? Is the other person working on something else?)

3. **Decide whom to ask.**

   Discuss how to decide whether to ask a teacher, classmate, or someone else (e.g., the person isn't busy, the person is likely to know the information you need).

4. **Ask.**

   Explain that the information should be asked for in a respectful or friendly way, depending upon the person being asked.

SUGGESTED MODELING SITUATIONS

School: Your teacher is presenting a lesson in social studies and you want to know more about the country that is being presented.

Home: Your parent is painting a room and you want to know why certain things are being done.

Peer group: A friend is talking about a trip he took and you want to know more about the place he visited.

Community: You want to order something at a restaurant, but you want to know what the ingredients are first.

COMMENTS

This skill is an extension of Asking a Question About the Topic (Skill 4) and should be taught after the learner has a good understanding of asking questions related to a specific topic.

From *Skillstreaming Children and Youth with High-Functioning Autism: A Guide for Teaching Prosocial Skills,* © 2016 by E. McGinnis and R. L. Simpson. Champaign, IL: Research Press (www.researchpress.com, 800-519-2707).

Skill 75: Asking for Information

Name_____Date_____

SKILL STEPS

1. What relevant information do I want or need?

2. Is this a good time?

3. Decide whom to ask.

4. Ask.

FILL IN NOW

With whom will I try this? _____

When? _____

_____

SUPPORTS

☐ Coaching with *(name)* _____

☐ With supportive peer *(name)* _____

☐ Other *(specify)* _____

☐ None

FILL IN AFTER YOU PRACTICE THE SKILL

What happened? _____

_____

How did I do? *(circle the number)*	4	3	2	1
	Really good!	Pretty good.	So-So.	I need to try again.

Why did I circle this? _____

_____

From *Skillstreaming Children and Youth with High-Functioning Autism: A Guide for Teaching Prosocial Skills,* © 2016 by E. McGinnis and R. L. Simpson. Champaign, IL: Research Press (www.researchpress.com, 800-519-2707).

Skill 75: Asking for Information

Name_____Date_____

SKILL STEPS

1. What relevant information do I want or need?

2. Is this a good time?

3. Decide whom to ask.

4. Ask.

When did I practice?	How did I do? *(circle the number)*			
	Really Good!	Pretty good.	So-So.	I need to try again.
1. _____	4	3	2	1
2. _____	4	3	2	1
3. _____	4	3	2	1

SUPPORTS

	Practice Situation *(circle)*		
With prompting	1	2	3
With coaching	1	2	3
With supportive peer	1	2	3
Other support *(specify)* _____	1	2	3
_____			
None	1	2	3

.**Skillstreaming**

Skill 76: Organizing Materials

SKILL STEPS

1. **What materials do you need?**

    If needed, have the learner write the materials needed for the class in a planner.

2. **Gather the materials together.**

    The learner may want to check off each material listed in the planner. If the skill is used in school, remind learners to bring only the materials needed for the class.

3. **Ask, "Do I have everything I need?"**

4. **Recheck your materials and pack them up.**

SUGGESTED MODELING SITUATIONS

School: You are getting materials from your locker for the next class.

Home: You are getting your backpack ready for school the next day.

Peer group: You are going to a friend's birthday party.

Community: You are going swimming with friends.

COMMENTS

You may provide additional strategies to help learners stay organized. For example, provide a different colored folder for each class. Have learners write down what is needed to bring to school the next day. Communicate this with parents so they may review the list at home and assist the learner in checking off the items to put in the backpack.

From *Skillstreaming Children and Youth with High-Functioning Autism: A Guide for Teaching Prosocial Skills,* © 2016 by E. McGinnis and R. L. Simpson. Champaign, IL: Research Press (www.researchpress.com, 800-519-2707).

Skill 76: Organizing Materials

Name_____Date_____

SKILL STEPS

1. What materials do you need?

2. Gather the materials together.

3. Ask, "Do I have everything I need?"

4. Recheck your materials and pack them up.

FILL IN NOW

With whom will I try this? _____

When? _____

_____

SUPPORTS

☐ Coaching with *(name)* _____

☐ With supportive peer *(name)* _____

☐ Other *(specify)* _____

☐ None

FILL IN AFTER YOU PRACTICE THE SKILL

What happened? _____

_____

How did I do? *(circle the number)*   4   3   2   1

Really good!   Pretty good.   So-So.   I need to try again.

Why did I circle this? _____

_____

Skillstreaming

Skill 76: Organizing Materials

Name_____Date_____

SKILL STEPS

1. What materials do you need?

2. Gather the materials together.

3. Ask, "Do I have everything I need?"

4. Recheck your materials and pack them up.

When did I practice?	How did I do? *(circle the number)*			
	Really Good!	Pretty good.	So-So.	I need to try again.
1. _____	4	3	2	1
2. _____	4	3	2	1
3. _____	4	3	2	1

SUPPORTS

	Practice Situation *(circle)*		
With prompting	1	2	3
With coaching	1	2	3
With supportive peer	1	2	3
Other support *(specify)* _____	1	2	3
None	1	2	3

From *Skillstreaming Children and Youth with High-Functioning Autism: A Guide for Teaching Prosocial Skills,* © 2016 by E. McGinnis and R. L. Simpson. Champaign, IL: Research Press (www.researchpress.com, 800-519-2707).

Skill 77: Making Corrections

SKILL STEPS

1. **Look at the first correction.**

   Explain that sometimes it is overwhelming to look at all of the corrections. Looking at one correction at a time will lessen frustration.

2. **Try to make the correction on your own.**

3. **If you are not successful, ask someone.**

   Inform learners of rules regarding asking classmates for help or explain that they will need to ask the teacher when available. Review or teach the skill of Asking for Information (Skill 75) or Asking a Favor (Skill 13), if needed.

4. **Make the correction.**

5. **Go on to the next correction.**

SUGGESTED MODELING SITUATIONS

School: You have corrections to make in your most difficult subject.

Home: You have corrections to make as your homework assignment.

Peer group: You made something for a friend, but it didn't turn out right.

Community: You worked on a project, but your part doesn't look the way you wanted it to.

COMMENTS

This skill is most useful for assignments that are completed carelessly, not for assignments beyond the learner's skills. If many errors are made on an assignment, it is important for teachers to analyze these errors and reteach necessary academic skills.

From *Skillstreaming Children and Youth with High-Functioning Autism: A Guide for Teaching Prosocial Skills,* © 2016 by E. McGinnis and R. L. Simpson. Champaign, IL: Research Press (www.researchpress.com, 800-519-2707).

Skill 77: Making Corrections

Name_____Date_____

SKILL STEPS

1. Look at the first correction.

2. Try to make the correction on your own.

3. If you are not successful, ask someone.

4. Make the correction.

5. Go on to the next correction.

FILL IN NOW

With whom will I try this? _____

When? _____

_____

SUPPORTS

☐ Coaching with *(name)* _____

☐ With supportive peer *(name)* _____

☐ Other *(specify)* _____

☐ None

FILL IN AFTER YOU PRACTICE THE SKILL

What happened? _____

_____

How did I do? *(circle the number)*   4   3   2   1

                                 Really good!   Pretty good.   So-So.   I need to try again.

Why did I circle this? _____

_____

From *Skillstreaming Children and Youth with High-Functioning Autism: A Guide for Teaching Prosocial Skills,* © 2016
by E. McGinnis and R. L. Simpson. Champaign, IL: Research Press (www.researchpress.com, 800-519-2707).

Skill 77: Making Corrections

Name_____Date_____

SKILL STEPS

1. Look at the first correction.

2. Try to make the correction on your own.

3. If you are not successful, ask someone.

4. Make the correction.

5. Go on to the next correction.

	How did I do? (circle the number)			
When did I practice?	Really Good!	Pretty good.	So-So.	I need to try again.
1. _____	4	3	2	1
2. _____	4	3	2	1
3. _____	4	3	2	1

SUPPORTS

	Practice Situation (circle)		
With prompting	1	2	3
With coaching	1	2	3
With supportive peer	1	2	3
Other support (specify) _____	1	2	3
_____			
None	1	2	3

.Skillstreaming

From *Skillstreaming Children and Youth with High-Functioning Autism: A Guide for Teaching Prosocial Skills,* © 2016 by E. McGinnis and R. L. Simpson. Champaign, IL: Research Press (www.researchpress.com, 800-519-2707).

Skill 78: Preparing for Class

SKILL STEPS

1. **Ask yourself, "Is my assignment done?"**

   Learners should make sure the completed assignment is in their folder or backpack.

2. **Ask yourself, "Do I have the materials I need?"**

   Review or teach the skill of Organizing Materials (Skill 76) as needed. Explain that if learners do not have the necessary materials, they will need to get these organized.

3. **Say to yourself, "Okay, I'm ready for class."**

4. **Plan to turn in your assignment when you get to class.**

   Explain that this is often the very first thing learners will do when they get to class. When no assignment has been given, they will skip this step.

SUGGESTED MODELING SITUATIONS

Situations are provided for school settings only.

You are preparing for a scheduled class the next day.

You are preparing for a special class that is usually not on your schedule.

COMMENTS

If time is needed for learners to complete their assignments, they should use this skill a day or so before the assignment is due.

Skill 78: Preparing for Class

Name_____Date_____

SKILL STEPS

1. Ask yourself, "Is my assignment done?"

2. Ask yourself, "Do I have the materials I need?"

3. Say to yourself, "Okay, I'm ready for class."

4. Plan to turn in your assignment when you get to class.

FILL IN NOW

With whom will I try this?_____

When?_____

_____

SUPPORTS

☐ Coaching with *(name)* _____

☐ With supportive peer *(name)* _____

☐ Other *(specify)* _____

☐ None

FILL IN AFTER YOU PRACTICE THE SKILL

What happened? _____

_____

How did I do? *(circle the number)*   4   3   2   1

                              Really good!   Pretty good.   So-So.   I need to try again.

Why did I circle this? _____

_____

Skillstreaming

From *Skillstreaming Children and Youth with High-Functioning Autism: A Guide for Teaching Prosocial Skills,* © 2016
by E. McGinnis and R. L. Simpson. Champaign, IL: Research Press (www.researchpress.com, 800-519-2707).

Skill 78: Preparing for Class

Name_____Date_____

SKILL STEPS

1. Ask yourself, "Is my assignment done?"

2. Ask yourself, "Do I have the materials I need?"

3. Say to yourself, "Okay, I'm ready for class."

4. Plan to turn in your assignment when you get to class.

When did I practice?	How did I do? *(circle the number)*			
	Really Good!	Pretty good.	So-So.	I need to try again.
1. _____	4	3	2	1
2. _____	4	3	2	1
3. _____	4	3	2	1

SUPPORTS

	Practice Situation *(circle)*		
With prompting	1	2	3
With coaching	1	2	3
With supportive peer	1	2	3
Other support *(specify)* _____	1	2	3
None	1	2	3

From *Skillstreaming Children and Youth with High-Functioning Autism: A Guide for Teaching Prosocial Skills,* © 2016 by E. McGinnis and R. L. Simpson. Champaign, IL: Research Press (www.researchpress.com, 800-519-2707).

Skill 79: Dealing with Transitions

SKILL STEPS

1. **Say to yourself, "It's time to change. I need to get ready."**

   Learners may need to repeat this to themselves more than once.

2. **Take three deep breaths and relax.**

   Additional self-control strategies may be added if learners find particular ones most useful. Refer to Skill 39 (Using Self-Control).

3. **Get ready for the change.**

   Discuss routines that would be helpful to the learner, such as putting materials away, getting materials ready for the next class or to go home, and waiting quietly for directions. Some learners may want to use a stress ball or other item to help them wait quietly.

4. **Say to yourself, "I'm ready for the change."**

SUGGESTED MODELING SITUATIONS

School: You are going from one classroom to another.

Home: You are getting ready to leave for school.

Peer group: You are supposed to walk home with a friend after school.

Community: You are attending a community event and changing activities.

COMMENTS

Transitions are often particularly challenging for this population. Advance preparation in transitions is helpful, particularly if the transition is a change in the typical routine or schedule.

.Skillstreaming

From *Skillstreaming Children and Youth with High-Functioning Autism: A Guide for Teaching Prosocial Skills,* © 2016 by E. McGinnis and R. L. Simpson. Champaign, IL: Research Press (www.researchpress.com, 800-519-2707).

Skill 79: Dealing with Transitions

Name_____Date_____

SKILL STEPS

1. Say to yourself, "It's time to change. I need to get ready."

2. Take three deep breaths and relax.

3. Get ready for the change.

4. Say to yourself, "I'm ready for the change."

FILL IN NOW

With whom will I try this?_____

When?_____

_____

SUPPORTS

☐ Coaching with *(name)*_____

☐ With supportive peer *(name)*_____

☐ Other *(specify)*_____

☐ None

FILL IN AFTER YOU PRACTICE THE SKILL

What happened?_____

_____

How did I do? *(circle the number)*   4   3   2   1

                      Really good!   Pretty good.   So-So.   I need to try again.

Why did I circle this?_____

_____

From *Skillstreaming Children and Youth with High-Functioning Autism: A Guide for Teaching Prosocial Skills,* © 2016 by E. McGinnis and R. L. Simpson. Champaign, IL: Research Press (www.researchpress.com, 800-519-2707).

Skill 79: Dealing with Transitions

Name_____Date_____

SKILL STEPS

1. Say to yourself, "It's time to change. I need to get ready."
2. Take three deep breaths and relax.
3. Get ready for the change.
4. Say to yourself, "I'm ready for the change."

	How did I do? *(circle the number)*			
When did I practice?	Really Good!	Pretty good.	So-So.	I need to try again.
1. _____	4	3	2	1
2. _____	4	3	2	1
3. _____	4	3	2	1

SUPPORTS

	Practice Situation *(circle)*		
With prompting	1	2	3
With coaching	1	2	3
With supportive peer	1	2	3
Other support *(specify)* _____	1	2	3
_____			
None	1	2	3

Skillstreaming

From *Skillstreaming Children and Youth with High-Functioning Autism: A Guide for Teaching Prosocial Skills,* © 2016 by E. McGinnis and R. L. Simpson. Champaign, IL: Research Press (www.researchpress.com, 800-519-2707).

Skill 80: Interrupting

SKILL STEPS

1. **Decide if you need to interrupt.**

   Discuss appropriate times to interrupt (e.g., when the person you need help from is looking at you).

2. **Walk up to the person.**

   Make sure that this is allowed in the classroom setting. Otherwise, learners should raise their hands.

3. **Wait quietly.**

   Emphasize the importance of waiting until the person has finished talking.

4. **Say to the person, "Excuse me."**

5. **Ask or tell.**

   Explain the importance of waiting until the person is ready to listen to you (e.g., the person looks at you, the person says something to you).

SUGGESTED MODELING SITUATIONS

School: You want help from the teacher, but she is helping another student.

Home: Your parent is on the phone, but there is someone at the door.

Peer group: Your friend is talking to someone, but you want to let your friend know that it's time to leave.

Community: Your ride is waiting for you and you want to tell the coach that you have to leave.

COMMENTS

It will be important to discuss situations in which learners should not interrupt (e.g., to ask a question that could wait until later) and situations in which they should interrupt immediately (e.g., in an emergency). It may be helpful to define for learners situations that are emergencies.

Skill 80: Interrupting

Name_____Date_____

SKILL STEPS

1. Decide if you need to interrupt.
2. Walk up to the person.
3. Wait quietly.
4. Say to the person, "Excuse me."
5. Ask or tell.

FILL IN NOW

With whom will I try this? _____

When? _____

_____

SUPPORTS

☐ Coaching with *(name)* _____

☐ With supportive peer *(name)* _____

☐ Other *(specify)* _____

☐ None

FILL IN AFTER YOU PRACTICE THE SKILL

What happened? _____

_____

How did I do? *(circle the number)*   4   3   2   1

                 Really good!   Pretty good.   So-So.   I need to try again.

Why did I circle this? _____

_____

From *Skillstreaming Children and Youth with High-Functioning Autism: A Guide for Teaching Prosocial Skills,* © 2016
by E. McGinnis and R. L. Simpson. Champaign, IL: Research Press (www.researchpress.com, 800-519-2707).

Skill 80: Interrupting

Name_____Date_____

SKILL STEPS

1. Decide if you need to interrupt.
2. Walk up to the person.
3. Wait quietly.
4. Say to the person, "Excuse me."
5. Ask or tell.

	How did I do? *(circle the number)*			
When did I practice?	Really Good!	Pretty good.	So-So.	I need to try again.
1. _____	4	3	2	1
2. _____	4	3	2	1
3. _____	4	3	2	1

SUPPORTS

	Practice Situation *(circle)*		
With prompting	1	2	3
With coaching	1	2	3
With supportive peer	1	2	3
Other support *(specify)* _____	1	2	3
None	1	2	3

Program Forms and Checklists

TEACHER/STAFF CHECKLIST

Learner name_____ Class/age_____

Teacher/staff_____ Date_____

Instructions: Listed below are important skills that learners may be more or less proficient in using. This checklist will help you evaluate how well the learner uses the various skills and identify target skills for instruction. Please rate his/her use of each skill, based on your observations.

Circle 1 if the learner is *almost never* good at using the skill.

Circle 2 if the learner is *seldom* good at using the skill.

Circle 3 if the learner is *sometimes* good at using the skill.

Circle 4 if the learner is *often* good at using the skill.

Circle 5 if the learner is *almost always* good at using the skill.

Please rate the learner on all skills listed. If you know of a situation in which the learner has particular difficulty using the skill well, please note it briefly in the space marked "Problem situation."

	Almost never	Seldom	Sometimes	Often	Almost always
1. **Listening Without Interrupting:** Does the learner appear to listen when someone is speaking, make an effort to understand what is said, and refrain from interrupting?	1	2	3	4	5
Problem situation:					
2. **Greeting Others:** Does the learner greet others in appropriate ways?	1	2	3	4	5
Problem situation:					
3. **Responding to a Greeting:** When someone greets the learner, does he/she greet the person back?	1	2	3	4	5
Problem situation:					
4. **Asking a Question About the Topic:** Does the learner stay on topic when asking questions?	1	2	3	4	5
Problem situation:					

From *Skillstreaming Children and Youth with High-Functioning Autism: A Guide for Teaching Prosocial Skills,* © 2016 by E. McGinnis and R. L. Simpson. Champaign, IL: Research Press (www.researchpress.com, 800-519-2707).

5. **Staying on Topic:** Does the learner stay on topic during conversations or discussions?

        1   2   3   4   5

Problem situation:

6. **Responding to Questions:** Does the learner answer questions with appropriate responses?

        1   2   3   4   5

Problem situation:

7. **Taking Turns:** Does the learner take turns when appropriate?

        1   2   3   4   5

Problem situation:

8. **Complimenting Others:** Does the learner tell others that he/she likes something about them or something they have done?

        1   2   3   4   5

Problem situation:

9. **Helping Others:** Does the learner help others at appropriate times and in appropriate ways?

        1   2   3   4   5

Problem situation:

10. **Encouraging Others:** Does the learner encourage others when they feel sad or frustrated?

        1   2   3   4   5

Problem situation:

11. **Cooperating with Others:** Does the learner cooperate with others?

        1   2   3   4   5

Problem situation:

12. **Sharing:** Does the learner share with others?

        1   2   3   4   5

Problem situation:

The rating scale header reads (diagonally): Almost never, Seldom, Sometimes, Often, Almost always

13. **Asking a Favor:** Does the learner know how and when to ask a favor of someone?   1   2   3   4   5

Problem situation:

14. **Starting a Conversation:** Does the learner know how and when to start a conversation with someone?   1   2   3   4   5

Problem situation:

15. **Continuing a Conversation:** When having a conversation, does the learner keep the conversation going?   1   2   3   4   5

Problem situation:

16. **When to Introduce a New Topic:** When having a conversation, does the learner know when to introduce a new topic?   1   2   3   4   5

Problem situation:

17. **Accepting a Topic Change:** Does the learner accept a change in topics during discussions or conversations?   1   2   3   4   5

Problem situation:

18. **Ending a Conversation:** Does the learner end a conversation in a timely and appropriate manner?   1   2   3   4   5

Problem situation:

19. **Responding to Offers to Join In:** Does the learner join in activities or games with others when invited?   1   2   3   4   5

Problem situation:

	Almost never	Seldom	Sometimes	Often	Almost always

20. **Asking to Join In:** Does the learner ask to join in activities or games with others?

        1   2   3   4   5

Problem situation:

21. **Communicating Preferences:** Does the learner tell others in respectful ways about what he/she likes to do?

        1   2   3   4   5

Problem situation:

22. **Accepting Another's Opinion:** Does the learner accept others' opinions without becoming upset or frustrated?

        1   2   3   4   5

Problem situation:

23. **Reading Others:** Does the learner look at others' faces and gestures and try to understand them, even if the person doesn't say anything?

        1   2   3   4   5

Problem situation:

24. **Reading the Environment:** Does the learner behave appropriately in a variety of settings (e.g., responding appropriately to contextual and environmental signs)?

        1   2   3   4   5

Problem situation:

25. **Using a Friendly Voice:** Does the learner speak to others (e.g., peers) in a friendly manner?

        1   2   3   4   5

Problem situation:

26. **Using a Respectful Voice:** Does the learner speak to adults using a respectful voice and words?

        1   2   3   4   5

Problem situation:

	Almost never	Seldom	Sometimes	Often	Almost always

27. **Giving Information Nonverbally:** Does the learner understand what his/her facial expressions and gestures say to others?   1   2   3   4   5

Problem situation:

28. **Attending to a Model:** Does the learner watch and listen to others to see how they do things?   1   2   3   4   5

Problem situation:

29. **Respecting Another's Boundaries:** Does the learner show respect of others' boundaries or physical space?   1   2   3   4   5

Problem situation:

30. **Showing Interest in Others:** Does the learner watch others to see what they are interested in doing?   1   2   3   4   5

Problem situation:

31. **Understanding Differences:** Does the learner seem to accept differences among people, including opinions, traits, and mannerisms?   1   2   3   4   5

Problem situation:

32. **Taking Another's Perspective:** Does the learner understand how and why another person might feel a certain way?   1   2   3   4   5

Problem situation:

33. **Regulating Your Attention:** Does the learner pay attention when he/she is supposed to?   1   2   3   4   5

Problem situation:

	Almost never	Seldom	Sometimes	Often	Almost always

34. **Recognizing Anxiety:** Does the learner recognize when he/she is feeling anxious? — 1 2 3 4 5

   Problem situation:

35. **Deciding What Causes Your Anxiety:** Can the learner determine specific situations that create anxiety for him/her? — 1 2 3 4 5

   Problem situation:

36. **Dealing with Anxiety:** Does the learner deal with his/her anxiety in appropriate ways? — 1 2 3 4 5

   Problem situation:

37. **Checking Your Voice and Interests:** Does the learner monitor his/her voice tone and interests in certain topics, recognizing boredom or other feelings in the listener? — 1 2 3 4 5

   Problem situation:

38. **No Means No:** Does the learner understand situations where he/she should not touch someone or say something about their body? — 1 2 3 4 5

   Problem situation:

39. **Using Self-Control:** Does the learner control his/her own behavior in a variety of situations? — 1 2 3 4 5

   Problem situation:

40. **Dealing with Change:** Does the learner accept change in routine without losing control or becoming upset? — 1 2 3 4 5

   Problem situation:

	Almost never	Seldom	Sometimes	Often	Almost always

41. **Dealing with Boredom:** Does the learner stay with an activity until it is finished even though he/she may feel bored?

        1   2   3   4   5

Problem situation:

42. **Responding to Authority:** Does the learner follow the rules when told to do so by someone in authority?

        1   2   3   4   5

Problem situation:

43. **Checking Your Behavior:** Does the learner monitor his/her own behavior in a variety of situations and settings?

        1   2   3   4   5

Problem situation:

44. **Affirming Yourself:** Does the learner make positive statements about himself/herself?

        1   2   3   4   5

Problem situation:

45. **Determining Private Information:** Does the learner resist sharing information that is private and shouldn't be shared?

        1   2   3   4   5

Problem situation:

46. **Understanding Rules of Swearing:** Does the learner resist swearing in situations and settings where this isn't appropriate?

        1   2   3   4   5

Problem situation:

47. **Understanding Rules of Touch:** Does the learner know when it is appropriate to touch someone or something and when it is not?

        1   2   3   4   5

Problem situation:

48. **Planning for Stressful Situations:** When the learner knows a stressful situation is coming up, does he/she make an effective plan to deal with this?

    Problem situation:

    | 1 | 2 | 3 | 4 | 5 |

49. **Defining a Problem:** When a problem occurs, does the learner accurately assess what caused it?

    Problem situation:

    | 1 | 2 | 3 | 4 | 5 |

50. **Considering Alternatives:** Does the learner think of good choices to solve a problem?

    Problem situation:

    | 1 | 2 | 3 | 4 | 5 |

51. **Choosing an Alternative:** Does the learner choose an alternative and follow through with this choice?

    Problem situation:

    | 1 | 2 | 3 | 4 | 5 |

52. **When to Change Strategies:** When one choice doesn't work to solve a problem, does the learner change to a different choice?

    Problem situation:

    | 1 | 2 | 3 | 4 | 5 |

53. **When a Rule Doesn't Work:** When a rule doesn't apply to a given situation, does the learner handle this in appropriate ways?

    Problem situation:

    | 1 | 2 | 3 | 4 | 5 |

54. **Giving Feedback:** Does the learner notice when someone does a good job and tell him/her specifically what the person did that was good?

    Problem situation:

    | 1 | 2 | 3 | 4 | 5 |

	Almost never	Seldom	Sometimes	Often	Almost always

55. **Seeking Attention:** Does the learner seek attention in appropriate ways?   1   2   3   4   5

Problem situation:

56. **Accepting Attention:** Does the learner accept the attention of others in desirable way?   1   2   3   4   5

Problem situation:

57. **Making a Complaint:** Does the learner make a complaint to the appropriate person in an appropriate manner and at a good time?   1   2   3   4   5

Problem situation:

58. **When You Don't Understand:** When the learner doesn't understand a social situation (e.g., why he/she must wait or isn't allowed to do something), does he/she deal with this in appropriate ways?   1   2   3   4   5

Problem situation:

59. **Knowing Your Feelings:** Can the learner identify how he/she feels in a variety of situations?   1   2   3   4   5

Problem situation:

60. **Feeling Different:** If the learner feels different from others, does he/she deal appropriately with this feeling?   1   2   3   4   5

Problem situation:

61. **Expressing Your Feelings:** Does the learner express his/her feelings in appropriate ways?   1   2   3   4   5

Problem situation:

	Almost never	Seldom	Sometimes	Often	Almost always

62. **Calming Your Feelings:** Does the learner deal with things that bother him/her (e.g., touch, loud noises) in good ways?   1   2   3   4   5

Problem situation:

63. **Showing Affection:** Does the learner let others know in acceptable ways that he/she cares about them?   1   2   3   4   5

Problem situation:

64. **Recognizing Another's Feelings:** Does the learner seem to understand how someone else is feeling?   1   2   3   4   5

Problem situation:

65. **Showing Concern for Another:** Does the learner show concern for others in appropriate ways and at appropriate times?   1   2   3   4   5

Problem situation:

66. **Understanding Another's Intentions:** Does the learner seem to correctly interpret the intentions and motivations of others?   1   2   3   4   5

Problem situation:

67. **Dealing with Another's Anger:** When someone is angry, does the learner deal with this anger in good ways?   1   2   3   4   5

Problem situation:

68. **Asking for Help:** Does the learner ask for assistance when needed in appropriate ways and at good times?   1   2   3   4   5

Problem situation:

69. **Ignoring Distractions:** Does the learner ignore distractions in class in order to complete his/her task?

    Problem situation:

    1   2   3   4   5

70. **Contributing to Discussions:** Does the learner contribute to discussions in desirable ways and at appropriate times?

    Problem situation:

    1   2   3   4   5

71. **Taking a Break:** Does the learner take breaks when needed in an appropriate manner?

    Problem situation:

    1   2   3   4   5

72. **Setting a Goal:** Does the learner set goals and work toward achieving these goals?

    Problem situation:

    1   2   3   4   5

73. **Completing Assignments:** Does the learner complete and turn in assignments on time?

    Problem situation:

    1   2   3   4   5

74. **Following Adult Directions:** Does the learner follow adult directions related to his/her behavior or a task?

    Problem situation:

    1   2   3   4   5

75. **Asking for Information:** Does the learner ask for needed and relevant information in an appropriate manner?

    Problem situation:

    1   2   3   4   5

	Almost never	Seldom	Sometimes	Often	Almost always

76. **Organizing Materials:** Does the learner organize needed materials for particular activities?

   Problem situation:

   1 2 3 4 5

77. **Making Corrections:** Does the learner make the necessary corrections on assignments without becoming overly frustrated?

   Problem situation:

   1 2 3 4 5

78. **Preparing for Class:** Does the learner bring needed materials to classes?

   Problem situation:

   1 2 3 4 5

79. **Dealing with Transitions:** Does the learner handle transitions from one activity or setting to another without acting out?

   Problem situation:

   1 2 3 4 5

80. **Interrupting:** Does the learner interrupt others only when necessary and in an appropriate way?

   Problem situation:

   1 2 3 4 5

PARENT CHECKLIST

Name_____Date_____

Child's name_____Date of birth_____

Instructions: Listed below are important skills that children and youth may be more or less proficient in using. This checklist will help you evaluate how well your child uses the various skills and identify target skills for instruction. Please rate his/her use of each skill, based on your observations.

Circle 1 if your child is *almost never* good at using the skill.

Circle 2 if your child is *seldom* good at using the skill.

Circle 3 if your child is *sometimes* good at using the skill.

Circle 4 if your child is *often* good at using the skill.

Circle 5 if your child is *almost always* good at using the skill.

Please rate your child on all skills listed. If you know of a situation in which your child has particular difficulty using the skill well, please note it briefly in the space marked "Problem situation."

	Almost never	Seldom	Sometimes	Often	Almost always
1. **Listening Without Interrupting:** Does your child appear to listen when someone is speaking, make an effort to understand what is said, and refrain from interrupting? Problem situation:	1	2	3	4	5
2. **Greeting Others:** Does your child greet others in appropriate ways? Problem situation:	1	2	3	4	5
3. **Responding to a Greeting:** When someone greets your child, does he/she greet the person back? Problem situation:	1	2	3	4	5
4. **Asking a Question About the Topic:** Does your child stay on topic when asking questions? Problem situation:	1	2	3	4	5

From *Skillstreaming Children and Youth with High-Functioning Autism: A Guide for Teaching Prosocial Skills,* © 2016 by E. McGinnis and R. L. Simpson. Champaign, IL: Research Press (www.researchpress.com, 800-519-2707).

5. **Staying on Topic:** Does your child stay on topic during conversations or discussions? — 1   2   3   4   5

   Problem situation:

6. **Responding to Questions:** Does your child answer questions with appropriate responses? — 1   2   3   4   5

   Problem situation:

7. **Taking Turns:** Does your child take turns when appropriate? — 1   2   3   4   5

   Problem situation:

8. **Complimenting Others:** Does your child tell others that he/she likes something about them or something they have done? — 1   2   3   4   5

   Problem situation:

9. **Helping Others:** Does your child help others at appropriate times and in appropriate ways? — 1   2   3   4   5

   Problem situation:

10. **Encouraging Others:** Does your child encourage others when they feel sad or frustrated? — 1   2   3   4   5

    Problem situation:

11. **Cooperating with Others:** Does your child cooperate with others? — 1   2   3   4   5

    Problem situation:

12. **Sharing:** Does your child share with others? — 1   2   3   4   5

    Problem situation:

13. **Asking a Favor:** Does your child know how and when to ask a favor of someone?

       1   2   3   4   5

Problem situation:

14. **Starting a Conversation:** Does your child know how and when to start a conversation with someone?

       1   2   3   4   5

Problem situation:

15. **Continuing a Conversation:** When having a conversation, does your child keep the conversation going?

       1   2   3   4   5

Problem situation:

16. **When to Introduce a New Topic:** When having a conversation, does your child know when to introduce a new topic?

       1   2   3   4   5

Problem situation:

17. **Accepting a Topic Change:** Does your child accept a change in topics during discussions or conversations?

       1   2   3   4   5

Problem situation:

18. **Ending a Conversation:** Does your child end a conversation in a timely and appropriate manner?

       1   2   3   4   5

Problem situation:

19. **Responding to Offers to Join In:** Does your child join in activities or games with others when invited?

       1   2   3   4   5

Problem situation:

	Almost never	Seldom	Sometimes	Often	Almost always

20. **Asking to Join In:** Does your child ask to join in activities or games with others? 　　　1　2　3　4　5

Problem situation:

21. **Communicating Preferences:** Does your child tell others in respectful ways about what he/she likes to do? 　　　1　2　3　4　5

Problem situation:

22. **Accepting Another's Opinion:** Does your child accept others' opinions without becoming upset or frustrated? 　　　1　2　3　4　5

Problem situation:

23. **Reading Others:** Does your child look at others' faces and gestures and try to understand them, even if the person doesn't say anything? 　　　1　2　3　4　5

Problem situation:

24. **Reading the Environment:** Does your child behave appropriately in a variety of settings (for example, responding appropriately to contextual and environmental signs)? 　　　1　2　3　4　5

Problem situation:

25. **Using a Friendly Voice:** Does your child speak to others (for example, peers) in a friendly manner? 　　　1　2　3　4　4

Problem situation:

26. **Using a Respectful Voice:** Does your child speak to adults using a respectful voice and words? 　　　1　2　3　4　5

Problem situation:

27. **Giving Information Nonverbally:** Does your child understand what his/her facial expressions and gestures say to others?

   Problem situation:

   1 2 3 4 5

28. **Attending to a Model:** Does your child watch and listen to others to see how they do things?

   Problem situation:

   1 2 3 4 5

29. **Respecting Another's Boundaries:** Does your child show respect of others' boundaries or physical space?

   Problem situation:

   1 2 3 4 5

30. **Showing Interest in Others:** Does your child watch others to see what they are interested in doing?

   Problem situation:

   1 2 3 4 5

31. **Understanding Differences:** Does your child seem to accept differences among people, including opinions, traits, and mannerisms?

   Problem situation:

   1 2 3 4 5

32. **Taking Another's Perspective:** Does your child understand how and why another person might feel a certain way?

   Problem situation:

   1 2 3 4 5

33. **Regulating Your Attention:** Does your child pay attention when he/she is supposed to?

   Problem situation:

   1 2 3 4 5

	Almost never	Seldom	Sometimes	Often	Almost always

34. **Recognizing Anxiety:** Does your child recognize when he/she is feeling anxious?   1   2   3   4   5

   Problem situation:

35. **Deciding What Causes Your Anxiety:** Can your child determine specific situations that create anxiety for him/her?   1   2   3   4   5

   Problem situation:

36. **Dealing with Anxiety:** Does your child deal with his/her anxiety in appropriate ways?   1   2   3   4   5

   Problem situation:

37. **Checking Your Voice and Interests:** Does your child monitor his/her voice tone and interests in certain topics, recognizing boredom or other feelings in the listener?   1   2   3   4   5

   Problem situation:

38. **No Means No:** Does your child understand situations where he/she should not touch someone or say something about the person's body?   1   2   3   4   5

   Problem situation:

39. **Using Self-Control:** Does your child control his/her own behavior in a variety of situations?   1   2   3   4   5

   Problem situation:

40. **Dealing with Change:** Does your child accept change in routine without losing control or becoming upset?   1   2   3   4   5

   Problem situation:

	Almost never	Seldom	Sometimes	Often	Almost always

41. **Dealing with Boredom:** Does your child stay with an activity until it is finished even though he/she may feel bored? 1 2 3 4 5

Problem situation:

42. **Responding to Authority:** Does your child follow the rules when told to do so by someone in authority? 1 2 3 4 5

Problem situation:

43. **Checking Your Behavior:** Does your child monitor his/her own behavior in a variety of situations and settings? 1 2 3 4 5

Problem situation:

44. **Affirming Yourself:** Does your child make positive statements about himself/herself? 1 2 3 4 5

Problem situation:

45. **Determining Private Information:** Does your child resist sharing information that is private and shouldn't be shared? 1 2 3 4 5

Problem situation:

46. **Understanding Rules of Swearing:** Does your child resist swearing in situations and settings where this isn't appropriate? 1 2 3 4 5

Problem situation:

47. **Understanding Rules of Touch:** Does your child know when it is appropriate to touch someone or something and when it is not? 1 2 3 4 5

Problem situation:

48. **Planning for Stressful Situations:** When your child knows a stressful situation is coming up, does he/she make an effective plan to deal with this?

    1   2   3   4   5

Problem situation:

49. **Defining a Problem:** When a problem occurs, does your child accurately assess what caused it?

    1   2   3   4   5

Problem situation:

50. **Considering Alternatives:** Does your child think of good choices to solve a problem?

    1   2   3   4   5

Problem situation:

51. **Choosing an Alternative:** Does your child choose an alternative and follow through with this choice?

    1   2   3   4   5

Problem situation:

52. **When to Change Strategies:** When one choice doesn't work to solve a problem, does your child change to a different choice?

    1   2   3   4   5

Problem situation:

53. **When a Rule Doesn't Work:** When a rule doesn't apply to a given situation, does your child handle this in appropriate ways?

    1   2   3   4   5

Problem situation:

54. **Giving Feedback:** Does your child notice when someone does a good job and tell him/her specifically what the person did that was good?

    1   2   3   4   5

Problem situation:

	Almost never	Seldom	Sometimes	Often	Almost always

55. **Seeking Attention:** Does your child seek attention in appropriate ways?

        1   2   3   4   5

Problem situation:

56. **Accepting Attention:** Does your child accept the attention of others in desirable ways?

        1   2   3   4   5

Problem situation:

57. **Making a Complaint:** Does your child make a complaint to the appropriate person in an appropriate manner and at a good time?

        1   2   3   4   5

Problem situation:

58. **When You Don't Understand:** When your child doesn't understand a social situation (for example, why he/she must wait or isn't allowed to do something), does he/she deal with this in appropriate ways?

        1   2   3   4   5

Problem situation:

59. **Knowing Your Feelings:** Can your child identify how he/she feels in a variety of situations?

        1   2   3   4   5

Problem situation:

60. **Feeling Different:** If your child feels different from others, does he deal appropriately with this feeling?

        1   2   3   4   5

Problem situation:

61. **Expressing Your Feelings:** Does your child express his/her feelings in appropriate ways?

        1   2   3   4   5

Problem situation:

	Almost never	Seldom	Sometimes	Often	Almost always

62. **Calming Your Feelings:** Does your child deal with things that bother him/her (for example, touch, loud noises) in good ways?　　1　2　3　4　5

　　Problem situation:

63. **Showing Affection:** Does your child let others know in acceptable ways that he/she cares about them?　　1　2　3　4　5

　　Problem situation:

64. **Recognizing Another's Feelings:** Does your child seem to understand how someone else is feeling?　　1　2　3　4　5

　　Problem situation:

65. **Showing Concern for Another:** Does your child show concern for others in appropriate ways and at appropriate times?　　1　2　3　4　5

　　Problem situation:

66. **Understanding Another's Intentions:** Does your child seem to correctly interpret the intentions and motivations of others?　　1　2　3　4　5

　　Problem situation:

67. **Dealing with Another's Anger:** When someone is angry, does your child deal with this anger in good ways?　　1　2　3　4　5

　　Problem situation:

68. **Asking for Help:** Does your child ask for assistance when needed in appropriate ways and at good times?　　1　2　3　4　5

　　Problem situation:

	Almost never	Seldom	Sometimes	Often	Almost always

69. **Ignoring Distractions:** Does your child ignore distractions in class in order to complete his/her task?

    Problem situation:

    1   2   3   4   5

70. **Contributing to Discussions:** Does your child contribute to discussions in desirable ways and at appropriate times?

    Problem situation:

    1   2   3   4   5

71. **Taking a Break:** Does your child take breaks when needed in an appropriate manner?

    Problem situation:

    1   2   3   4   5

72. **Setting a Goal:** Does your child set goals and work toward achieving these goals?

    Problem situation:

    1   2   3   4   5

73. **Completing Assignments:** Does your child complete and turn in assignments on time?

    Problem situation:

    1   2   3   4   5

74. **Following Adult Directions:** Does your child follow adult directions related to his/her behavior or a task?

    Problem situation:

    1   2   3   4   5

75. **Asking for Information:** Does your child ask for needed and relevant information in an appropriate manner?

    Problem situation:

    1   2   3   4   5

	Almost never	Seldom	Sometimes	Often	Almost always

76. **Organizing Materials:** Does your child organize needed materials for particular activities?　　1　2　3　4　5

Problem situation:

77. **Making Corrections:** Does your child make the necessary corrections on assignments without becoming overly frustrated?　　1　2　3　4　5

Problem situation:

78. **Preparing for Class:** Does your child bring needed materials to classes?　　1　2　3　4　5

Problem situation:

79. **Dealing with Transitions:** Does your child handle transitions from one activity or setting to another without acting out?　　1　2　3　4　5

Problem situation:

80. **Interrupting:** Does your child interrupt others only when necessary and in an appropriate way?　　1　2　3　4　5

Problem situation:

LEARNER CHECKLIST

Learner _____ Date _____

Instructions: Each of the questions will ask you about how well you do something. Next to each question is a number.

Circle number 1 if you *almost never* do what the question asks.

Circle number 2 if you *seldom* do it.

Circle number 3 if you *sometimes* do it.

Circle number 4 if you do it *often.*

Circle number 5 if you *almost always* do it.

	Almost never	Seldom	Sometimes	Often	Almost always
1. Is it easy for me to listen when someone is talking and not interrupt?	1	2	3	4	5
2. Is it easy for me to say hello to people?	1	2	3	4	5
3. When someone says hello to me, do I greet the person back?	1	2	3	4	5
4. When I ask a question, do I stay on the topic?	1	2	3	4	5
5. Do I stay on the topic when having a conversation?	1	2	3	4	5
6. Do I answer questions with an appropriate (for example, brief) response?	1	2	3	4	5
7. Is it easy for me to take turns?	1	2	3	4	5
8. Do I tell others what they have done well?	1	2	3	4	5
9. Do I notice when someone needs help and try to help the person?	1	2	3	4	5
10. Do I encourage others when they feel sad or frustrated?	1	2	3	4	5
11. Is it easy for me to work with others?	1	2	3	4	5
12. Is it easy for me to share with others?	1	2	3	4	5
13. Is it easy for me to ask for help from someone?	1	2	3	4	5
14. Do I know how and when to start a conversation with someone?	1	2	3	4	5
15. When I am having a conversation, can I keep the conversation going?	1	2	3	4	5
16. When I am having a conversation, do I know when to introduce a new topic?	1	2	3	4	5

	Almost never	Seldom	Sometimes	Often	Almost always
17. When I am having a conversation and the other person changes the topic, can I ask a question or make a comment about the new topic?	1	2	3	4	5
18. Is it easy for me to end a conversation in an appropriate way?	1	2	3	4	5
19. Do I join in activities or games with others when invited?	1	2	3	4	5
20. Do I ask to join in activities or games when I want to?	1	2	3	4	5
21. Do I tell others in good ways about what I like to do?	1	2	3	4	5
22. When someone says something that's different from what I think, can I handle it?	1	2	3	4	5
23. Do I look at other people's faces and gestures to try to understand them, even if they don't say anything?	1	2	3	4	5
24. Do I have good behavior in lots of different places?	1	2	3	4	5
25. Do I talk to classmates and friends in a friendly way?	1	2	3	4	5
26. Do I talk to adults in a respectful voice and using respectful words?	1	2	3	4	5
27. Do I understand what my facial expressions and gestures say to others?	1	2	3	4	5
28. Do I watch and listen to others to see how they do something?	1	2	3	4	5
29. Do I show respect to others by not standing too close or touching the person?	1	2	3	4	5
30. Do I watch others to see what they are interested in?	1	2	3	4	5
31. Do I accept that everyone is different and unique?	1	2	3	4	5
32. Is it easy for me to understand how someone else might feel or think?	1	2	3	4	5
33. Is it easy for me to keep paying attention when I'm supposed to?	1	2	3	4	5
34. Can I tell when I am getting anxious?	1	2	3	4	5
35. Do I know what causes me to become anxious?	1	2	3	4	5
36. Do I deal with feeling anxious in good ways?	1	2	3	4	5
37. Do I pay attention to how I talk, what I talk about, and if I talk too long?	1	2	3	4	5

	Almost never	Seldom	Sometimes	Often	Almost always
38. Do I understand situations where I should not touch someone or say something about the person's body?	1	2	3	4	5
39. Do I stay in control when I'm angry or frustrated?	1	2	3	4	5
40. Is it easy for me to handle change when things aren't the way I thought they would be?	1	2	3	4	5
41. When I'm supposed to do an activity, can I stick with it even though I'm bored?	1	2	3	4	5
42. Can I follow the rules when someone in authority tells me to?	1	2	3	4	5
43. Do I pay attention to how I act and try to change if I'm not acting in a good way?	1	2	3	4	5
44. Do I say positive things to myself about myself?	1	2	3	4	5
45. Do I understand when information is private and I shouldn't talk about it?	1	2	3	4	5
46. Do I know when it's okay to swear and when it isn't okay?	1	2	3	4	5
47. Do I know when it's okay to touch someone or something and when it isn't okay?	1	2	3	4	5
48. When I know something stressful is coming up, can I make a plan to deal with it?	1	2	3	4	5
49. When a problem occurs, can I figure out what caused it?	1	2	3	4	5
50. Can I think of good choices to solve a problem?	1	2	3	4	5
51. Do I follow through with a choice to solve the problem?	1	2	3	4	5
52. If that choice didn't work out, can I change to a different choice?	1	2	3	4	5
53. Can I handle it when a rule doesn't apply to every situation?	1	2	3	4	5
54. Do I notice when someone does a good job and tell the person specifically what he/she did that was good?	1	2	3	4	5
55. Do I seek attention in good ways?	1	2	3	4	5
56. Do I accept the attention of others in good ways?	1	2	3	4	5
57. When I think something is unfair, do I complain to the right person at a good time and in a good way?	1	2	3	4	5
58. When I don't understand why I have to wait or when I can't do something I want to do, can I ask in a respectful way?	1	2	3	4	5

	Almost never	Seldom	Sometimes	Often	Almost always
59. Do I know how I feel about different things that happen?	1	2	3	4	5
60. If I feel different from others, do I know how to deal with this feeling?	1	2	3	4	5
61. Do I let others know what I am feeling and do it in a good way?	1	2	3	4	5
62. Do I deal with things that bother me (for example, touch or loud noises) in good ways?	1	2	3	4	5
63. When I like someone, can I tell or show the person in a good way and at a good time?	1	2	3	4	5
64. Is it easy for me to tell how someone else is feeling?	1	2	3	4	5
65. When someone is having a problem, do I show concern for them in appropriate ways and at a good time?	1	2	3	4	5
66. Is it easy for me to decide why someone might have done something?	1	2	3	4	5
67. When someone is angry, do I know how to deal with this?	1	2	3	4	5
68. Is it easy for me to ask for help in good ways and at a good time?	1	2	3	4	5
69. Is it easy for me to ignore distractions?	1	2	3	4	5
70. Do I contribute (make good comments and ask appropriate questions) to class discussions?	1	2	3	4	5
71. Do I take a break at good times and in a good way?	1	2	3	4	5
72. Can I set goals for myself and work toward these goals?	1	2	3	4	5
73. Do I finish assignments and turn these in on time?	1	2	3	4	5
74. Is it easy for me to understand and follow adult directions?	1	2	3	4	5
75. Do I ask for information I need in a good way and at a good time?	1	2	3	4	5
76. Do I get together the materials I need for a class or activity?	1	2	3	4	5
77. Do I fix mistakes on my work without getting upset?	1	2	3	4	5
78. Do I bring needed materials to class?	1	2	3	4	5
79. Do I handle going from one activity or place to another without getting upset?	1	2	3	4	5
80. Do I interrupt others only when I need to and in a good way?	1	2	3	4	5

SKILL CHECKLIST SUMMARY

Learner _____ Dates _____

Skillstreaming leader _____

	Teacher/Staff	Parent	Learner	Average Score
Group I: Relationship Skills				
1. Listening Without Interrupting				
2. Greeting Others				
3. Responding to a Greeting				
4. Asking a Question About the Topic				
5. Staying on Topic				
6. Responding to Questions				
7. Taking Turns				
8. Complimenting Others				
9. Helping Others				
10. Encouraging Others				
11. Cooperating with Others				
12. Sharing				
13. Asking a Favor				
14. Starting a Conversation				
15. Continuing a Conversation				
16. When to Introduce a New Topic				
17. Accepting a Topic Change				
18. Ending a Conversation				
19. Responding to Offers to Join In				
20. Asking to Join In				
21. Communicating Preferences				
22. Accepting Another's Opinion				
Group II: Social Comprehension				
23. Reading Others				
24. Reading the Environment				
25. Using a Friendly Voice				
26. Using a Respectful Voice				
27. Giving Information Nonverbally				
28. Attending to a Model				
29. Respecting Another's Boundaries				
30. Showing Interest in Others				
31. Understanding Differences				

	Teacher/Staff	Parent	Learner	Average Score
32. Taking Another's Perspective				
Group III: Self-Regulation				
33. Regulating Your Attention				
34. Recognizing Anxiety				
35. Deciding What Causes Your Anxiety				
36. Dealing with Anxiety				
37. Checking Your Voice and Interests				
38. No Means No				
39. Using Self-Control				
40. Dealing with Change				
41. Dealing with Boredom				
42. Responding to Authority				
43. Checking Your Behavior				
44. Affirming Yourself				
Group IV: Problem Solving				
45. Determining Private Information				
46. Understanding Rules of Swearing				
47. Understanding Rules of Touch				
48. Planning for Stressful Situations				
49. Defining a Problem				
50. Considering Alternatives				
51. Choosing an Alternative				
52. When to Change Strategies				
53. When a Rule Doesn't Work				
54. Giving Feedback				
55. Seeking Attention				
56. Accepting Attention				
57. Making a Complaint				
58. When You Don't Understand				
Group V: Understanding Emotions				
59. Knowing Your Feelings				
60. Feeling Different				
61. Expressing Your Feelings				
62. Calming Your Feelings				
63. Showing Affection				
64. Recognizing Another's Feelings				
65. Showing Concern for Another				

	Teacher/Staff	Parent	Learner	Average Score
66. Understanding Another's Intentions				
67. Dealing with Another's Anger				
Group VI: School-Related Skills				
68. Asking for Help				
69. Ignoring Distractions				
70. Contributing to Discussions				
71. Taking a Break				
72. Setting a Goal				
73. Completing Assignments				
74. Following Adult Directions				
75. Asking for Information				
76. Organizing Materials				
77. Making Corrections				
78. Preparing for Class				
79. Dealing with Transitions				
80. Interrupting				

SKILL GROUPING CHART

Group _____

Skillstreaming leader _____

Instructions: Mark the specific skills each learner needs to develop (for example, score of 1 or 2 on the Skill Checklist Summary).

	student names							
Group I: Relationship Skills								
1. Listening Without Interrupting								
2. Greeting Others								
3. Responding to a Greeting								
4. Asking a Question About the Topic								
5. Staying on Topic								
6. Responding to Questions								
7. Taking Turns								
8. Complimenting Others								
9. Helping Others								
10. Encouraging Others								
11. Cooperating with Others								
12. Sharing								
13. Asking a Favor								
14. Starting a Conversation								
15. Continuing a Conversation								
16. When to Introduce a New Topic								
17. Accepting a Topic Change								
18. Ending a Conversation								
19. Responding to Offers to Join In								
20. Asking to Join In								
21. Communicating Preferences								
22. Accepting Another's Opinion								
Group II: Social Comprehension								
23. Reading Others								
24. Reading the Environment								
25. Using a Friendly Voice								
26. Using a Respectful Voice								

Skillstreaming

	student names							
27. Giving Information Nonverbally								
28. Attending to a Model								
29. Respecting Another's Boundaries								
30. Showing Interest in Others								
31. Understanding Differences								
32. Taking Another's Perspective								
Group III: Self-Regulation								
33. Regulating Your Attention								
34. Recognizing Anxiety								
35. Deciding What Causes Your Anxiety								
36. Dealing with Anxiety								
37. Checking Your Voice and Interests								
38. No Means No								
39. Using Self-Control								
40. Dealing with Change								
41. Dealing with Boredom								
42. Responding to Authority								
43. Checking Your Behavior								
44. Affirming Yourself								
Group IV: Problem Solving								
45. Determining Private Information								
46. Understanding Rules of Swearing								
47. Understanding Rules of Touch								
48. Planning for Stressful Situations								
49. Defining a Problem								
50. Considering Alternatives								
51. Choosing an Alternative								
52. When to Change Strategies								
53. When a Rule Doesn't Work								
54. Giving Feedback								
55. Seeking Attention								
56. Accepting Attention								
57. Making a Complaint								
58. When You Don't Understand								

	student names								
Group V: Understanding Emotions									
59. Knowing Your Feelings									
60. Feeling Different									
61. Expressing Your Feelings									
62. Calming Your Feelings									
63. Showing Affection									
64. Recognizing Another's Feelings									
65. Showing Concern for Another									
66. Understanding Another's Intentions									
67. Dealing with Another's Anger									
Group VI: School-Related Skills									
68. Asking for Help									
69. Ignoring Distractions									
70. Contributing to Discussions									
71. Taking a Break									
72. Setting a Goal									
73. Completing Assignments									
74. Following Adult Directions									
75. Asking for Information									
76. Organizing Materials									
77. Making Corrections									
78. Preparing for Class									
79. Dealing with Transitions									
80. Interrupting									

HOMEWORK REPORT I

Name _____ Date _____

Skill _____

SKILL STEPS

FILL IN NOW

With whom will I try this? _____

When? _____

_____

SUPPORTS

☐ Coaching with *(name)* _____

☐ With supportive peer *(name)* _____

☐ Other *(specify)* _____

☐ None

FILL IN AFTER YOU PRACTICE THE SKILL

What happened? _____

_____

How did I do? *(circle the number)*   4   3   2   1

                           Really good!   Pretty good.   So-So.   I need to try again.

Why did I circle this? _____

From *Skillstreaming Children and Youth with High-Functioning Autism: A Guide for Teaching Prosocial Skills,* © 2016 by E. McGinnis and R. L. Simpson. Champaign, IL: Research Press (www.researchpress.com, 800-519-2707).

HOMEWORK REPORT 2

Name_____Date_____

Skill _____

SKILL STEPS

	How did I do? *(circle the number)*			
When did I practice?	Really Good!	Pretty good.	So-So.	I need to try again.
1. _____	4	3	2	1
2. _____	4	3	2	1
3. _____	4	3	2	1

SUPPORTS

	Practice Situation *(circle)*		
With prompting	1	2	3
With coaching	1	2	3
With supportive peer	1	2	3
Other support *(specify)* _____	1	2	3
_____			
None	1	2	3

Skillstreaming

From *Skillstreaming Children and Youth with High-Functioning Autism: A Guide for Teaching Prosocial Skills,* © 2016 by E. McGinnis and R. L. Simpson. Champaign, IL: Research Press (www.researchpress.com, 800-519-2707).

HOMEWORK REPORT 3

Name_____Date_____

Situation *(describe)* _____

_____

With whom will I try this? _____

When? _____

SKILLS NEEDED AND SKILL STEPS

Skill _____	Skill _____	Skill _____
_____	_____	_____
Steps	Steps	Steps

SUPPORTS

☐ Coaching with *(name)* _____

☐ With supportive peer *(name)* _____

☐ Other *(specify)* _____

☐ None

FILL IN AFTER YOU PRACTICE THE SKILL

What happened? _____

_____

How did I do? *(circle the number)*   4   3   2   1

Really good!   Pretty good.   So-So.   I need to try again.

Why did I circle this? _____

From *Skillstreaming Children and Youth with High-Functioning Autism: A Guide for Teaching Prosocial Skills,* © 2016 by E. McGinnis and R. L. Simpson. Champaign, IL: Research Press (www.researchpress.com, 800-519-2707).

HOMEWORK DATA RECORD

Learner _____ Skillstreaming leader _____

Skill or skill sequence _____

Date	Homework completed	Evaluation	Supports provided (list)	Comments
	Report 1 2 3	4 3 2 1		
	Report 1 2 3	4 3 2 1		
	Report 1 2 3	4 3 2 1		
	Report 1 2 3	4 3 2 1		

Date	Homework completed	Evaluation	Supports provided (list)	Comments
	Report 1 2 3	4 3 2 1		
	Report 1 2 3	4 3 2 1		
	Report 1 2 3	4 3 2 1		
	Report 1 2 3	4 3 2 1		

Date	Homework completed	Evaluation	Supports provided (list)	Comments
	Report 1 2 3	4 3 2 1		
	Report 1 2 3	4 3 2 1		
	Report 1 2 3	4 3 2 1		
	Report 1 2 3	4 3 2 1		

Skillstreaming

From *Skillstreaming Children and Youth with High-Functioning Autism: A Guide for Teaching Prosocial Skills,* © 2016 by E. McGinnis and R. L. Simpson. Champaign, IL: Research Press (www.researchpress.com, 800-519-2707).

GROUP SELF-REPORT CHART

Name of group member	Skill _____	Skill _____	Skill _____	Skill _____	Skill _____	Skill _____

Name of group member	Skill _____	Skill _____	Skill _____	Skill _____	Skill _____	Skill _____

SKILLSTREAMING RUBRIC

Learner _____ Date _____

Instructions: This rubric may be used by the Skillstreaming leader or staff, parent, or learner to assess skill use and evaluate progress. Younger children and those with reading difficulties may require assistance in understanding and choosing the correct evaluation choices.

Skill 1: Listening Without Interrupting

1 – Difficulty listening to others without interrupting or trying to talk about something else.

2 – With help and reminders, usually able to listen to others without interrupting or trying to talk about something else.

3 – Most of the time, and usually without help, listens to others without interrupting or trying to talk about something else.

4 – Almost always listens to others without interrupting or trying to talk about something else.

Skill 2: Greeting Others

1 – Has difficulty looking at people, smiling, saying hello, and talking to others.

2 – With help looks at people, smiles, says hello, and talks to others.

3 – Most of the time, and usually without help, looks at people, smiles, say hello, and talks to others

4 – Almost always looks at people, smiles, says hello, and talks to others

Skill 3: Responding to a Greeting

1 – Rarely, if ever, responds to a greeting in an appropriate manner.

2 – Sometimes responds to a greeting in an appropriate manner.

3 – Most of the time, with some help, responds to a greeting in an appropriate manner.

4 – Almost always and without any help responds to a greeting appropriately.

Skill 4: Asking a Question About the Topic

1 – Has difficulty asking questions about topics others are talking about.

2 – With help and reminders, asks questions about topics others are talking about.

3 – Most of the time, and usually without reminders, asks questions about topics others are talking about.

4 – Almost always asks questions about topics others are talking about.

Skill 5: Staying on Topic

1 – Has difficulty staying on topic during a conversation or discussion.

2 – With help and reminders, stays on topic during a conversation or discussion.

3 – Most of the time, and usually without help, stays on topic during a conversation or discussion.

4 – Almost always stays on topic during a conversation or discussion.

From *Skillstreaming Children and Youth with High-Functioning Autism: A Guide for Teaching Prosocial Skills,* © 2016 by E. McGinnis and R. L. Simpson. Champaign, IL: Research Press (www.researchpress.com, 800-519-2707).

Skill 6: Responding to Questions

1 – Has great difficulty responding to questions with an appropriate (for example, brief) response.

2 – With help and reminders, responds to questions with an appropriate response.

3 – Most of the time, and usually without reminders, responds to questions with an appropriate response.

4 – Almost always responds to questions with an appropriate response.

Skill 7: Taking Turns

1 – Has difficulty taking turns during games and activities.

2 – With help, is able to wait for a turn during games and activities.

3 – Most of the time, and usually without help, able to wait for a turn during games and activities.

4 – Almost never has problems waiting for a turn during games and activities.

Skill 8: Complimenting Others

1 – Has difficulty knowing when and how to compliment others.

2 – With help, knows when and how to compliment others in an appropriate way.

3 – Most of the time and usually without reminders, knows when and how to compliment others in an appropriate way.

4 – Almost always knows when and how to compliment others in an appropriate way.

Skill 9: Helping Others

1 – Rarely attempts to help others, such as deciding if someone needs help and giving help in a good and friendly way.

2 – With help, knows when and how to help others in a good and friendly way.

3 – Most of the time and usually without reminders, knows when and how to help others in a good and friendly way.

4 – Almost always knows when and how to help others in a good and friendly way.

Skill 10: Encouraging Others

1 – Has difficulty knowing when and how to encourage others.

2 – With help, knows when and how to encourage others in an appropriate way.

3 – Most of the time and usually without reminders, knows when and how to encourage others in an appropriate way.

4 – Almost always knows when and how to encourage others in an appropriate way.

Skill 11: Cooperating with Others

1 – Has difficulty listening to and following directions and waiting for a turn.

2 – With help, is able to listen for and follow directions and wait for a turn.

3 – Most of the time, and usually without reminders, listens for and follows directions and waits for a turn.

4 – Almost always listens for and follows directions and waits for a turn.

Skill 12: Sharing

1 – Has difficulty sharing with others.

2 – With help, is able to share with others in a friendly way.

3 – Most of the time and usually without reminders, is able to share with others in a friendly way.

4 – Almost always is able to share with others in a friendly way.

Skill 13: Asking a Favor

1 – Has difficulty knowing when to ask a favor, whom to ask, and how to ask for a favor in a desirable way.

2 – With help, knows when to ask a favor, whom to ask, and how to ask for a favor in a desirable way.

3 – Most of the time and usually without reminders, knows when to ask a favor, whom to ask, and how to ask for a favor in a desirable way.

4 – Almost always knows when to ask a favor, whom to ask, and how to ask for a favor in a desirable way.

Skill 14: Starting a Conversation

1 – Has difficulty knowing when and how to start a conversation with peers or adults.

2 – Often needs help in knowing when and how to start a conversation.

3 – Most of the time, and usually without help, knows when and how to start a conversation.

4 – Almost always knows when and how to start a conversation with peers and adults.

Skill 15: Continuing a Conversation

1 – Has difficulty keeping a conversation going.

2 – Often needs help in keeping a conversation going.

3 – Most of the time, and usually without help, can keep a conversation going.

4 – Almost always can keep a conversation going.

Skill 16: When to Introduce a New Topic

1 – During a conversation, has difficulty knowing when and how to introduce a new topic.

2 – With help and reminders, knows when and how to introduce a new topic during a conversation.

3 – Most of the time, and usually without help, knows when and how to introduce a new topic during a conversation.

4 – Almost always knows when and how to introduce a new topic during a conversation.

Skill 17: Accepting a Topic Change

1 – Often becomes angry and upset when people begin talking about new topics.

2 – With help and reminders, doesn't get angry and upset when people begin talking about new topics.

3 – Most of the time, and usually without help, accepts when people begin talking about new topics.

4 – Almost never gets upset when people begin talking about new topics.

Skill 18: Ending a Conversation

1 – Has difficulty knowing when and how to end a conversation in a desirable way.

2 – Often needs help in knowing when and how to end a conversation in a desirable way.

3 – Most of the time, and usually without help, knows when and how to end a conversation in a desirable way.

4 – Almost always knows when and how to end a conversation in a desirable way.

Skill 19: Responding to Offers to Join In

1 – When asked to join in, has trouble knowing when and how to join others appropriately.

2 – When invited and with help, knows when and how to join others appropriately.

3 – Most of the time, and usually without help, when invited knows when and how to join others appropriately.

4 – When invited, almost always knows when and how to join others appropriately.

Skill 20: Asking to Join In

1 – Rarely asks to join in a game or activity when wanting to play.

2 – With help, knows when and how to ask to join in.

3 – Most of the time, and usually without help, knows when and how to ask to join in.

4 – Almost always knows when and how to ask to join in.

Skill 21: Communicating Preferences

1 – Has difficulty telling others about dislikes and what is preferred in an appropriate way.

2 – With help, is able to tell others dislikes and preferences in an appropriate way.

3 – Most of the time, and usually without help, is able to tell others about dislikes and preferences in an appropriate way.

4 – Almost always tells others dislikes and preferences in an appropriate way.

Skill 22: Accepting Another's Opinion

1 – Becomes easily upset and interrupts when disagreeing with what others are saying.

2 – With help and reminders, is able to avoid getting upset and interrupting when disagreeing with what others are saying.

3 – Most of the time, and usually without help, does not get upset or interrupt when disagreeing with what others are saying.

4 – Almost always listens without getting upset or interrupting, even when disagreeing with what others are saying.

Skill 23: Reading Others

1 – Has difficulty understanding what others are thinking and feeling by looking at their faces and bodies.

2 – Sometimes, and with help, understands what others are thinking and feeling by looking at faces and bodies.

3 – Most of the time, with some help, understands what others are thinking and feeling by looking at faces and bodies.

4 – Without any help, understands what others are thinking and feeling by looking at faces and bodies.

Skill 24: Reading the Environment

1 – Has difficulty figuring out what is going on and how to behave appropriately based on what is occurring.

2 – With help, figures out what is going on and how to behave appropriately based on what is occurring.

3 – Most of the time and usually without help, figures out what is going on and how to behave appropriately based what is occurring.

4 – Almost always figures out what is going on and how to behave appropriately in most settings.

Skill 25: Using a Friendly Voice

1 – Has difficulty talking with others using a friendly face, voice, and body.

2 – With help and reminders, talks with others using a friendly face, voice, and body.

3 – Most of the time, and usually without help, talks with others using a friendly face, voice, and body.

4 – Almost always talks to others using a friendly face, voice, and body.

Skill 26: Using a Respectful Voice

1 – Has difficulty using a respectful voice when talking with adults.

2 – With help and reminders is able to use a respectful voice when talking to adults.

3 – Most of the time, and usually without help, uses a respectful voice when talking to adults.

4 – Almost always uses a respectful voice when talking to adults.

Skill 27: Giving Information Nonverbally

1 – Has difficulty understanding what facial expressions, voice tone, and gestures say to others.

2 – With help, can understand what facial expressions, voice tone, and gestures say to others.

3 – Most of the time and usually without help, understands what facial expressions, voice tone, and gestures say to others.

4 – Almost always understands what facial expressions, voice tone, and gestures say to others.

Skill 28: Attending to a Model

1 – Has difficulty learning from others by watching and listening to them.

2 – With help, learns from others by watching and listening to them.

3 – Most of the time and usually without help, learns from others by watching and listening to them.

4 – Almost always, when appropriate, learns from others by watching and listening to them.

Skill 29: Respecting Another's Boundaries

1 – Has difficulty respecting other people's property and boundaries. These problems include touching the property of others and standing or sitting too close to other people.

2 – With help, is able to respect other people's property and boundaries. Reminders are sometimes needed to help know when and how to appropriately touch the property of others and how close to stand and sit around other people.

3 – Most of the time, and usually without help, is able to respect people's property and boundaries. Knowing when and how to appropriately touch the property of others and how close to stand and sit around other people is usually not a problem.

4 – Almost always respects other people's property and boundaries. Knowing when and how to appropriately touch the property of others and how close to stand and sit around other people is not a problem.

Skill 30: Showing Interest in Others

1 – Has difficulty noticing others and their interests.

2 – With help, notices others and their interests.

3 – Most of the time and usually without reminders, notices others and their interests.

4 – Almost always, when appropriate, notices others and their interests.

Skill 31: Understanding Differences

1 – Rarely accepts that everyone is different and unique without becoming upset.

2 – With help, is able to accept that everyone is different and unique without becoming upset.

3 – Most of the time, and usually without help, is able to accept that everyone is different and unique without becoming upset.

4 – Almost always accepts that everyone is different and unique and does not become upset due to these differences.

Skill 32: Taking Another's Perspective

1 – Rarely understands how someone else might feel or think.

2 – With help, understands how someone else might feel or think.

3 – Most of the time, and usually without help, understands how someone else might feel or think.

4 – Almost always, when appropriate, shows understanding of how someone else might think or feel.

Skill 33: Regulating Your Attention

1 – Has difficulty paying attention when it is expected.

2 – With help, maintains attention as expected.

3 – Most of the time, and usually without help, keeps attending to the task or activity.

4 – Almost always is able to maintain attention when expected.

Skill 34: Recognizing Anxiety

1 – Often becomes anxious and loses control. Is unaware of the physical cues related to anxiety.

2 – With help, maintains control and understands the physical cues related to anxiety.

3 – Most of the time, and usually without help, understands the physical cues of anxiety.

4 – Almost always recognizes when anxious in a variety of situations and settings.

Skill 35: Deciding What Causes Your Anxiety

1 – Does not identify any situations that cause anxiety.

2 – With help, identifies some situations that create anxiety.

3 – Most of the time, and usually without help, identifies situations that create anxiety.

4 – Almost always is able to define situations that create anxiety.

Skill 36: Dealing with Anxiety

1 – When anxious, is unable to use any strategies to stay in control.

2 – When anxious, with help sometimes uses strategies to deal with the anxiety and stay in control.

3 – When anxious, most of the time and usually without help uses desirable strategies to deal with the anxiety and stay in control.

4 – When anxious, almost always and without help uses desirable strategies to deal with the anxiety and stay in control.

Skill 37: Checking Your Voice and Interests

1 – Is unaware of voice tone and shares interests excessively, often boring others.

2 – With help, sometimes is able to monitor voice tone and sharing of interests.

3 – Most of the time, and usually without help, is able to monitor voice tone and sharing of interests.

4 – Almost always, and without help, is able to monitor voice tone and sharing of interests.

Skill 38: No Means No

1 – Does not understand situations and actions that are dangerous or highly inappropriate and does the action anyway.

2 – With help, understands some situations and actions that are dangerous or highly inappropriate and, occasionally, stops the action.

3 – Most of the time, and even without help or reminders, understands situations and actions that are dangerous or highly inappropriate and stops the action.

4 – Almost always, and without help, understands situations and actions that are dangerous or inappropriate and refrains from engaging in these actions.

Skill 39: Using Self-Control

1 – Is unable to use self-control, often becoming angry or upset.

2 – With help, is able to have self-control and keep from becoming angry and upset.

3 – Most of the time, and usually without help, uses self-control and does not become angry or upset.

4 – Rarely has problems with self-control.

Skill 40: Dealing with Change

1 – Most of the time, becomes upset when routines and schedules change, even with notice.

2 – With help and notice, sometimes accepts routine and schedule changes without becoming upset.

3 – Most of the time, and usually without help or notice, accepts routine and schedule changes without becoming upset.

4 – Almost always, without help or notice, accepts routine and schedule changes without becoming upset.

Skill 41: Dealing with Boredom

1 – When uninterested in an activity, almost always is unable to stick with it and finish.

2 – When uninterested in an activity, with help can sometimes stick with it and finish.

3 – When uninterested in an activity, most of the time and usually without help can stay with it until it's finished.

4 – When uninterested in an activity, almost always stays with it until it's finished.

Skill 42: Responding to Authority

1 – Has difficulty listening to and following the directions of adults who are in authority positions, such as teachers.

2 – With help, listens to and follows the directions of adults who are in authority positions, such as teachers.

3 – Most of the time, and usually without help, listens to and follows the directions of adults who are in authority positions.

4 – Almost always listens to and follows the directions of adults who are in authority positions.

Skill 43: Checking Your Behavior

1 – Rarely attends to own behaviors.

2 – With help and reminders, sometimes attends to own behaviors and tries to change if not acting appropriately.

3 – Most of the time, and usually without help, attends to own behaviors and tries to change if not acting appropriately.

4 – Almost always attends to own behaviors and tries to change if not acting appropriately.

Skill 44: Affirming Yourself

1 – Makes many negative comments about self; makes no positive comments about self.

2 – Sometimes makes positive comments about self and makes few negative comments.

3 – Most of the time makes positive instead of negative comments about self.

4 – Makes positive self-statements and refrains from making negative self-statements.

Skill 45: Determining Private Information

1 – Has no idea what private information is and freely shares this information.

2 – Has a basic understanding of information that is private and shouldn't be shared; tries to refrain from sharing this information.

3 – Most of the time accurately assesses information that is private and rarely shares this information.

4 – Has a good understanding of private information and consistently resists sharing this information.

Skill 46: Understanding Rules of Swearing

1 – Frequently swears at inappropriate times.

2 – Has a basic understanding of when and where it is inappropriate to swear and tries to control swearing in these situations and at these times.

3 – Most of the time, and usually without help, refrains from inappropriate swearing.

4 – Independently controls inappropriate swearing.

Skill 47: Understanding Rules of Touch

1 – Does not understand when it's okay or not okay to touch someone or something.

2 – With help and reminders, resists touching someone or something.

3 – Most of the time, and with little help, resists touching someone or something when it's inappropriate.

4 – Almost always resists touching someone or something when it's inappropriate.

Skill 48: Planning for Stressful Situations

1 – Does not develop a plan for handling upcoming stressful situations.

2 – With help and reminders, can sometimes develop a plan for handling upcoming stressful situations and sometimes is successful following this plan.

3 – Most of the time, and usually without help, develops plans for handling upcoming stressful situations and most of the time follows this plan.

4 – Almost always independently develops plans for handling upcoming stressful situations and consistently follows these plans.

Skill 49: Defining a Problem

1 – When a problem occurs, has no idea how to figure out what caused it.

2 – Sometimes, and with help, is able to identify what caused a problem.

3 – Most of the time, and usually without help, is able to identify what caused or contributed to a problem.

4 – Almost always is able to identify what caused or contributed to a problem independently.

Skill 50: Considering Alternatives

1 – Is unable to generate any alternatives to solve any problem.

2 – With help, is able to identify good options for dealing with problems.

3 – Most of the time, and usually without help, is able to identify good options for dealing with problems.

4 – Almost always independently identifies good options for dealing with problems.

Skill 51: Choosing an Alternative

1 – Is unable to choose a good alternative to solve a problem.

2 – With help, identifies a good alternative to solve a problem.

3 – Most of the time, and usually without help, identifies a good alternative to solve a problem.

4 – Almost always independently identifies a good alternative to solve a problem.

Skill 52: When to Change Strategies

1 – Consistently stays with one strategy to solve a problem, even if it's not effective.

2 – With help, is able to consider changing strategies if one strategy isn't effective.

3 – Most of the time, with some help is able to change strategies if one strategy isn't effective.

4 – Consistently and independently is able to change strategies if one strategy is unsuccessful.

Skill 53: When a Rule Doesn't Work

1 – When a rule isn't applied in all situations and places, easily becomes upset or angry; doesn't try to understand that a rule may not always apply.

2 – With help, is beginning to understand why rules don't apply to every situation and tries to control feelings about this.

3 – Most of the time, with some help is able to understand why rules don't apply to every situation and resists becoming angry or upset.

4 – Consistently shows understanding of why some rules don't apply to every situation and does not become angry or upset.

Skill 54: Giving Feedback

1 – Does not know when and how to give helpful feedback to others.

2 – With help sometimes understands when and how to give helpful feedback to others.

3 – Most of the time with help gives helpful feedback to others in desirable ways.

4 – Almost always gives helpful feedback at appropriate times and in appropriate ways.

Skill 55: Seeking Attention

1 – Rarely tries to get attention from others in good ways.

2 – With help, sometimes seeks attention from others in good ways.

3 – Most of the time, and with some help, seeks attention from others in good ways.

4 – Almost always seeks attention from others in good ways.

Skill 56: Accepting Attention

1 – Does not understand how to return or react to the attention of others in acceptable ways.

2 – With help, sometimes returns or reacts to the attention of others in acceptable ways.

3 – Most of the time, and usually without help, returns or reacts to the attention of others in acceptable ways.

4 – Almost always returns or reacts to the attention of others in desirable ways.

Skill 57: Making a Complaint

1 – Does not understand when or how to make a complaint in an acceptable way.

2 – With help, sometimes makes a complaint in an acceptable way.

3 – Most of the time, and usually without help, makes a complaint in an acceptable way and at a good time.

4 – Almost always independently makes a complaint in an acceptable way and at a good time.

Skill 58: When You Don't Understand

1 – When confused about an action or event, easily becomes upset.

2 – Often needs help to know how to deal with feeling confused about an action or event.

3 – Most of the time, with little help, asks respectfully for an explanation when confused about an event or action.

4 – Almost always asks respectfully for an explanation when confused about an event or action.

Skill 59: Knowing Your Feelings

1 – Does not identify or seem to understand own feelings in different situations. Often becomes upset without understanding why.

2 – Sometimes, with help, is able to identify and understand own feelings in a variety of situations.

3 – Most of the time, and usually without help, is able to identify and understand own feelings in a variety of situations.

4 – Almost always identifies and understands own feelings in almost all situations.

Skill 60: Feeling Different

1 – Feels different from others but has no idea how to deal with this.

2 – Sometimes, with help, is able to verbally express feeling different from others and generate ideas about how to deal with this.

3 – Most of the time, with some help, generates and follows ideas about how to deal with feeling different from others.

4 – Almost always generates and follows ideas about how to deal with feeling different from others.

Skill 61: Expressing Your Feelings

1 – Does not let others know of own feelings in good ways.

2 – Sometimes, with help, lets others know of own feelings in good ways.

3 – Most of the time, with little help, lets others know of own feelings in good ways.

4 – Almost always independently lets others know of own feelings in good ways.

Skill 62: Calming Your Feelings

1 – When having intense feelings, does not have strategies to calm self down.

2 – When having intense feelings, with help, sometimes can calm self down.

3 – When having intense feelings, with little help, most times can calm self down.

4 – When having intense feelings, independently and almost always can calm self down.

Skill 63: Showing Affection

1 – Does not understand when and how to show affection in acceptable ways.

2 – With help, sometimes is able to show affection in acceptable ways and at appropriate times.

3 – Most of the time, and with little help, is able to show affection in acceptable ways and at appropriate times.

4 – Almost always is able to show affection in acceptable ways and at appropriate times independently.

Skill 64: Recognizing Another's Feelings

1 – Is unable to figure out how someone else might be feeling.

2 – With help, sometimes is able to figure out how someone else might be feeling.

3 – Most of the time, and with little help, is able to figure out how someone else might be feeling.

4 – Almost always is able to tell how someone else might be feeling in most situations.

Skill 65: Showing Concern for Another

1 – Does not show concern for others appropriately.

2 – With help, shows concern for others in appropriate ways and at good times.

3 – Most of the time, shows concern for others in appropriate ways and at good times.

4 – Almost always shows concern for others in appropriate ways and at good times.

Skill 66: Understanding Another's Intentions

1 – Does not understand why someone may have done something in almost any situation.

2 – With help, sometimes can understand why someone may have done something in some situations.

3 – Most of the time, and with little help, can understand why someone may have done something in most situations.

4 – Seems to understand why someone may have done something in almost all situations.

Skill 67: Dealing with Another's Anger

1 – When someone is angry, does not deal with another's anger in desirable ways.

2 – With help, can sometimes deal with another's anger in desirable ways.

3 – Most of the time, and with little help, can deal with another's anger in desirable ways.

4 – Almost always deals with another's anger in desirable ways.

Skill 68: Asking for Help

1 – When needing help or assistance, does not seek this in good ways or at appropriate times.

2 – When needing help or assistance, sometimes seeks this in a good way and at an appropriate time.

3 – When needing help or assistance, most times seeks this in a good way and at an appropriate time.

4 – When needing help or assistance, almost always seeks this in a good way and at an appropriate time.

Skill 69: Ignoring Distractions

1 – Does not ignore distractions or stay focused in class.

2 – With help, is able to ignore distractions and stay focused in class.

3 – Most of the time, and usually without help, is able to ignore distractions and stay focused in class.

4 – Has no difficulty ignoring distractions and staying focused in class.

Skill 70: Contributing to Discussions

1 – Does not participate in class discussions, such as making comments, asking questions about topics, and listening without interrupting others.

2 – With help and reminders, is able to participate in class discussions, such as making comments, asking questions about topics, and listening without interrupting others.

3 – Most of the time, and usually without help, is able to participate in class discussions, such as making comments, asking questions about topics, and listening without interrupting.

4 – Almost always participates in class discussions by making comments, asking questions about topics, and listening without interrupting others.

Skill 71: Taking a Break

1 – Does not recognize when needing to take a break; when prompted, does not take a break in a desirable way.

2 – Sometimes, with help, recognizes when a break is needed; when prompted, sometimes takes a break in a desirable way.

3 – Most of the time, with a little help, recognizes when a break is needed; when prompted, most of the time takes a break in a desirable way.

4 – Almost always recognizes when a break is needed; when prompted, almost always takes a break in a desirable way.

Skill 72: Setting a Goal

1 – Is unable to set goals or work toward achieving a goal.

2 – With help and reminders, sometimes can set a goal and work toward achieving a goal.

3 – Most of the time, with some help, can set a goal and work toward achieving a goal.

4 – Almost always can set a goal and work toward achieving this goal.

Skill 73: Completing Assignments

1 – Rarely completes and turns in class assignments on time.

2 – With help, is able to complete and turn in class assignments on time.

3 – Most of the time, and usually without help, is able to complete and turn in class assignments on time.

4 – Consistently completes and turns in class assignments on time.

Skill 74: Following Adult Directions

1 – Rarely is able to follow adult directions.

2 – With help, is able to understand and follow adult directions.

3 – Most of the time, and usually without help, is able to understand and follow adult directions.

4 – Almost always understands and follows adult directions.

Skill 75: Asking for Information

1 – Does not understand how to get needed information, such as knowing whom to ask and how to ask.

2 – Sometimes, with help, understands how to get needed information, such as knowing whom to ask and how to ask.

3 – Most of the time, with little help, understands how to get needed information, such as knowing whom to ask and how to ask.

4 – Almost always understands how to get needed information, such as knowing whom to ask and how to ask.

Skill 76: Organizing Materials

1 – Does not remember or organize materials and other things needed for classes.

2 – With help and reminders, remembers and organizes materials and other things needed for classes.

3 – Most of the time, and usually without help or reminders, remembers and organizes materials and other things needed for classes.

4 – Consistently remembers and organizes materials and other things needed for classes.

Skill 77: Making Corrections

1 – Consistently becomes upset when asked to make corrections on assignments.

2 – With help, sometimes is able to make corrections on assignments when asked to do so without becoming upset.

3 – Most of the time, and usually without help, is able to make corrections on assignments when asked to do so without becoming upset.

4 – Almost always makes corrections on assignments when asked to do so without becoming upset.

Skill 78: Preparing for Class

1 – Is rarely prepared for class, such as having completed assignments and needed materials.

2 – With help, is sometimes prepared for class, such as having completed assignments and needed materials.

3 – Most of the time, and usually without help, is prepared for class, such as having completed assignments and needed materials.

4 – Almost always is well-prepared for class, including having completed assignments and needed materials.

Skill 79: Dealing with Transitions

1 – Typically becomes upset when asked to change classes and move to a different location at school.

2 – With help, is able to change classes and move to a different location at school without becoming upset.

3 – Most of the time, and usually without help, is able to change classes and move to a different location at school without becoming upset.

4 – Is consistently able to change classes and move to a different location at school without becoming upset.

Skill 80: Interrupting

1 – Frequently interrupts others.

2 – With help and reminders, is sometimes able to avoid interrupting others. When it is necessary to interrupt, sometimes is able to do so in appropriate ways and at the appropriate times.

3 – Most of the time and with little help, is able to avoid interrupting others. When it is necessary to interrupt, most of the time is able to do so in appropriate ways and at the appropriate times.

4 – Almost always is able to avoid interrupting others. When it is necessary to interrupt, is consistently able to do so in appropriate ways and at the appropriate times.

LEADER'S SESSION IMPLEMENTATION CHECKLIST

Leader _____

Date of session _____ Time of session _____

Instructions: Complete this checklist at the conclusion of the Skillstreaming group session by marking "yes" or "no" relative to each procedure implemented.

	Yes	No
Step 1: Define the skill		
1. The skill to be taught was defined, and the group understood its meaning.	☐	☐
2. Skill steps were presented and discussed (via skill poster or skill cards).	☐	☐
(For all sessions after initial learning takes place)	☐	☐
3. Skill homework was discussed.	☐	☐
4. Appropriate reinforcement was provided for completed homework.	☐	☐
Step 2: Model the skill		
5. Modeling supports were put in place as needed.	☐	☐
6. Two examples of the skill were modeled.	☐	☐
7. Each skill step was identified as the modeling unfolded.	☐	☐
8. Modeling displays were relevant to the learner's real-life circumstances.	☐	☐
9. The learner was directed to watch for the steps being modeled.	☐	☐
10. The model was friendly and helpful.	☐	☐
11. A coping model was presented, if indicated.	☐	☐
12. The model used self-talk to illustrate the steps and thinking about skill performance.	☐	☐
13. The modeling display depicted positive outcomes.	☐	☐
14. The model was rewarded for skill performance (following the skill steps).	☐	☐
Step 3: Establish learner skill need		
15. Each learner's need for skill use was defined (when, where, and with whom) and listed.	☐	☐
Step 4: Select the first role-player		
16. The main actor was selected for role-play (for example, "Who would like to go first?").	☐	☐
Step 5: Set up the role-play		
17. Role-play supports were put in place as needed.	☐	☐
18. Main actor selected a coactor who reminded him/her most of the real life person with whom he/she has the skill need.	☐	☐
19. Main actor described the physical setting, events preceding the problem, mood/manner of the person, and any other relevant information.	☐	☐

	Yes	No

Step 6: Conduct the role-play

20. Group members were assigned specific step(s) to observe. ☐ ☐

21. Main actor was instructed to follow the behavioral steps. ☐ ☐

22. Main actor was reminded to "think aloud." ☐ ☐

23. The coactor was reminded to stay in the role of the other person. ☐ ☐

24. One-to-one coaching was provided as needed to ensure accurate enactment of the skill steps. ☐ ☐

25. *(Initial)* The coaching focused on gradually shaping the learner's performance closer to that of the model. ☐ ☐

26. *(Subsequent)* The coaching included and accentuated social nuances. ☐ ☐

Step 7: Provide feedback

27. Coactor was asked to provide feedback (for example, how he/she felt, how well the main actor enacted the steps). ☐ ☐

28. Group members were asked if the main actor followed each step. ☐ ☐

29. Leaders provided appropriate feedback (praise, approval, encouragement), identifying specific aspects of the main actor's performance. ☐ ☐

30. Reinforcement in an amount consistent with the quality of role-play was provided. ☐ ☐

31. Main actor was invited to give comments. ☐ ☐

Step 8: Select the next role-player

32. Volunteers were asked to be the main actor in the next role-play. (Steps 5 through 7 followed for each.) ☐ ☐

33. All group members were given a chance to role-play or plans were made to role-play for those who did not participate as the main actor. ☐ ☐

Step 9: Assign skill homework

34. Skill homework was assigned to each main actor who learned the skill. ☐ ☐

35. Assistance was provided as needed in identifying the day, place, with whom the skill will be used, and so forth. ☐ ☐

36. For learners who did not appear ready to try the skill via a homework assignment, additional coaching or practice was planned. ☐ ☐

Total yes_____   Total no_____

OBSERVER'S SESSION IMPLEMENTATION CHECKLIST

Leader_____ Observer_____

Date of session_____ Time of session_____

Instructions: A highly skilled observer may complete this observation checklist as the Skillstreaming session is taking place. The observer will note whether the leader completed each procedure with a low level of competence (score 1), medium proficiency (score 2), or a high level of skill (score 3). At the conclusion of the observation, the observer may provide the leader with recommendations for specific steps needing improvement.

	Proficiency Level		
	1	2	3
Step 1: Define the skill			
1. The skill to be taught was defined and the group understood its meaning.	☐	☐	☐
2. Skill steps were presented and discussed (via poster or skill cards).	☐	☐	☐
(For all sessions after initial learning takes place)	☐	☐	☐
3. Skill homework was discussed.	☐	☐	☐
4. Appropriate reinforcement was provided for completed homework.	☐	☐	☐
Step 2: Model the skill			
5. Modeling supports were put in place as needed.	☐	☐	☐
6. Two examples of the skill were modeled.	☐	☐	☐
7. Each skill step was identified as the modeling unfolded.	☐	☐	☐
8. Modeling displays were relevant to the learner's real-life circumstances.	☐	☐	☐
9. The learner was directed to watch for the steps being modeled.	☐	☐	☐
10. The model was friendly and helpful.	☐	☐	☐
11. A coping model was presented, if indicated.	☐	☐	☐
12. The model used self-talk to illustrate the steps and thinking about skill performance.	☐	☐	☐
13. The modeling display depicted positive outcomes.	☐	☐	☐
14. The model was rewarded for skill performance (following the skill steps).	☐	☐	☐
Step 3: Establish learner skill need			
15. Each learner's need for skill use was defined (when, where, and with whom) and listed.	☐	☐	☐

From *Skillstreaming Children and Youth with High-Functioning Autism: A Guide for Teaching Prosocial Skills,* © 2016 by E. McGinnis and R. L. Simpson. Champaign, IL: Research Press (www.researchpress.com, 800-519-2707).

	Proficiency Level		
	1	**2**	**3**

Step 4: Select the first role-player

16. The main actor was selected for role-play (e.g., "Who would like to go first?"). ☐ ☐ ☐

Step 5: Set up the role-play

17. Role-play supports were put in place as needed. ☐ ☐ ☐

18. Main actor selected a coactor who reminded him/her most of the real life person with whom he/she has the skill need. ☐ ☐ ☐

19. Main actor described the physical setting, events preceding the problem, mood/manner of the person, and any other relevant information. ☐ ☐ ☐

Step 6: Conduct the role-play

20. Group members were assigned specific step(s) to observe. ☐ ☐ ☐

21. Main actor was instructed to follow the behavioral steps. ☐ ☐ ☐

22. Main actor was reminded to "think aloud." ☐ ☐ ☐

23. The coactor was reminded to stay in the role of the other person. ☐ ☐ ☐

24. One-to-one coaching was provided as needed to ensure accurate enactment of skill steps. ☐ ☐ ☐

25. *(Initially)* Coaching focused on gradually shaping the learner's performance closer to that of the model. ☐ ☐ ☐

26. *(Later)* Coaching included and accentuated social nuances. ☐ ☐ ☐

Step 7: Provide feedback

27. Coactor was asked to provide feedback (e.g., how he/she felt, how well the main actor enacted the steps). ☐ ☐ ☐

28. Group members were asked if the main actor followed each step. ☐ ☐ ☐

29. Leaders provided appropriate feedback (praise, approval, encouragement), identifying specific aspects of the main actor's performance. ☐ ☐ ☐

30. Reinforcement in an amount consistent with the quality of role-play was provided. ☐ ☐ ☐

31. Main actor was invited to give comments. ☐ ☐ ☐

Step 8: Select the next role-player

32. Volunteers were asked to be the main actor in the next role-play. (Repeated Steps 5 through 7.) ☐ ☐ ☐

33. All group members were given a chance to role-play or plans were made to role-play for those who did not participate as the main actor. ☐ ☐ ☐

	Proficiency Level		
	1	**2**	**3**

Step 9: Assign skill homework

34. Skill homework was assigned to each main actor who learned the skill.	☐	☐	☐
35. Assistance was provided as needed in identifying the day, place, with whom the skill will be used, and so forth.	☐	☐	☐
36. For learners who did not appear ready to try the skill via a homework assignment, additional coaching or practice was planned.	☐	☐	☐

TOTAL _____ /108)

95–108 points	Mastery of intervention demonstrated.
94–84 points	Consultation with master leader available.
83–73 points	Continued monitoring of instruction necessary.
72 points or below	Group leader intervention needed.

Strengths:

Suggestions for improvement:

Other comments:

APPENDIX B

Sample Skillstreaming Sessions

This appendix presents examples of Skillstreaming group sessions with youth with high-functioning autism disorders. The first group consists of four elementary-age learners who all have the social goal of improving their social comprehension and who are learning Skill 29, Respecting Another's Boundaries. The second group includes five high-school age youth who first learned the skill of Listening Without Interrupting (Skill 1); then, as a skill sequence, are learning Accepting Another's Opinion (Skill 22). Both groups have been oriented to the learning procedures and the group expectations. The nine steps in Skillstreaming instruction, as presented in Table 3 in this book, are illustrated in each group.

ELEMENTARY SKILLSTREAMING INSTRUCTION: RESPECTING ANOTHER'S BOUNDARIES (SKILL 29)

Step 1: Define the Skill

Ms. M: Today we're going to learn another very important skill to help us get along better with others. Our skill today is Respecting Another's Boundaries. What do you think a "boundary" is?

Isabella: Like the boundary of the playground?

Charlie: Yes, you have to stay inside the boundary.

Ms. M: Good! A boundary can be around a playground that you have to stay inside. How do you know the playground has a boundary?

Henry: It has a fence so we don't run into the street.

Ms. M: Yes, a fence shows us where the boundary of the playground is. And we need to stay inside this boundary to stay safe. People also have boundaries, but there is no fence to let us know another's boundary.

Sammi: An invisible boundary.

Ms. M: Correct! Our personal boundaries are invisible, but we can feel it when someone crosses our boundary. I'm going to stand up, and Mr. Jackson is going to slowly walk toward me. When he reaches my personal boundary, I'm going to hold up my hand for him to stop.

Mr. Jackson, the co-leader, walks toward Ms. M. until she holds up her hand.

Ms. M: I held up my hand when Mr. Jackson reached my personal boundary. Now he's going to take one step closer to me. *(Mr. Jackson does so.)* This feels very uncomfortable to me. Why do you think it's uncomfortable?

Henry: Mr. Jackson crossed your boundary.

Ms. M: Exactly! I know that some of you get upset when someone bumps you when you're standing in line. Why do you think someone might get upset about this?

Isabella: Someone crossed a boundary.

Ms. M: Yes, that is very likely the reason. Someone crossed a personal boundary.

Ms. M: So here are the steps to the skill of Respecting Another's Boundaries. (*Ms. M. shows a poster with the skill steps*).

Skill 29: Respecting Another's Boundaries

1. Decide how far away.

2. Ask, "Do I touch the person?"

3. Decide what to do instead.

Ms. M: Let's look at the first step: Decide how far away you should be from another person. It's typical to stay an arm's length away from another, like I'm doing now with Mr. Jackson (*Ms. M. reaches out her arm and moves an arm's length away from Mr. Jackson.*) Do you think your mother has the same personal boundary that I have?

Charlie: (*Shrugs.*) But my mom is my mother.

Ms. M: Exactly, Charlie. Different people have different boundaries. You probably hug your mom without having to ask, right?

Charlie: (*Nods.*)

Ms. M: But hugging someone you don't know well, like a classmate new to the school, would cross that person's personal boundary, right?

Ms. M: Let's look at the second step: Ask, "Do I touch the person?" Do any of you not like to be touched by someone you don't know very well? (*Sammi and Henry raise their hands.*) Yes, it's important to think about whether or not the person wants to be touched, and many people don't like it. Let's list some people on the easel pad and decide if it would be okay to touch them.

The group completes this activity.

Ms. M: Now, let's look at Step 3: Decide what to do instead of touching the person. What could you do instead of touching someone?

Charlie: You could start a discussion with them. I like to talk about trains, so I would start a discussion with them about trains. (*The leader resists being distracted by Charlie's need to learn an additional skill but makes a note of this need.*)

Ms. M: Okay. You could talk to them instead of touching them.

Step 2: Model the Skill

Ms. M: These three steps, in this order, make up a good way to respect another's boundaries. Now, Mr. Jackson and I are going to model the skill: We're going to show you how to follow these steps. Just like a coach, we'll show you the skill being done well. Please watch for each step as we model the skill. Here is the situation. I walk into the library, and I want to look for a book in the science section, but someone else is already there.

Mr. Jackson moves to a shelf and pretends to look for a book.

> **Ms. M:** Okay, I want to find a book, but I need to respect the other person's boundaries. (*Points to the first step on the chart.*) So, first I need to decide how far away to be from the other person. Since I don't know him, I'd better stand an arm's length away from him. (*Ms. M. does so, then points to the second step.*) Then I need to ask myself if I should touch the person. No, I shouldn't because I don't know him. And the third step is to decide what to do instead. I think I'll just say "Hi" and then look for my book. (*Ms. M. then moves to the center and follows her plan.*)

Ms. M. and Mr. Jackson model the skill again, using a different scenario.

Step 3: Establish Learner Skill Need

> **Ms. M:** Let's think of some times in your real lives when it's important to respect someone else's boundaries but it's difficult for you to do this. I'll write your names and the situation where this is hard for you on the easel pad so we can remember the situations. Who can think of a time when it's hard to respect someone else's boundaries?

> **Sammi:** Sometimes the teachers wear silky clothes, and I like to feel this fabric.

> **Ms. M:** Okay, that's a good situation. Who else has a situation?

> **Henry:** Um, when I touch classmates I get in trouble.

The list continues as each learner identifies a situation for skill use.

Step 4: Select the First Role-Player

> **Ms. M:** You all came up with really good situations where you could use this skill. Who would like to try this skill first? Who would like to role-play first? (*Henry volunteers.*) Okay, Henry.

Step 5: Set Up the Role-Play

> **Ms. M:** All right, Henry. Could you tell us more about the situation so we can help you feel like you are in this situation?

> **Henry:** I just like to touch classmates.

> **Ms. M:** Where are you when you want to touch a peer?

> **Henry:** Um, in the hall. I got in trouble when I touched Rebecca's hair.

> **Ms. M:** Is this a situation that is likely to happen again?

> **Henry:** (*Nods yes.*)

> **Ms. M:** Okay, when is this likely to happen?

> **Henry:** Before school starts for the day.

> **Ms. M:** Henry, who in the group reminds you most of the girl you want to touch?

> **Henry:** (*Points to Isabella.*)

> **Ms. M:** Isabella, would you be willing to help us out with this and be the coactor in the role-play?

Isabella stands up and walks to the front of the group.

> **Ms. M:** Thank you, Isabella. Let's move some of the chairs out of the way so this area looks more like a hallway.

Ms. M: Henry, what are you and the class-mate doing when you want to touch her?

Henry: She's at her locker.

Ms. M: Okay, then. This will be her locker. *(Pulls a chair to the center to represent the locker.) (To the group)* Before we get started with the actual role-play, I need each of you to watch for a certain step of the skill. Sammi, will you watch and see if Henry follows the first step, if he decides how far away to be from his classmate? Charlie, will you watch and see if he asks himself if it's okay to touch her? And Sammi, will you also watch for the third step, if he decides to do something else instead? Remember, when the role-play is over, you will give Henry and the rest of us your feedback and tell us what he did and how well he followed the skill steps.

Step 6: Conduct the Role-Play

Ms. M: Henry, remember to talk aloud what you are thinking so we know you are following the skill steps. And, Isabella, your job is to stay in the role of Henry's classmate and be at your locker. Is everyone ready? Okay, we're in the school hallway before school starts for the day.

Henry: *(Walks toward Isabella and stops.)*

Ms. M: Henry, look at the first step, "Decide how far away." And think aloud.

Henry: I see Rebecca. She's getting her books from her locker. How far away? I need to stand an arm's length away.

Ms. M: *(Nods and points to the second step on the poster.)*

Henry: Do I touch her? No, I shouldn't touch her. *(Looks at Step 3 on the poster.)* Decide what to do instead. I will say hello. *(Walks toward Isabella, holds out his arm, and stops.)* Hello.

Isabella: Hi.

Ms. M: Okay, Henry!

Step 7: Provide Feedback

Order of feedback is coactor, observers, main actor, leaders.

Ms. M: Let's get some feedback for Henry. Isabella, if you were the real classmate, how would you react to what Henry did?

Isabella: He said hello. That was good.

Ms. M: So it felt good to you that he said hello to you?

Isabella: Yes.

Ms. M.: Thank you, Isabella. Thanks for helping out with the role-play, too. Who watched to see if Henry followed the first step and if he decided how far away he should be from his classmate?

Sammi: He did. He put out his arm.

Ms. M: Thank you, Sammi. You saw that he put out his arm to let him know when to stop. Who watched to see if he followed the second step, if he asked himself if he should touch the classmate?

Charlie: I did. He did it.

Ms. M: How do you know Henry followed this step?

Charlie: He used think aloud.

Ms. M: Good watching and listening. Yes, we heard him use his words to think through this step. And Step 3? Did he decide what to do instead? Sammi?

Sammi: (*Nods.*)

Ms. M: And what did he decide to do instead?

Sammi: He said hello to the classmate.

Ms. M: Thank you, Sammi. Henry, how did it feel to follow these skill steps?

Henry: It's hard not to touch.

Ms. M: Yes, but you didn't touch her! I know it's hard to do. But, did it feel good to you that you followed all the skill steps?

Henry: Yes.

Ms. M: I thought you did a good job, and so did others in the group. You did each and every step of the skill. I also knew what you were thinking because you said your thinking out loud. I was also impressed that you decided to say hello to your classmate, too. I think this was a very good choice. Thank you, Henry.

Step 8: Select the Next Role-Player

Ms. M: Who would like to role-play the skill next?

Step 9: Assign Skill Homework

Although the leader was pleased Henry followed all of the skill steps, she was concerned that it would look odd for Henry to hold out his arm to signal to himself when to stop as he approached the classmate. Therefore, prior to assigning homework to Henry following this session, she provided coaching to him to learn to assess an appropriate distance without putting up his arm and in using nonverbal behaviors (facial expression, manner in which he walked to the peer). Then supportive peers were included in the group for additional

practice and reinforcement. She then planned homework with Henry.

Ms. M: Henry, you've role-played this skill a few times. Are you ready to try this in real life?

Henry: (*Shrugs.*)

Ms. M: You seem a bit unsure. Would you feel more comfortable if you had a someone to help coach you?

Henry: That would be good. I will try it. When can I try it?

Ms. M: Will you see this classmate in the hallway tomorrow?

Henry: I can do this tomorrow. Will Mr. Jackson be there to coach me?

Ms. M: Let's look at the homework report. We'll check the box for a coach and write in Mr. Jackson's name. Now will you write your name and the date here? The name of the skill and the skill steps are listed for you. Now with whom will you try the skill? Please write her name in this blank. (*Henry does so.*) Good. Now, when will you try the skill?

Henry: In the morning before school starts.

Ms. M: Okay, go ahead and write "before school" on the next line. Then after you try out the skill, you'll write what happened and how you did by choosing one of these options. Mr. Jackson will help you evaluate this if you'd like. Are you ready to try your homework?

ADOLESCENT SKILLSTREAMING INSTRUCTION: ACCEPTING ANOTHER'S OPINION (SKILL 22)

Ms. Sanchez: Good morning! I'm so glad you are all here for our group today!

Last week, we all worked very hard on the skill of Listening Without Interrupting (Skill 1). Who completed a homework assignment on this skill? (*All raise their hands.*) Great!

All group members report on their homework assignments and receive encouragement and reinforcement from Ms. Sanchez and the other group members.

Step 1: Define the Skill

Ms. Sanchez: Today we are going to work on another very important skill called Accepting Another's Opinion. What is an opinion?

DeShawn: An opinion is what someone thinks.

Tom: Yeah, that's what an opinion is.

Ms. Sanchez: Right. It's what someone thinks about something, like an idea or activity. Is an opinion the same as a fact?

Carlita: An opinion is not the same as a fact.

Ms. Sanchez: How are they different?

Devon: Well, a fact is truth. An opinion is just, just what you think.

Ms. Sanchez: Okay, I think I understand what you're saying, Devon. Let's think about this example: There is a basketball game at school tonight. Fact or opinion?

Tom: It is true so it is a fact.

Ms. Sanchez: Correct. Now, what is your opinion about basketball games?

Tom: I am going with my brother. I like basketball.

Ms. Sanchez: Okay, so your opinion of basketball is that you like it. Does anyone else have an opinion about basketball games?

Elizabeth: Basketball is foolish. It's stupid.

Ms. Sanchez: Okay, so Elizabeth, your opinion is that you don't like basketball, right?

Elizabeth: Yes.

Ms. Sanchez: So, one person likes basketball and the other person thinks it's kind of a silly game. So, we have two different opinions about the same thing. Is this okay?

DeShawn: You don't have to play in a game if you don't like it.

Devon: Yes, it's okay that Elizabeth doesn't like it, but it's also okay that Tom likes basketball.

Ms. Sanchez: Great! Two people don't have to have the very same opinion. It's okay to think differently about things. So, let's look at the steps to this skill (*shows the chart*): The first step is to… (*reads each of the skill steps*).

Skill 22: Accepting Another's Opinion

1. Listen without interrupting.

2. Think about what is said.

3. Say to yourself, "Everyone can have a different opinion. It's okay."

4. Answer or comment in a respectful way.

Ms. Sanchez: Let's talk a little more about Step 4. What does it mean to comment in a respectful way?

Elizabeth: Be nice.

Ms. Sanchez: Yes, say it in a nice or respectful way and use nice or respectful words. Mr. Jacobs (*the co-leader*) has another chart that lists some respectful comments that you might want to use. (*Mr. Jacobs displays this chart.*) Let's look at these comments.

Mr. Jacobs reads the statements.

Respectful Comments

If I agree:

   I think I understand what you are saying.

   I agree with what you are saying.

   Nod my head up and down.

If I don't agree:

   Continue to listen and don't say anything.

   I can understand why you think that.

   I understand, but I think…(politely state your opinion).

Mr. Jacobs: By using this skill, it doesn't mean that you can't say what you think. That wouldn't be fair. But it is expected that you give your opinion in a respectful way. These are respectful ways, while telling them their idea is stupid is not respectful. Do you have any questions about these comments? (*No response.*) So when you get to Step 4 of this skill, feel free to look at this chart.

Ms. Sanchez: Tom, will you give everyone a skill card please? (Tom hands out skill cards.)

Step 2: Model the Skill

Ms. Sanchez: Now Mr. Jacobs and I are going to model this skill. Your job is to watch and see how I follow each of the skill steps. The situation is that Mr. Jacobs likes to go bike riding, but it's not something I enjoy doing. So first I'm going to (*points to each skill step as she comments*): Listen without interrupting. I really do want to hear what Mr. Jacobs has to say. Then, Step 2, I'm going to think about what he is saying. Then, I'll say to myself, "Everyone can have a different opinion." And, finally, I'll make a respectful comment.

Mr. Jacobs walks up to Ms. Sanchez.

Mr. Jacobs: Hi, how are you?

Ms. Sanchez: I'm doing well. And you?

Mr. Jacobs: Just fine. I just went to a bike show and saw some really cool bikes. I like to go riding on the trails and am thinking about getting a new bike. The trails here are just beautiful, and riding is so much fun.

Ms. Sanchez: (*Thinking aloud*) First I need to listen without interrupting. Sometimes it's hard not to interrupt when someone is talking about something that doesn't interest me, but I can do it. I'll think about what he is talking about. He's talking about maybe getting a new bike because he likes to ride on the beautiful trails. I don't like bike riding, but "everyone can have a different opinion." Now I need to comment in a respectful way. (*Ms. Sanchez moves closer to Mr. Jacobs.*)

It's nice that you have something you like to do for fun. I don't enjoy riding. I would much rather walk the trails.

Ms. Sanchez: *(To the group)* Did I follow the skill steps? Did I follow the first step? Did I listen without interrupting? *(Learners respond.)* Then did I think about what was being said? *(Learners respond.)* How do you know? *(Learners respond: You repeated what he said.)* Then did I say to myself "everyone can have a different opinion?" *(Learners respond.)* And finally, did I comment in a respectful way? *(Learners respond.)* What did I say that was respectful?

Carlita: You said you were happy he liked bike riding but you liked to walk.

Ms. Sanchez: Yes, I think I did a good job following the skill steps. Good for me!

Mr. Jacobs: And good listening and watching, everyone.

For the second modeling display, the group views a brief video of supportive peers talking about their favorite TV shows and hobbies (a very effective form of modeling for this group). When making the video, the Skillstreaming leader showed the peers the skill steps and prompted them to be sure to listen carefully to each other.

Ms. Sanchez: *(Referring to the video)* Watch to see how Sue is looking at Brad when he is telling her about the TV shows he likes to watch. Sue is doing a great job of carefully listening to what he is saying and trying to understand.

Elizabeth: Yeah, but that show is stu... *(stops in mid-sentence)*. I guess it's okay if he likes it, though.

Ms. Sanchez: Yes, it's okay for someone to like a certain show. It doesn't mean that you have to like it. Let's talk about the steps Sue followed. Did Sue listen without interrupting? *(Learners respond.)* Did she seem to think about what is being said? *(Learners respond.)* Yes, we didn't hear her say she was doing this, but how could you tell she was following this step?

Tom: She knew what he was saying. She asked questions.

Ms. Sanchez: Good. Now, did she follow Step 3? Did she say to herself, "Everyone can have a different opinion?"

Devon: I didn't hear her say it.

Ms. Sanchez: Good listening. No, she didn't say it aloud. Do you think she thought this, though?

DeShawn: Maybe. 'Cause she was respectful.

Ms. Sanchez: Yes. When you first learn this skill you'll think aloud what normally you would say to yourself. Sue seems to have had a lot of practice with this skill, so maybe she said it to herself. And Step 4: Did she comment in a respectful way?

Carlita: Yeah. She said she didn't watch that show but it sounded interesting.

Ms. Sanchez: Yes, her comment was very respectful. Let's talk about how Sue and Brad appear to be feeling. Looks to me like both are enjoying their talk. Why do you think they are enjoying talking to each other?

Tom: They are smiling.

Elizabeth: And laughing.

Ms. Sanchez: Exactly. They are taking turns talking about what they like to do. And the person they are talking with is listening and paying attention. I hear them saying they have different favorite TV shows and hobbies, but that's okay. They understand it's okay to like different things.

DeShawn: Yeah. I think I like Brad's shows better. I don't know the shows Sue is talking about and don't plan to watch them. But Sue's okay. She's a neat girl.

Ms. Sanchez: So, you agree that it's okay for Sue to like something that Brad doesn't enjoy? (*Learners agree.*)

Step 3: Establish Learner Skill Need

Ms. Sanchez: That was our modeling of the skill. Now let's think of some times in your real lives when it's challenging for you to accept another's opinion. I'll write your names on the easel pad and your situation beside it so that we can remember the situations. Who can think of a time when accepting another's opinion is hard for you?

Elizabeth: Lots of times, I guess.

Ms. Sanchez: Can you think of one situation in particular?

Elizabeth: When my brother plays stu…oops. When he plays video games.

Ms. Sanchez: Thank you, Elizabeth. Someone else?

Tom: When I go to my cousin's house after school. I don't like the activities he does.

The list continues as each learner identifies a situation for skill use.

Step 4: Select the First Role-Player

Ms. Sanchez: You all came up with really good examples of situations when it's hard for you to accept another's opinion. Who would like to try the skill first? Who would like to role-play? (*Carlita volunteers.*) Okay, Carlita. It sounds like accepting another's opinion when working in a group in school is creating problems for you.

Step 5: Set Up the Role-Play

Mr. Jacobs: Carlita, could you tell us a little more about the situation so that we can help you feel more like you are in it?

Carlita: Mostly in English class when we have to fill out those sheets with the plot of the story and stuff. We have to agree before we can write it down.

Mr. Jacobs: Good description. Is there someone in the group that reminds you most of one of the peers you work with on this assignment?

Carlita: Tom, I guess.

Mr. Jacobs: Tom, are you okay with being the coactor for Carlita? (*Tom stands.*) Let's use this small table, and I have a sheet of paper that can represent the assignment. (Carlita and Tom sit at the table.) Is there a particular book or story you are reading now in English?

Carlita: *The Book Thief.*

Mr. Jacobs: Good. Tom, any questions about what you are to do as coactor? Now who would like to watch to see if Carlita follows the first step, if she listens without interrupting? Devon. Step 2, if she thinks about what is being said? DeShawn. Step 3, if she says "Everyone can have a different opinion?" Elizabeth. And Step 4, if she comments in a respectful way? Elizabeth.

Step 6: Conduct the Role-Play

Ms. Sanchez: Carlita, I'll be up at the skill poster to help remind you of the steps, or you can look at your skill card. You will need to talk aloud about what you are thinking so we know you are following each skill step. When you turn away from the table, we will know you are thinking aloud, okay? Ready?

Tom: We have to talk about the book. I just read the first chapter, but I don't like it. I don't want to read it. I told Mr. Todd I wanted to read a book about science.

Ms. Sanchez: Okay, Carlita. You followed the first step, you listened without interrupting. Now, Step 2…

Carlita: Tom said he doesn't like *The Book Thief,* but he only read one chapter.

Ms. Sanchez: Step 3…

Carlita: I say, "Everyone can have a different opinion."

Ms. Sanchez: Good.

Carlita: *(Looking at the skill poster)* Comment in a respectful way. I will say…I will say… *(Looking at the chart of respectful comments)* I understand what you are saying, but I like the book.

Ms. Sanchez: Okay, go ahead and say this to Tom.

Step 7: Provide Feedback

Order of feedback is coactor, observers, main actor, leaders.

Ms. Sanchez: Let's get some feedback for Carlita. Tom, how did it feel when Carlita listened to you?

Tom: Good. She listened to what I said.

Ms. Sanchez: And how did it feel when she made the comment?

Tom: It was good, too.

Ms. Sanchez: So, Tom, it felt good to you when Carlita used the skill.

Tom: Yes.

Ms. Sanchez: Let's go on to the observers. Did Carlita follow the first step, did she listen without interrupting? Devon?

Devon: She did a good job listening and didn't interrupt.

Ms. Sanchez: Step 2? DeShawn?

DeShawn: Yeah. She knew what he said.

Ms. Sanchez: And Step 3? Elizabeth.

Elizabeth: She did it.

Ms. Sanchez: How do you know she followed this step?

Elizabeth: She said, "Everybody can have a different opinion."

Ms. Sanchez: And Step 4? Was her comment respectful?

Elizabeth: Yes, it was respectful. It was nice.

Ms. Sanchez: Carlita, the group had great things to say about how you role-played the skill. How do you think you did?

Carlita: It was hard. I forgot one time.

Ms. Sanchez: Yes, but you recovered! And you followed all of the skill steps. In particular, your comment was very respectful to Tom. Good job.

Step 8: Select the Next Role-Player

Mr. Jacobs: Who would like to role-play the skill next?

Step 9: Assign Skill Homework

The group leaders work individually with those who have role-played the skill and who seem ready to try the skill in their real lives through the same process next described for Carlita.

Ms. Sanchez: Carlita, let's plan your homework assignment. You role-played the skill twice in group and once with a supportive peer. Are you ready to try this in real life?

Carlita: I will do it.

Ms. Sanchez: Good. Thanks for your commitment! Write your name and the date here on the homework report. The name of the skill and the skill steps are listed for you. Now, with whom will you try the skill?

Carlita: The English group.

Ms. Sanchez: Write that here. Now, let's decide when you will try the skill.

Carlita: (*Sighs*) In English.

Ms. Sanchez: Go ahead and write "in English class." Then, after you try the skill, you'll write what happened. Then you'll decide how you did by circling one of the numbers. You'll choose number 4 if you followed all of the steps. You'll choose number 4 even if the skill didn't work out the way you wanted but you still followed all of the steps. Choose 3 if you followed three of the steps and 2 if you followed two of the steps. Choose 1 if you didn't use the skill at all. Then, on the last line, you'll explain why you circled the number you chose. Questions?

Carlita: I get it.

Ms. Sanchez: Now, you role-played with Amanda, a supportive peer. Would you like Amanda to be there when you try this for the first time?

Carlita: Yes I would.

Ms. Sanchez: Then we'll mark the coaching support and write Amanda's name here.

References

American Psychiatric Association. (2000). *Diagnostic and statistical manual of mental disorders* (DSM-IV-TR; 4th ed., text revision). Washington, DC: Author.

American Psychiatric Association. (2013). *Diagnostic and statistical manual of mental disorders* (DSM-V; 5th ed.). Washington, DC: Author.

Asperger, H. (1944). Die "Autistischen Psychopathen" im Kindesalter ["Autistic psychopathy" in childhood]. *Archiv fur Psychiatrie ud Nervenkrankheiten, 17,* 76–136.

Attwood, (2007). *The compete guide to Asperger syndrome.* Philadelphia: Jessica Kingsley.

Baker, J. (2004). *Social skills training for children and adolescents with Asperger Syndrome and social communication problems.* Shawnee Mission, KS: Autism Asperger Publishing.

Bandura, A. (1973). *Aggression: A social learning analysis.* Englewood Cliffs, NJ: Prentice Hall.

Barnhill, G. P. (2001). Social attribution and depression in adolescents with Asperger Syndrome. *Focus on Autism and Other Developmental Disabilities, 16,* 46–53.

Baron-Cohen, S. (1995). *Mindblindess: An essay on autism and theory of mind.* Cambridge, MA: MIT Press.

Baron-Cohen, S. (2001, December 1). Think different? An interview with Oliver Morton. *Wired,* 185–187.

Baron-Cohen, S., Golan, O., Wheelwright, S., & Hill, J. (2004). *Mind reading: The interactive guide to emotions.* London: Jessica Kingsley.

Baron-Cohen, S., Leslie, A., & Frith, U. (1985). Does the autistic child have a theory of mind? *Cognition, 25,* 37–46.

Batesko, M. L. (2007). Creating a positive elementary environment for Asperger children. *Journal of College Teaching and Learning, 4*(10), 63–66.

Bellini, S. (2006). *Building social relationships: A systematic approach to teaching social interaction skills to children and adolescents with autism spectrum disorders and other social difficulties.* Shawnee Mission, KS: Autism Asperger Publishing.

Bolick, T. (2001). *Asperger syndrome and adolescence.* Gloucester, MA: Fair Winds Press.

Bregman, J., & Higdon, C. (2012). Definitions and clinical characteristics of autism spectrum disorders. In D. Zager, M. Wehmeyer, & R. Simpson, *Educating students with autism spectrum disorders* (pp. 13–45). New York: Routledge.

Cesaroni, L., & Garber, M. (1991). Exploring the experience of autism through firsthand accounts. *Journal of Autism and Developmental Disorders, 21,* 303–313.

Chan, J., Lang, R., Rispoli, M., O'Reilly, M., Sigafoos, J., & Cole, H. (2009). Use of peer mediated interventions in the treatment of autism spectrum disorders: A systematic review. *Research in Autism Spectrum Disorders, 3,* 876–889.

Chapman, W. E. (1977). *Roots of character education.* Schenectady, NY: Character Research Press.

Church, C., Alisanski, S., & Amanullah, S. (2000). The social, behavioral, and academic experiences of children with Asperger Syndrome. *Focus on Autism and Other Developmental Disabilities, 15,* 15–20.

Cotugno, A. (2009). Social competence and social skills training and intervention for children with autism spectrum disorders. *Journal of Autism and Developmental Disorders, 39*(9), 1268–1277.

Dewey, J. (1938). *Experience and education.* New York: Collier.

Dunn, W. (2008). A sensory-processing approach to supporting students with autism spectrum disorders. In R. Simpson & B. Myles (Eds.), *Educating children and youth with autism* (pp. 299–356). Austin, TX: Pro-Ed.

Ehlers, S., Nyden, A., Gillberg, B., Sandburg, A., Dehlgren, S., Hjelmquist, E., & Oden, A. (1997). Aspergers Syndrome, autism and attention deficit disorders: A comparative study of cognitive profiles of 120 children. *Journal of Child Psychology and Psychiatry and Allied Disciplines, 38,* 207–217.

Flavell, J. H., Miller, P. H., & Miller, S. A. (1993). *Cognitive development* (3rd ed.). Englewood Cliffs, NJ: Prentice Hall.

Foley, B. E., & Staples, A. H. (2003). Developing augmentative and alternative communication (AAC) and literacy interventions in a supported employment setting. *Topics in Language Disorders, 23*(4), 325–343.

Frankel, F., Myatt, R., Sugar, C., Whitham, C., Gorospe, C. M., & Laugeson, E. (2010). A randomized controlled study of parent-assisted children's friendship training with children having autism spectrum disorders. *Journal of Autism and Developmental Disorders, 40*(7), 827–842.

Frith, U. (1991). *Autism and Asperger Syndrome.* Cambridge, UK: Cambridge University Press.

Ganz, J. (2007). Classroom structuring methods and strategies for children and youth with autism spectrum disorders. *Exceptionality, 15*(4), 249–260.

Garcia Winner, M. (2008). *Think social: A social thinking curriculum for school-age students.* San Jose, CA: Think Social.

Gerhardt, P., & Crimmins, D. (2013). *Social skills and adaptive behavior in learners with autism spectrum disorders.* Baltimore: Paul H. Brookes.

Ghaziuddin, M., Weidmer-Mikhail, E., & Ghaziuddin, N. (1998). Comorbidity of Asperger Sysndrome: A preliminary report. *Journal of Intellectual Disability Research, 42*(4), 279–283.

Goldstein, A. P. (1973). *Structured Learning Therapy: Toward a psychotherapy for the poor.* New York: Academic.

Goldstein, A. P., & McGinnis, E. (1997). *Skillstreaming the adolescent: New strategies and perspectives for teaching prosocial skills* (Rev. ed.). Champaign, IL: Research Press.

Goldstein, A. P., Sprafkin, R. P., Gershaw, N. J., & Klein, P. (1980). *Skillstreaming the adolescent: A structured learning approach to teaching prosocial skills.* Champaign, IL: Research Press.

Goleman, D. (2006). *Social intelligence: The new science of human relationships.* New York: Random House.

Griswold, D., Barnhill, G. P., Myles, B. S., Hagiwara, T., & Simpson, R. L. (2002). Asperger Syndrome and academic achievement. *Focus on Autism and Other Developmental Disabilities, 17*(2), 94–102.

Grizenko, J., Zappitelli, M., Langevin, J. P., Hrychko, S., El-Messidi, A., Kaminester, D., Pawliuk, N., & Stepanian, M. T. (2000). Effectiveness of a social skills training program using self/other perspective-taking: A nine month follow-up. *American Journal of Orthopsychiatry, 70*(4), 501–509.

Harpur, J., Lawlor, M., & Fitzgerald, M. (2004). *Succeeding in college with Asperger Syndrome: A student guide.* London, UK: Jessica Kingsley.

Heflin, J., & Alaimo, D. (2007). *Students with autism spectrum disorders: Effective instructional practices.* Upper Sadder River, NJ: Pearson/Merrill Prentice Hall.

Jones, E. A., & Carr, E. G. (2004). Joint attention in children with autism: Theory and intervention. *Focus on Autism and Other Developmental Disabilities, 19*(1), 13–26.

Jones, K.M., Young, M.M., & Friman, P.C. (2000). Increasing peer praise of socially rejected delinquent youth: Effects on cooperation and acceptance. *School Psychology Review, 15,* 30–39.

Kanner, L. (1943). Autistic disturbances of affective content. *The Nervous Child, 2,* 217–250.

Koegel, S.K., Kuriakose, S., Singh, A.K., & Koegel, R.L. (2012). Improving generalization of peer socialization gains in inclusive school settings using initiations training. *Behavior Modification, 36,* 361–377.

Kohlberg, L. (Ed.). (1973). *Collected papers on moral development and moral education.* Cambridge, MA: Harvard University, Center for Moral Education.

Lane, K.L., Menies, H.M., Barton-Arwood, S.M., Doukas, G.L., & Munton, S.M. (2005). Designing, implementing, and evaluating social skills interventions for elementary students: Step-by-step procedures based on actual school-based investigations. *Preventing School Failure, 49*(2), 18–26.

Lee, S., Odom, S., & Loftin, R. (2007). Social engagement with peers and stereotypic behavior of children with autism. *Journal of Positive Behavior Interventions, 9,* 67–79.

Lincoln, A., Courchesne, E., Kilman, B., Elmasian, R., & Allen, M. (1988). A study of intellectual ability in high-functioning people with autism. *Journal of Autism and Developmental Disorders, 18,* 505–524.

Lopata, C., Thomeer, M.L., Volker, M.A., & Nida, R.E. (2006). Effectiveness of a cognitive-behavioral treatment on the social behaviors of children with Asperger Disorder. *Focus on Autism and Other Developmental Disabilities, 21*(4), 237–244.

Lopata, C., Thomeer, M., Volker, M.A., Nida, R.E., & Lee, G.K. (2008). Effectiveness of a manualized summer social treatment program for high functioning children with autism spectrum disorders. *Journal of Autism and Developmental Disorders, 38,* 890–904.

Mann, J.H. (1956). Experimental evaluations of role playing. *Psychological Bulletin, 53,* 227–234.

Matson, J.L., Matson, M.L., & Rivet, T.T. (2007). Social-skills treatments for children with autism spectrum disorders. *Behavior Modification, 31,* 682–707.

McGinnis, E. (2012a). *Skillstreaming the adolescent: A guide for teaching prosocial skills* (3rd ed.). Champaign, IL: Research Press.

McGinnis, E. (2012b). *Skillstreaming in early childhood: A guide for teaching prosocial skills* (3rd ed.). Champaign, IL: Research Press.

McGinnis, E. (2012c). *Skillstreaming the elementary school child: A guide for teaching prosocial skills* (3rd ed.). Champaign, IL: Research Press.

McGinnis, E., & Goldstein, A.P. (1984). *Skillstreaming the elementary school child: A guide for teaching prosocial skills.* Champaign, IL: Research Press.

McGinnis, E. & Goldstein, A.P. (1990). *Skillstreaming in early childhood: Teaching prosocial skills to the preschool and kindergarten child.* Champaign, IL: Research Press.

McGinnis, E., & Goldstein, A.P. (1997). *Skillstreaming the elementary school child: New strategies and perspectives for teaching prosocial skills* (Rev. ed.). Champaign, IL: Research Press.

McGinnis, E., & Goldstein, A.P. (2003). *Skillstreaming in early childhood: New strategies and perspectives for teaching prosocial skills* (Rev. ed.). Champaign, IL: Research Press.

Mesibov, G.B., Shea, V., & Adams, L. (2001). *Understanding Asperger syndrome and high functioning autism.* New York: Kluwer Academic/Plenum Publishing.

Miller, J.P. (1976). *Humanizing the classroom.* New York: Praeger.

Moroz, K.B., & Jones, K.M. (2002). The effects of positive peer reporting on children's social involvement. *School Psychology Review, 31*(2) 235–245.

Moyes, R.A. (2001). *Incorporating social goals in the classroom: A guide for teachers and parents of children with high-functioning autism and Asperger syndrome.* Philadelphia: Jessica Kingsley.

Mundy, P., Block, J., Vaughan Van Hecke, A., Delgado, C., Parlade, M., & Palmeras, Y. (2007). Individual differences in the development of joint attention in infancy. *Child Development, 78,* 938–954.

Myles, B. S., Cook, K. T., Miller, N. E., Rinner, L., & Robbins, L. A. (2000). *Asperger Syndrome and sensory issues: Practical solutions for making sense of the world.* Shawnee Mission, KS: Autism Asperger Publishing Company.

Myles, B. S., & Simpson, R. L. (1998). *Asperger's syndrome: A guide for educators and parents.* Austin, TX: Pro-Ed.

Myles, B. S., & Southwick, J. (1999). *Asperger syndrome and difficult moments: Practical solutions for tantrums, rage, and meltdowns.* Shawnee Mission, KS: Autism Asperger Publishing Company.

Owen-DeSchryver, J. S., Carr, E. G., Cale, S. I., & Blakeley-Smith, A. (2008). Promoting social interactions between students with autism spectrum disorders and their peers in inclusive school settings. *Focus on Autism and Other Developmental Disabilities, 23,* 15–28.

Ozonoff, S., & Miller, J. (1995). Teaching theory of mind: A new approach to social skills training for individuals with autism. *Journal of Autism and Developmental Disorders, 25,* 415–433.

Polirstok, S. R., & Houghteling, L. (2006). Asperger syndrome: A primer for behavioral interventionists. *Journal of Early and Intensive Behavior Intervention, 3*(2), 187–195.

Rosaler, M. (2004). *Coping with Asperger syndrome.* New York: Rosen Publishing Group.

Safran, S. P., Safran, J. S., & Ellis, K. (2003). Intervention ABCs for children with Asperger syndrome. *Top Language Disorders, 23*(2), 154–165.

Schall, C. M., & McDonough, J. T. (2010). Autism spectrum disorders in adolescence and early adulthood: characteristics and issues. *Journal of Vocational Rehabilitation, 32*(2), 81–88.

Seltzer, M. M., Krauss, M. W., Shattuck, P. T., Orsmond, G., Swe, A., & Lord, C. (2003). The symptoms of autism spectrum disorders in adolescence and adulthood. *Journal of Autism and Developmental Disorders, 33*(6), 565–581.

Shonkoff, J. P., & Bales, S. N. (2011). Science does not speak for itself: Translating child development research for the public and its policymakers. *Child Development, 82*(1), 17–32.

Shore, S. (2003). *Beyond the wall: Personal experiences with autism and Asperger syndrome* (2nd ed.). Shawnee Mission, KS: Autism Asperger Publishing.

Siegel, D., Minshew, N., & Goldstein, G. (1996). Wechsler IQ profiles in diagnosis of high-functioning autism. *Journal of Autism and Developmental Disorders, 26,* 389–406.

Simon, S. G., Howe, L. W., & Kirshchenbaum, H. (1972). *Values clarification.* New York: Hart.

Simpson, R., Ganz, J., & Mason, R. (2012). Social skill interventions and programming for learners with autism spectrum disorders. In D. Zager, M. Wehmeyer, & R. Simpson (Eds.), *Educating students with autism spectrum disorders* (pp. 207–226). New York: Routledge.

Simpson, R., & Myles, B. (2011). *Asperger syndrome and high-functioning autism.* Austin, TX: Pro-Ed.

Skinner, C. H., Cashwell, T. H., & Skinner, A. L. (2000). Increasing tootling: Effects of a peer-monitored group contingency program on students' reports of peers' prosocial behaviors. *Psychology in the Schools, 37,* 263–270.

Smith, I. (2000). Motor functioning in Asperger Syndrome. In A. Klin, F. Volkmar, & S. Sparrow (Eds.), *Asperger syndrome* (pp. 97–124). New York: Guilford.

Smith, I., & Bryson, S. (1994). Imitation and action in autism: A critical review. *Psychological Bulletin, 116,* 259–273.

Stichter, J. P., O'Connor, K. V., Herzog, M. J., Lierheimer, K., & McGhee, S. D. (2012). Social competence intervention for elementary students with Asperger Syndrome and high functioning autism. *Journal of Autism and Developmental Disorders, 42,* 354–366.

Tantam, D. (2000). Adolescence and adulthood of individuals with Asperger syndrome. In A. Klin, F. Volkmar, & S. Sparrow (Eds.), *Asperger syndrome* (pp. 367–399). New York: Guilford.

Thieman, K., & Kamps, D. (2008). Promoting social-communicative competence of children with autism in integrated environments. In R. Simpson & B. Myles (Eds.), *Educating children and youth with autism* (pp. 267–298). Austin, TX: Pro-Ed.

Thompson, T. (2007). *Making sense of autism*. Baltimore: Paul H. Brookes.

Todd, T., & Reid, G. (2007). Increasing physical activity in individuals with autism. *Focus on Autism and Other Developmental Disabilities, 21*(3), 167–176.

Tse, J., Strulovitch, J., Tagalakis, V., Linyan, M., & Rombonne, E. (2007). Social skills training for adolescents with Asperger Syndrome and High Functioning Autism. *Journal of Autism and Developmental Disorders, 37,* 1960–1968.

Volkmar, F., & Klin, A. (2000). Diagnostic issues. In A. Klin, F. Volkmar, & S. Sparrow (Eds.), *Asperger syndrome* (pp. 25–71). New York: Guilford.

Weiss, M.J. (2013). Behavior analytic interventions for developing social skills in individuals with autism. In P.F. Gerhardt & D. Crimmins (Eds.), *Social skills and adaptive behavior in learners with autism spectrum disorders* (pp. 33–52). Baltimore, MD: Paul H. Brookes.

Wechsler, D. (1989). *Wechsler Preschool and Primary Scale of Intelligence–Revised*. San Antonio, TX: Psychological Corporation.

Weschler, D. (1991). *Wechsler Intelligence Scale for Children* (3rd ed.). San Antonio, TX: Psychological Corporation.

Wetherby, A., & Prizant, B. (2000). *Autism spectrum disorders: A transactional developmental perspective*. Baltimore: Paul H. Brookes.

Wing, L. (1981). Asperger's Syndrome: A clinical account. *Psychological Medicine, 11,* 115–130.

Wood, B.K., Umbreit, J., Liaupsin, C.J., & Gresham, F.M. (2007). A treatment integrity analysis of function-based interventions. *Education and Treatment of Children, 30*(4), 105–120.

World Health Organization. (2007). *International statistical classification of diseases and related health problems* (10th ed.). Geneva, Switzerland: Author.

Zager, D., & Dreyfus, F. (2012). Academic development through integrated behavioral experiential teaching. In D. Zager, M. Wehmeyer, & R. Simpson (Eds.), *Educating students with autism spectrum disorders* (pp. 113–125). New York: Routledge.

Zager, D., Wehmeyer, M., & Simpson, R. (Eds.). (2012). *Educating students with autism spectrum disorders*. New York: Routledge.

About the Authors

Ellen McGinnis, PhD, holds degrees in elementary education, special education, and school administration. She has taught elementary and secondary students in the public schools and has served as special education consultant in both public and hospital schools, school principal, special education director, and executive director of student support services. Dr. McGinnis recently retired as the mental health and dispute resolution consultant from the Iowa Department of Education and now works as an author and private consultant. The author of numerous articles on identifying and teaching youth with emotional/behavioral disorders, she collaborated with Dr. Arnold P. Goldstein on early Skillstreaming books and is author of the most recently released editions of *Skillstreaming in Early Childhood, Skillstreaming the Elementary School Child,* and *Skillstreaming the Adolescent.*

Richard L. Simpson, EdD, is professor emeritus at the University of Kansas. He has directed numerous demonstration programs for the University of Kansas and the University of Kansas Medical Center for students with autism spectrum disorders and has coordinated a variety of federal grants related to students with disabilities. He has also worked as a special education teacher, school psychologist, and coordinator of a community mental health outreach program. He has authored numerous books, articles, and tests on a variety of topics related to students with disabilities. Dr. Simpson is the former senior editor of the professional journal *Focus on Autism and Other Developmental Disabilities.*